Approaches to Teaching
the Writings of Emilia Pardo Bazán

Approaches to Teaching the Writings of Emilia Pardo Bazán

Edited by

Margot Versteeg

and

Susan Walter

Modern Language Association of America
New York   2017

MLA and the MODERN LANGUAGE ASSOCIATION are trademarks
owned by the Modern Language Association of America.
For information about obtaining permission to reprint material from
MLA book publications, send your request by mail (see address below)
or e-mail (permissions@mla.org).

Library of Congress Cataloging-in-Publication Data:

Names: Versteeg, Margot, editor. | Walter, Susan (Susan Jean) editor.
Title: Approaches to teaching the writings of Emilia Pardo Bazán / edited by
Margot Versteeg, Susan Walter.
Description: New York : The Modern Language Association of America, 2017. |
Series: Approaches to teaching world literature, ISSN 1059-1133 ; 147 |
Includes bibliographical references and index. |
Identifiers: LCCN 2017038780 (print) |
LCCN 2017045142 (e-book) | ISBN 9781603293242 (EPub) |
ISBN 9781603293259 (Kindle) | ISBN 9781603293228 (hardback) | ISBN 9781603293235 (paper)
Subjects: LCSH: Pardo Bazán, Emilia, condesa de, 1852–1921—Study and teaching (Higher) |
BISAC: Language Arts & Disciplines / Study & Teaching. | Literary Criticism / European /
Spanish & Portuguese. | Literary Criticism / Women Authors.
Classification: LCC PQ6629.A7 (e-book) | LCC PQ6629.A7 Z555 2017 (print) |
DDC 863/.5—dc23

Approaches to teaching the writings of Emilia Pardo Bazán /
edited by Margot Versteeg and Susan Walter.

Approaches to Teaching World Literature 147
ISSN 1059-1133

Cover illustration of the paperback and electronic editions:
The White Slave Trade, 1895, by Joaquín Sorolla y Bastida (1863–1923).
Oil on canvas. Museo Sorolla, Madrid, Spain / Index / Bridgeman Images.

Published by The Modern Language Association of America
85 Broad Street, suite 500, New York, New York 10004-2434
www.mla.org

CONTENTS

PREFACE

Emilia Pardo Bazán (1851–1921) was the most prolific and influential woman writer of late-nineteenth-century Spain. Her literary career spanned more than fifty years, during which she published twenty novels, twenty-one novellas, close to six hundred short stories, a collection of poetry, seven plays, two cookbooks, and countless essays on topics ranging from literary criticism to social commentary. She also directed a book series and founded a cultural magazine of which she was the sole author. In a culture that presented few opportunities for women, Pardo Bazán actively engaged with the most pressing literary, cultural, and social debates of her time. She was instrumental in introducing Spanish literary and intellectual circles to foreign literary models, such as French naturalism and Russian spiritual realism, and made critical contributions to contemporary discourses on gender, nation, and empire. Pardo Bazán's literary production is complex and sophisticated, and readers today often enjoy discovering the author's highly critical messages about Spain.

The present volume is a guide to teaching the works of Pardo Bazán. It offers a series of pedagogical tools to explore the multidimensionality of the author's diverse oeuvre and addresses the rewards and challenges of teaching Pardo Bazán's literary production, whether in Spanish or in translation. There are ample possibilities to incorporate Pardo Bazán's works in the classroom, but teachers and students may need multiple theoretical and conceptual frameworks to fully understand the works' variety and complexity. Naturalism has traditionally been the focus for teaching Pardo Bazán, but her contributions to the literary landscape of her time go well beyond naturalism; no single label accurately describes the richness of her vast production. More recent scholarship, for example, has portrayed Pardo Bazán as a perceptive observer of gender dynamics and of the society of her time.

This volume offers fresh and original suggestions for teaching the naturalist novels *Los pazos de Ulloa* (1886; "The House of Ulloa") and *La madre naturaleza* (1887; "Mother Nature") and provides guidance to instructors who want to teach Pardo Bazán's lesser-known novels. *Insolación* (1889; "Sunstroke"), *Memorias de un solterón* (1896; "Memoirs of a Confirmed Bachelor"), and the modernist novel *Dulce dueño* (1911; "Sweet Master") are exciting works that can facilitate the teaching of a variety of literary and cultural themes. Pardo Bazán's short fiction and essays, such as "La mujer española" (1890; "The Women of Spain"), reveal a consistent line of thought that Pardo Bazán developed in a fervent, dynamic dialogue with her (male) contemporaries. The volume also encourages instructors to try their hand at teaching Pardo Bazán's cookbooks, travel narratives, and plays.

This is a propitious time to publish a volume on teaching Pardo Bazán's writings. The author is popular both in the classroom and with literary scholars, evident from the ever-increasing body of secondary literature in English, Spanish, and other languages. Recent editions and anthologies of her work are readily available. This volume is structured around five clusters of topics—"Gendered Perspectives," "Science and Medicine," "Nation, Empire, and Geopolitics," "Realism, Naturalism, and Literary Connections," and "Interdisciplinary Approaches"—which show the various theoretical and interpretive lenses through which Pardo Bazán's work can be studied and taught. The essays, all written by specialists in the field, place Pardo Bazán in the cultural milieu of late-nineteenth- and early-twentieth-century Spain and address some of the contradictions in the author's work that make teaching her writings such a challenging and rewarding endeavor.

Part One

MATERIALS

In the following pages we aim to give both novice and veteran instructors of the works of Emilia Pardo Bazán an overview of the most useful resources, whether they are teaching Pardo Bazán in Spanish undergraduate or graduate classrooms or in world literature or gender studies courses. Our presentation of materials opens with brief descriptions of the biographies of Pardo Bazán. Then we review the most valuable and readily available editions of her texts, in Spanish and in English translations. The "Critical Resources" section introduces the book-length critical studies and collections of critical essays. In "Intellectual and Critical Contexts" we describe resources aimed at contextualizing Pardo Bazán's literary, historical, and social environment. The next section presents the vast audiovisual and online materials, first focusing on textual sources available on the sites *Biblioteca Virtual Miguel de Cervantes*, *Hemeroteca Digital*, and *Biblioteca Digital Ciudad Seva*, among others, followed by sites that have interesting visual materials that will aid instructors with the historical and social contextualization of Pardo Bazán's works. The last part of this section gives information on documentary films about the author and films based on her novels and short stories. "Organizations and Conferences" consists of information about the Casa-Museo Emilia Pardo Bazán and the Real Academia Galega. Pardo Bazán's conflicted relation with Galician literature and letters is explained in the section "Galician Studies." Finally, a literary-historical time line presents important events in Pardo Bazán's life and in Spain during her lifetime (1851–1921).

Biographical Resources

First published in 1962, Carmen Bravo-Villasante's classic biography, *Emilia Pardo Bazán: Vida y obra* ("Emilia Pardo Bazán: Life and Work"), is a basic but praiseworthy work; its last edition appeared in 1973. In 2001 Cristina Fernández Cubas published a short biography titled *Emilia Pardo Bazán*, an excellent overview of the author's life. In 2003 the historian Pilar Faus Sevilla published the monumental, two-volume *Emilia Pardo Bazán: Su época, su vida, su obra* ("Emilia Pardo Bazán: Her Time, Her Life, Her Work"), a worthy historical contextualization of the author's life and works. In Eva Acosta's well-written 2007 biography targeted at a general audience, *Emilia Pardo Bazán: La luz en la batalla* ("Emilia Pardo Bazán: A Guiding Light in the Struggle"), Acosta portrays Pardo Bazán as a female intellectual in a male-dominated world and highlights the author's combative manner.

Resources for Teaching

Pardo Bazán's Works

For faculty members conducting research, the three-volume Aguilar edition of Pardo Bazán's *Obras completas* ("Complete Works"), edited between 1957 and 1973 by Federico Carlos Sainz de Robles and Harry L. Kirby, Jr., is a popular choice because the volumes contain most of the author's published works and are readily available in most university libraries. However, these volumes are not ideal for use in the classroom because of their tiny print and limited footnotes and introductory materials.

The handsome edition of Pardo Bazán's works edited by Darío Villanueva and José Manuel González Herrán and published by the Fundación José Antonio de Castro between 1999 and 2011, also titled *Obras completas*, includes only the author's fiction. The twelve volumes in this edition have a normal type size and high-quality paper and are therefore appealing for classroom use; unfortunately, their high price is prohibitive for many. The first five volumes contain the novels, volume six the *novelas cortas* ("short novels") and *novelas ejemplares* ("exemplary novels"), and the last six volumes are short stories organized by the collections in which they were originally published.

An exceptional resource for teaching Pardo Bazán's short stories is Juan Paredes Núñez's four-volume edition of *Cuentos completos* ("Complete Stories"). For this edition, Paredes Núñez prepared several appendixes with complete publication information for all the stories he included. Each appendix offers a different organization of the stories: by publication date, alphabetically by story title, by the collection the stories were initially published in, and so on. Perhaps the most unique feature of this collection is the forty-five-page *censo de personajes* ("list of characters") at the end of the fourth volume.

Three American scholars have published editions for the undergraduate classroom of some of Pardo Bazán's most approachable works. Linda Willem's 2010 edition of a collection of short stories, *"Naúfragas" y otros cuentos* ("'Castaways' and Other Stories"), and Jennifer Smith's 2011 edition of *Insolación* ("Sunstroke") include useful features for second-language learners of Spanish, such as a substantial Spanish-English glossary of the more difficult lexical items and footnotes that explain literary, historical, and social references. The introductions of both volumes are in English and have concise historical and biographical overviews that help students contextualize the narratives within the cultural milieu in which they were produced. Likewise, Joyce Tolliver's 1996 edition of *"El encaje roto" y otros cuentos* ("'Torn Lace' and Other Stories") contains a useful introduction in English about Pardo Bazán, her works, and bibliographical information that faculty members and students alike will find helpful. The sixteen stories in this volume are each preceded by brief English summaries of their primary themes.

The Cátedra editions of Pardo Bazán's novels include notes and introductory materials by some of the leading scholars of the author and her works. María de los Ángeles Ayala's editions of *Los pazos de Ulloa* (1997; "The House of Ulloa") and of *Memorias de un solterón* (2004; "Memoirs of a Confirmed Bachelor"), Ignacio Javier López's edition of *La madre naturaleza* (1999; "Mother Nature"), Ermitas Penas Varela's editions of *Morriña* (2007; "Homesickness") and of *Insolación* (2001), Marina Mayoral's edition of *La quimera* (1991; "The Chimera"), and Benito Varela Jácome's edition of *La Tribuna* (1975; "The Tribune") are all wonderful texts for the classroom. The 2006 Simancas editions of the novels *Una cristiana* ("A Christian Woman"), *El cisne de Vilamorta* ("The Swan of Vilamorta"), *La piedra angular* ("The Cornerstone"), and *La sirena negra* ("The Black Siren") are also worthy of note, as is Marisa Sotelo Vázquez's 2003 Alianza edition of *Un viaje de novios* ("A Wedding Trip"). Marina Mayoral's 1989 Castalia edition of *Dulce dueño* ("Sweet Master") remains definitive.

Although Pardo Bazán is best known for her novels and short stories, in the last two decades some valuable editions of her essays and plays have been published. In 2011 Íñigo Sánchez-Llama published *Obra crítica, 1888–1908* ("Critical Work, 1888–1908"), a collection of Pardo Bazán's essays, primarily those concerned with literary criticism and politics. The collection's extensive introduction offers insights into Pardo Bazán's stance on many literary and political topics, including the place of the Galician language within Spain's process of modernization, the author's role as a female intellectual, and her relation to the Generation of 1898, a group of writers and intellectuals who wrote extensively on Spain's national character during the turn of the century. Maria Luisa Pérez Bernardo recently published a most welcome edition of Pardo Bazán's essay collection *De siglo a siglo, 1896–1901* (2014; "From Century to Century"). Carlos Dorado's edition of the articles that Pardo Bazán published in her column La vida contemporánea in *La ilustración artística* is also an excellent resource (Pardo Bazán, *La vida*). For those interested in Pardo Bazán's feminist writings, we recommend Guadalupe Gómez-Ferrer's collection of several essays, *La mujer española y otros escritos* (1999; "The Women of Spain and Other Writings"). Tonina Paba's two volumes, *Viajes por España* ("Travels through Spain") and *Viajes por Europa* ("Travels through Europe"), include most of Pardo Bazán's travel writings and will undoubtedly invite scholars and students alike to study more closely this fascinating aspect of the author's journalistic production. Montserrat Ribao Pereira's edition of Pardo Bazán's plays, *Teatro completo* ("Complete Plays"), is a wonderful resource for instructors. Its introductory materials place Pardo Bazán's drama within the Spanish literary context of the time and give valuable insights into the primary themes that these works address.

Translations

Several translations are available for teaching Pardo Bazán's works in English. The first translations of many of the novels and novellas, by Mary Serrano, appeared in the late nineteenth century, including *A Wedding Trip* (*Un viaje de novios*) and *Homesickness* (*Morriña*) in 1891, *The Angular Stone* (*La piedra angular*) in 1892, and *A Galician Girl's Romance* (*Bucólica*) and *The Swan of Villamorta* (*El cisne de Vilamorta*) in 1900. Amparo Loring translated *Midsummer Madness* (*Insolación*) in 1907. Unfortunately, many of Serrano's translations are fairly liberal and don't do justice to Pardo Bazán's rich and sophisticated prose. Higher-quality translations of the novels are Walter Borenstein's *The Tribune of the People* (1999; *La Tribuna*) and *Mother Nature* (2010; *La madre naturaleza*). Lucía Graves and Paul O'Prey's 1990 translation of *The House of Ulloa* (*Los pazos de Ulloa*) has helped bring this foundational work to a wider audience. María Urruela's collection of translations of several of Pardo Bazán's short stories, "*Torn Lace*" *and Other Stories* (1996), is a fantastic volume for incorporating some of Pardo Bazán's rich short narratives into the classroom. Its introduction and notes, by Joyce Tolliver, make it valuable for instructors new to teaching Pardo Bazán.

Critical Resources

Two bibliographical studies cover the critical work focused on Pardo Bazán's oeuvre. The older is Robert M. Scari's 1982 *Bibliografía descriptiva de estudios críticos sobre la obra de Emilia Pardo Bazán* ("Descriptive Bibliography of Critical Studies of Emilia Pardo Bazán's Work"). A more recent study is José Manuel González Herrán's "Ediciones y estudios sobre la obra literaria de Emilia Pardo Bazán: Estado de la cuestión, 1921–2003" ("Editions and Studies on the Literary Work of Emilia Pardo Bazán: Current State of Criticism, 1921–2003").

Studies of Pardo Bazán's work range from those that attempt to encompass the author's entire oeuvre to approaches and interpretations limited to particular works or series of works. Originally published in French, Nelly Clémessy's two-volume *Emilia Pardo Bazán como novelista* (1982; "Emilia Pardo Bazán as a Novelist") is an important, extensive study of Pardo Bazán that offers instructors a wealth of detailed information on the author's life and work. Carmen Bravo-Villasante's *Emilia Pardo Bazán: Vida y obra* is also useful. More limited in scope is Walter Pattison's *Emilia Pardo Bazán* (1971).

Several collections of critical essays offer different viewpoints and approaches and also contain critical bibliographies. *Estudios sobre Emilia Pardo Bazán: In Memoriam Maurice Hemingway* (1997; "Studies on Emilia Pardo Bazán: In Memoriam Maurice Hemingway"), edited by José Manuel González Herrán, is a good starting point for instructors. Other options are *Estudios sobre la obra de Emilia Pardo Bazán: Actas de las jornadas conmemorativas de los 150 años de su nacimiento* (2003; "Studies of Emilia Pardo Bazán's Work: Proceedings of the Conference in Memory of the 150th Anniversary of Her Birth"), edited by Ana María Freire López, and the conference proceedings of the regular Pardo Bazán symposia published by the Real Academia Galega (González Herrán et al., *Actas del I Simposio*, *Actas del II Simposio*, *Actas del III Simposio*, and *Actas del IV Simposio*).

For many years Pardo Bazán was read and taught primarily for her literary naturalism, and several critical studies focus almost exclusively on this aspect of her corpus. These studies may still be helpful to instructors, though they are slightly dated. Pardo Bazán's naturalism is featured in Donald Fowler Brown's *The Catholic Naturalism of Pardo Bazán* (1957; 1971), in Fernando Barroso's *El naturalismo en la Pardo Bazán* (1973; "Naturalism in Pardo Bazán"), and in Mariano Baquero Goyanes's *La novela naturalista española: Emilia Pardo Bazán* (1986; "The Spanish Naturalist Novel: Emilia Pardo Bazán").

With *Emilia Pardo Bazán: The Making of a Novelist* (1983), Maurice Hemingway radically changed the field of Pardo Bazán studies by putting aside the notion that Pardo Bazán was foremost a naturalist. Hemingway's study examines the author's growth into maturity as a novelist and concentrates on four novels published between 1890 and 1896: *Una cristiana*, *La piedra angular*, *Doña Milagros*, and *Memorias de un solterón*. Francisca González Arias's *Portrait of a Woman as Artist: Emilia Pardo Bazán and the Modern Novel in France and Spain* (1992) traces Pardo Bazán's development as an intellectual and an artist by studying the intertextual relations between the author's novels and those of contemporary French and Spanish authors.

One of the earliest feminist approaches to Pardo Bazán's work is *El feminismo en la novela de la Condesa de Pardo Bazán* (1976; "Feminism in the Novels of the Countess of Pardo Bazán"), by Teresa Cook. Especially since the publication of Maryellen Bieder's 1993 article "Plotting Gender / Replotting the Reader: Strategies of Subversion in Stories by Pardo Bazán," many studies of the author's work have adopted a gender-based approach that is not exclusively focused on the novels. Adna Rosa Rodríguez, for instance, explores the feminist aspects of Pardo Bazán's essays in *La cuestión feminista en los ensayos de Emilia Pardo Bazán* (1991; "The Feminist Question in the Essays of Emilia Pardo Bazán").

In *Género, nación y literatura: Emilia Pardo Bazán en la literatura gallega y española* (2013; "Gender, Nation, and Literature: Emilia Pardo Bazán in Galician and Spanish Literature") Carmen Pereira-Muro studies Pardo Bazán's work in the context of competing Spanish and Galician nationalisms. Pereira-Muro argues that the author achieved her place in the Spanish national canon by manipulating a series of masculine cultural models (realism, prose, Castilian language). Pereira-Muro also attributes Pardo Bazán's thorny relation with emerging Galician naturalism to the author's transgressive gender performance as a woman writing in a man's world.

Pardo Bazán's short stories are classroom favorites and have received ample critical attention. Juan Paredes Núñez's *Los cuentos de Emilia Pardo Bazán*

(1979; "The Stories of Emilia Pardo Bazán") takes a traditional approach, arranging the stories in broad thematic categories, including psychological stories, stories that contain social criticism, stories on religious topics, patriotic stories, and feminist stories. Ángeles Quesada Novás's *El amor en los cuentos de Emilia Pardo Bazán* (2004; "Love in the Stories of Emilia Pardo Bazán") offers a detailed study of several groups of stories dealing with the theme of love. The 2006 issue of the journal *La Tribuna* is dedicated to Pardo Bazán's short fiction.

The recent resurgence of interest in the author's short fiction has resulted in a number of excellent critical studies that exemplify the successful combination of a feminist approach with contemporary narrative theory. Tolliver's *Cigar Smoke and Violet Water: Gendered Discourse in the Stories of Emilia Pardo Bazán* (1998) analyzes several of Pardo Bazán's short stories, exploring narrative voices and the role gender plays both in narrative dynamics and in the writer's engagement with her public. Tolliver probes deeply to question artificial categories and dismantle binary cultural constructions. Susan Walter's *From the Outside Looking In: Narrative Frames and Narrative Spaces in the Short Stories of Emilia Pardo Bazán* (2010) argues that Pardo Bazán used structural framing devices to create competing dialogues between narrators, call into question dominant social norms, and engage the reader in the process of interpretation. In *Crafting the Female Subject: Narrative Innovation in the Short Fiction of Emilia Pardo Bazán* (2009), Susan M. McKenna also examines Pardo Bazán's narrative techniques, analyzing four distinct literary devices that Pardo Bazán uses to disrupt narrative form and to explore nascent female sexuality.

Other critical studies focus on Pardo Bazán's nonfictional production. In *Poética de la novela en la obra crítica de Emilia Pardo Bazán* (1998; "Poetics of the Novel in Emilia Pardo Bazán's Critical Work"), Cristina Patiño Eirín analyzes the stylistics of Pardo Bazán's criticism. Eduardo Ruiz-Ocaña Dueñas's *La obra periodística de Emilia Pardo Bazán en* La ilustración artística *de Barcelona (1895–1916)* (2004; "The Journalistic Work of Emilia Pardo Bazán in *The Artistic Illustration* of Barcelona [1895–1916]") offers an excellent overview of Pardo Bazán's contributions to *La ilustración artística* and is helpful for instructors who wish to teach some of the author's journalism. Rocío Charques Gámez's *Emilia Pardo Bazán y su* Nuevo teatro crítico (2012; "Emilia Pardo Bazán and Her *New Critical Theater*") is an inventory of *Nuevo teatro crítico*, a cultural magazine that Pardo Bazán published from 1891 to 1893. The 2007 issue of the journal *La Tribuna* focuses entirely on her journalism.

Intellectual and Critical Contexts

There is a plenitude of material for contextualizing Pardo Bazán's literary, historical, and social environment, ranging from general studies about nineteenth- and early-twentieth-century history and culture to more specific social and scientific studies. A good overview of Spanish literature is *Historia de la literatura española:*

Siglo XIX (II) (1995; "History of Spanish Literature: The Nineteenth Century [II]"), coordinated by Leonardo Romero Tobar. For the history of Spain, we recommend José Álvarez Junco's *Mater dolorosa* (2001; "Our Lady of Sorrows") and Adrian Shubert and Álvarez Junco's *Spanish History since 1808* (2000). Instructors who aim to place Pardo Bazán's production in the context of imperial loss may find useful Sebastian Balfour's *The End of the Spanish Empire, 1898–1923* (1997) and Christopher Schmidt-Nowara's *The Conquest of History* (2006). Alda Blanco's *Cultura y conciencia imperial en la España del siglo XIX* (2012; "Culture and Imperial Conscience in Nineteenth-Century Spain") also offers important insights.

For Spanish cultural history, *1900 en España* (1991; "1900 in Spain"), edited by Serge Salaün and Carlos Serrano (originally published in French), collects many interesting essays on Spanish fin de siècle culture. *Spanish Cultural Studies: An Introduction* (1995), edited by Helen Graham and Jo Labanyi, and *The Cambridge Companion to Modern Spanish Culture* (1999), edited by David Gies, are excellent resources for cultural history. Instructors interested in discussions of race in Pardo Bazán's time may consult Joshua Goode's *Impurity of Blood: Defining Race in Spain (1870–1930)* (2009), while those interested in the impact of Darwinism on Spanish literature may wish to read Travis Landry's *Subversive Seduction: Darwin, Sexual Selection, and the Spanish Novel* (2012). *Intersections of Race, Class, Gender, and Nation in Fin-de-siècle Spanish Literature and Culture* (2017), edited by Jennifer Smith and Lisa Nalbone, contains several essays on Pardo Bazán, while *Modernity and Epistemology in Nineteenth-Century Spain: Fringe Discourses* (2016), edited by Ryan A. Davis and Alicia Cerezo, offers a welcome introduction to the epistemological richness of the nineteenth century. Instructors who would like to teach Pardo Bazán's work in combination with visual culture could consult *The Nineteenth-Century Visual Culture Reader*, edited by Vanessa Schwartz and Jeannene Przyblyski (2003), for an introduction to different aspects of this field. The essays in the volume *Visualizing Spanish Modernity* (2005), edited by Susan Larson and Eva Woods, deal specifically with visual culture in the Spanish context. *Fictions of the Feminine in the Nineteenth-Century Spanish Press* (1999), by Lou Charnon-Deutsch, introduces readers to representations of women in the press, while her more recent title, *Hold That Pose: Visual Culture in the Late-Nineteenth-Century Spanish Periodical* (2008), explores both the ideological impact and technological developments in images published in Spanish magazines during the Restoration period.

La mujer en los discursos de género: Textos y contextos en el siglo XIX (1998; "Women in Gender Discourses: Text and Contexts in the Nineteenth Century"), edited by Catherine Jagoe et al., is indispensable for any instructor who wants to teach Pardo Bazán through the lens of gender. The nineteenth-century primary sources included in the volume make it easy to elucidate for students the medical, legal, and educational contexts, with respect to gender, of Pardo Bazán's culture. Denise DuPont's *Writing Teresa: The Saint from Ávila at the Fin-de-siglo* (2011) offers an in-depth study of five major Spanish figures (among them

Pardo Bazán) in the turn-of-the-century explosion of literary treatments of Saint Teresa. In *Gender and Modernity in Spanish Literature, 1789–1920* (2014), Elizabeth Smith Rousselle, juxtaposing texts by female and male Spanish authors, explores how gender influenced writers' representations of what it meant to be a modern subject. Noël Valis's *The Culture of* Cursilería: *Bad Taste, Kitsch, and Class in Modern Spain* (2003) discusses *cursilería* ("bad taste"), a frequent topic in Pardo Bazán's work. Dorota Heneghan's *Striking Their Modern Pose* (2016) explores the importance of fashion in the construction and representation of gender and society in nineteenth-century Spanish narrative. Jesús Cruz's *The Rise of Middle-Class Culture in Nineteenth-Century Spain* (2011) deals with the growing middle classes, and Leigh Mercer's *Urbanism and Urbanity: The Spanish Bourgeois Novel and Contemporary Customs, 1845–1925* (2012) discusses the social options open to members of Spain's bourgeoisie.

Electronic and Audiovisual Resources

Under the charge of Ana María Freire López, the part of the *Biblioteca Virtual Miguel de Cervantes* Web site dedicated to Emilia Pardo Bazán offers many valuable resources ("Emilia Pardo Bazán"). These resources are offered exclusively in Spanish and include biographical information, complete electronic texts of most of Pardo Bazán's novels, extensive bibliographical information on her writings in all genres, complete electronic texts of many critical studies of her work, and, finally, a unique resource, "Videoteca," that includes several dozen short video recordings in which various Spanish scholars explain important literary concepts as well as information related specifically to Pardo Bazán's life and works ("Videoteca").

The *Biblioteca Digital Ciudad Seva*, founded by Puerto Rican author Luis López Nieves, offers the complete texts of more than two hundred of Pardo Bazán's short stories (."Emilia Pardo Bazán: Cuentos"). *HathiTrust Digital Library*, a partnership of academic and research institutions, offers a large number of digitized, original editions of titles by Pardo Bazán, made available by libraries around the world. Electronic resources related to Pardo Bazán's writings can be accessed from the Web site *Biblioteca Digital Hispánica*. Visitors to the *Project Gutenberg* Web site can download novels by Pardo Bazán and English translations of her works ("Books"). Many nineteenth-century journals and magazines can be accessed at the Web site *Hemeroteca Digital*, a part of the *Biblioteca Digital Hispánica* project, hosted by the Biblioteca Nacional de España.

The Biblioteca Nacional (BNE) houses a large collection of photographs, drawings, and advertising posters that can be used in the classroom to provide visual context for Pardo Bazán's texts. The BNE's collection of nineteenth-century advertising posters is divided into categories: circus, theater, bullfighting, fairs, festivities and exhibitions, travel and transport, freight haulage, horse racing, publications, dances, politics, and miscellaneous posters.

Another wonderful source of visual material that can be used to contextualize Pardo Bazán's work is the Museo del Prado. Its online gallery offers access to approximately five thousand works from the nineteenth century in the museum's collection. The Web site will eventually contain the museum's complete collection.

There are two high-quality documentary films about the life and works of Pardo Bazán. *Vida y obra literaria de Emilia Pardo Bazán* (2006; "Life and Literary Work of Emilia Pardo Bazán"), directed by Ricardo Groizard Moreno and written by Ana María Freire López and Margarita Almela Boix, is forty minutes long. Galicia's Secretaria Xeral de Iguadade created a Galician-language pedagogical guide, "A escaleira desigual" ("The Uneven Staircase"), for the film *Emilia Pardo Bazán: La condesa rebelde* (2011; "Emilia Pardo Bazán: The Rebellious Countess"), directed by María Ignacia Ceballos (Castelao).

Several films have been adapted from Pardo Bazán's novels and short stories. The most notable is *Los pazos de Ulloa* (1984; "The House of Ulloa"), directed by Gonzalo Suárez. It is based primarily on the novel *Los pazos de Ulloa* but includes some material from *La madre naturaleza*, the sequel to *Los pazos*. The film is available through the archive of the *Radio y Televisión Española* (*RTVE*) Web site. José Luis Sáenz de Heredia's *El indulto* (1960; "The Pardon") is based on the short story of the same name. *La sirena negra* (1947; "The Black Siren") was directed by Carlos Serrano de Osma; Fernando Fernán Gómez plays a leading role. *Un viaje de novios* (1947; "A Wedding Trip"), based on the novel of the same name, was made under the direction of Gonzalo P. Delgrás, and *Opera en Marineda* ("Opera in Marineda"), directed by Pilar Miró in 1974, is an adaptation of the short story "Por el arte" ("For Art's Sake").

Organizations and Conferences

Real Academia Galega and Casa-Museo Emilia Pardo Bazán

Both the Real Academia Galega (RAG) and the Casa-Museo Emilia Pardo Bazán are housed in Pardo Bazán's former home on the Rúa Tabernas, in A Coruña's Old Town. The RAG holds Pardo Bazán's personal archive, which includes handwritten and typewritten manuscripts as well as photographs, and the books of the author's personal library. The RAG and the Casa-Museo edit an open-access journal that is dedicated exclusively to the study of her works, *La Tribuna: Cadernos de estudos da Casa Museo Emilia Pardo Bazán*. A walking tour of places and monuments in Marineda and A Coruña that are mentioned in Pardo Bazán's writings is available on request from the Casa-Museo, which is free and open to the public.

Galician Studies

As a conservative who wrote in Spanish, Pardo Bazán occupies a fraught space in nationalist-identified Galician studies. Pereira-Muro's *Género, nación y literatura* discusses Spanish and Galician nationalisms in Pardo Bazán's work. Since the author did not write in *gallego* (Galician), critical engagement with her from a Galician studies perspective has been sparse, resulting in awkward critical voids: the field of Hispanic studies has tended to overlook Galician links in her work, and Galician studies has deliberately avoided engaging with the author's work so as to not grant her a place in the national literary canon. Helena Miguélez-Carballeira's essay in this volume is an effort to fill some of these gaps. Instructors interested in Pardo Bazán's work in the Galician context could consult *Emilia Pardo Bazán: Novelista de Galicia* (1944; "Emilia Pardo Bazán: Novelist of Galicia"), by Emilio González López. Kirsty Hooper explores the history of literature written by Galician women in "Girl, Interrupted: The Distinctive History of Galician Women's Narrative" (2003).

Several interesting books and articles may be of interest to instructors who are able to read *gallego*, such as *A sociedade galega da Restauración na obra literaria de Pardo Bazán, 1875–1900* (1987; "Galician Restoration Society in the Literary Work of Pardo Bazán, 1875–1900"), by Carlos Velasco Souto; "Análise da literatura española feita por galegos: D\u00aa Emilia, como exemplo" (1985; "Analysis of Spanish Literature Written by Galicians: The Case of Doña Emilia"), by Francisco Rodríguez; and "Unha conferencia inédita de Emilia Pardo Bazán sobre os problemas de Galicia" (2003; "An Unpublished Talk by Emilia Pardo Bazán about Galicia's Issues"), by Euloxio R. Ruibal. Other articles examine the place of Pardo Bazán in the context of the nineteenth-century Galician *Rexurdimento* (regionalist movement), such as "E. Pardo Bazán y su imagen del 'Rexurdimento' cultural gallego en la *Revista de Galicia*" (2004; "E. Pardo Bazán and Her Opinion of Galician's Cultural 'Rexurdimento' in the *Revista de Galicia*"), by Xoan González-Millán. Martha LaFollette Miller reads Pardo Bazán alongside Rosalía de Castro in "Mythical Conceptualizations of Galicia in Murguía and Pardo Bazán, Aspects of Rosalian Context" (1988), and Kerry Ann McKevitt reads Pardo Bazán with Ramón del Valle-Inclán in "O espazo simbólico: Pardo Bazán, Valle-Inclán e os pazos galegos señoriais" (2006; "Symbolic Space: Pardo Bazán, Valle-Inclán and Galician Stately Palaces"). More resources on Galician studies are offered by the triannual conference of the Asociación Internacional de Estudos Galegos (AIEG) and in *Galicia 21: Journal of Contemporary Galician Studies*, which was founded in 2009.

Literary-Historical Time Line for Emilia Pardo Bazán

1851   Emilia Pardo Bazán is born on 16 September in A Coruña, Spain, to a bourgeois family.

1859–60   The Hispano-Moroccan War takes place.

1868   Pardo Bazán marries José Quiroga Pérez Pinal, a law student.

1868   A military pronouncement by Generals Prim and Serrano leads to the Glorious Revolution. Queen Isabel II is dethroned and exiled to France.

1869   Pardo Bazán's father, José Pardo Bazán, is named a representative of the Progressive Party in the Spanish *Cortes* (National Assembly). The family, including Emilia and her new husband, moves to Madrid.

1870   José Pardo Bazán is given a papal title by Pope Pius IX.

1870   General Prim is assassinated. The Italian prince Amadeo de Saboya (the second son of King Victor Emmanuel) is elected king of Spain.

1871   Pardo Bazán, along with her husband and parents, travels to France, Italy, and England, where she learns English.

1873   The first Spanish Republic is declared. King Amadeo de Saboya abdicates the throne.

1873–76   The third Carlist War takes place.

1874   The Spanish monarchy is restored under King Alfonso XII. The Restoration period begins.

1877   Pardo Bazán publishes her essay *Reflexiones científicas contra el darwinismo* ("Scientific Reflections against Darwinism"), in which she refutes Darwin's ideas.

1878   She publishes her first novel, *Pascual López: Autobiografía de un estudiante de medicina* ("Pascual López: Autobiography of a Medical Student").

1879   The Partido Socialista Obrero Español (PSOE; Spanish Socialist Party) is founded.

1881   Pardo Bazán publishes *Un viaje de novios.*

1882   She begins frequent visits to the tobacco factory of A Coruña, which she observes as part of her preparation to write the novel *La Tribuna.*

1882   Pardo Bazán publishes *La cuestión palpitante* ("The Burning Question"), a study and critique of French naturalism, as a series of articles in the journal *La época.*

1883   After *La cuestión palpitante* is criticized by some of her contemporaries for its supposedly immoral nature, Pardo Bazán becomes separated from her husband in part because he is uncomfortable with the attention that some of her polemical writings have brought her.

1883   She publishes *La Tribuna.*

1884   She founds the Society of Galician Folklore.

1885   King Alfonso XII dies and the regency of his wife, María Cristina of Austria, begins.

1886   On an extended trip to Paris, Pardo Bazán attends the Goncourt brothers' salon and meets other important authors, including Émile Zola and Joris-Karl Huysmans.

1886   She writes and publishes *Los pazos de Ulloa.*

1886   King Alfonso XIII is born.

1887   Pardo Bazán publishes *La madre naturaleza*, the sequel to *Los pazos de Ulloa*.

1887   She is sent to Rome as a travel correspondent for *El imparcial*, where she publishes articles on a Catholic pilgrimage that are later published as a book titled *Mi romería* (1888; "My Pilgrimage").

1887   Pardo Bazán gives a series of presentations on the Russian novel at the Ateneo de Madrid, which are published later that year as the book *La revolución y la novela en Rusia* ("The Revolution and the Novel in Russia").

1889   She publishes her novel *Insolación.*

1889   She publishes her article "The Women of Spain" in the *Fortnightly Review*. The Spanish version of this essay will be published in 1890 as "La mujer española."

1890   Pardo Bazán's father dies, which upsets her greatly because of their close bond and his unwavering support of her intellectual pursuits.

1891   Pardo Bazán founds the cultural magazine *Nuevo teatro crítico* (1891–93). During the almost three years of its publication, she is the sole author of all its articles and short stories.

1892   She publishes *Cuentos de Marineda* ("Stories of Marineda").

1892   She establishes the book series La biblioteca de la mujer to educate Spanish women about feminism.

1894   She publishes *Doña Milagros*, the first novel of her Adam and Eve series.

1895   Uprising in Cuba, a Spanish colony at the time.

1896   Pardo Bazán publishes the novel *Memorias de un solterón*, the second novel of her Adam and Eve series.

1896	Uprising in the Philippines, a Spanish colony at the time.
1898	Spain loses the short Spanish-American War. The Treaty of Paris gives the United States control over Spain's last three remaining colonies: the Philippines, Puerto Rico, and Cuba.
1898	Pardo Bazán publishes her popular short story collection *Cuentos de amor* ("Love Stories") and the monologue play *El vestido de boda* ("The Wedding Dress").
1900	She publishes *Un destripador de antaño y otros cuentos* ("'The Heart Lover' and Other Stories") and *Historias y cuentos de Galicia* ("Stories and Tales of Galicia").
1902	She publishes *Cuentos de la patria* ("Patriotic Stories") and a collection of travel essays, *Por la Europa católica* ("Through Catholic Europe").
1902	She publishes the essay collection *De siglo a siglo, 1896–1901* with essays about the events of 1898 and Spain's colonial losses.
1906	Pardo Bazán is elected president of the literature section of the Ateneo de Madrid.
1906	She premieres her plays *Verdad* ("Truth") and *Cuesta abajo* ("Downhill").
1908	Pardo Bazán is given the title of *condesa* (countess) by King Alfonso XIII. She publishes the novel *La sirena negra*.
1910	She publishes the three-volume *La literatura francesa moderna* ("Modern French Literature").
1911	She publishes *Dulce dueño*.
1913	As part of her book series, La biblioteca de la mujer, Pardo Bazán publishes her first cookbook, *La cocina española antigua* ("Traditional Spanish Cuisine").
1914	World War I begins.
1914/17	Pardo Bazán publishes *La cocina española moderna* ("Modern Spanish Cuisine").
1916	Pardo Bazán is named professor of Romance literature at the Central University of Madrid.
1918	She starts to publish essays in the Spanish newspaper *ABC*.
1921	Pardo Bazán dies on 12 May in Madrid.

Part Two

APPROACHES

Introduction

Emilia Pardo Bazán's determined engagement with the most urgent literary, cultural, and social debates of her time earned her a consecrated place as one of the three most prominent authors of nineteenth-century Spain, together with her male counterparts Benito Pérez Galdós and Leopoldo Alas (also known as Clarín). Pardo Bazán's role as a female writer in a literary culture that presented few opportunities for women makes her work fertile ground for gendered and other critical approaches. However, her nuanced narrative style, sophisticated vocabulary, and ideological incongruities make her texts sometimes difficult to negotiate in the classroom. This volume offers instructors tools to fully explore the rich depths of Pardo Bazán's diverse oeuvre.

Pardo Bazán actively engaged with most of the literary trends of her time and contributed critically to contemporary discourses on gender, nation, and empire. Her textual production spans a succession of literary movements ranging from realism to modernism, and she was instrumental in introducing Spanish literary circles to French naturalism and Russian spiritual realism through her fiction and her essays. Engagement with foreign models brought Pardo Bazán plenty of criticism. She was often dismissed because of her gender and labeled an imitator by her male compatriots who believed that an authentic, national literary tradition was a masculine one. In her work Pardo Bazán questions not only Spain's literary models but the discursive construction of the nation itself, in particular its gendered spaces and clearly defined roles for each sex. In a period marked by major colonial losses and a resurgence in regionalist cultural identities on the Peninsula, the author often addressed the Spanish nation's struggle to reorient and redefine itself. Although Pardo Bazán promoted the Galician folklore tradition and other regionalist activities, her attitude toward the emerging Galician independence movement was distant. A full understanding of her literary production must consider her conflicted affiliation with her native Galicia.

The diversity and sophistication of Pardo Bazán's oeuvre is the reason that it is so popular in universities today. *Los pazos de Ulloa* (1886; "The House of Ulloa") and its sequel, *La madre naturaleza* (1887; "Mother Nature"), continue to appear on graduate reading lists, mainly because of their adherence to naturalist tenets, but Pardo Bazán is no longer read and taught primarily for her literary naturalism. Focus has shifted to her lesser-known novels: *Insolación* (1889; "Sunstroke"), *Memorias de un solterón* (1896; "Memoirs of a Confirmed Bachelor"), and the modernist *Dulce dueño* (1911; "Sweet Master") underscore Pardo Bazán's importance as a prominent observer of her time who developed an energetic dialogue with her contemporaries. In the last decade, considerable attention has been paid to Pardo Bazán's short fiction and to her essays, such as "La mujer española" (1890; first published by Pardo Bazán in English in 1889 as "The Women of Spain") and *De siglo a siglo, 1896–1901* (1902; "From Century to Century, 1896–1901"), a collection of essays about Spain's colonies and imperial losses. These texts facilitate the teaching of a variety of literary and cultural themes, and the essays in this volume will guide instructors through the critical frameworks necessary to integrate Pardo Bazán's works into university curricula.

In European scholarship—in Spain, the United Kingdom, and France—as well as that of North America, Pardo Bazán's writings have generated an ever-increasing body of secondary literature—in Spanish, English, and other languages—that focuses on the complexity of her texts. While the variety and complexity of her writings make teaching them so rewarding, multiple theoretical and conceptual frameworks are often necessary to fully understand the works. It is surprising that, despite the author's popularity in the classroom and with literary critics, few scholarly articles have addressed the pedagogical rewards and challenges of teaching Pardo Bazán, whether in Spanish or in translation. With the exception of an article by María Isabel Borda Crespo, which proposes ways to introduce students to Pardo Bazán's modernist prose, the scholarly articles written from a pedagogical perspective all deal with Pardo Bazán's short stories: they are the most widely taught part of the author's oeuvre and receive ample attention in this volume. Bonnie Gasior, for example, discusses how emphasizing the sociohistorical phenomenon of commoditization of women in early-twentieth-century Galicia can give students a fuller understanding of the frequently anthologized story "Las medias rojas" ("The Red Stockings"). Ángeles Quesada Novás has proposed, from an intertextual and comparative point of view, that instructors present Pardo Bazán's short stories to undergraduate students in thematic pairs ("Los cuentos"). The effectiveness of this approach is highlighted in the interdisciplinary textbook *Intrigras: Advanced Spanish through Literature and Film*, whose authors suggestively juxtapose Pardo Bazán's short story "El revolver" ("The Revolver") with films and short stories by other authors (Courtad et al. 98–105). Linda Willem, in the introduction to her anthology of stories by Pardo Bazán, "*Náufragas*" *y otros cuentos* (2010; "'Castaways' and Other Stories"), focuses on ways of engaging students in close reading when discussing the nineteenth-century vocabulary in Pardo Bazán's short fiction.

This volume offers a variety of much-needed resources that will directly facilitate both instructor preparation and student learning. Survey respondents requested, above all, practical techniques that can be easily implemented in the classroom; many contributors share original, classroom-tested teaching tools. Erika M. Sutherland, who shares a list of online resources, describes a series of projects she created to help students develop a tool kit of critical references and digital resources for exploring the naturalist-medical discourse in *Un viaje de novios* ("A Wedding Trip"). Carmen Pereira-Muro, who proposes reading the modernist novel *Dulce dueño* in dialogue with other art forms, describes the exercises she uses to familiarize students with the paintings, music, performing arts, design, and architecture of the period. Linda Willem outlines a sequence of steps for teaching *Los pazos de Ulloa* and *La madre naturaleza* in conjunction with their adaptation for television. Zachary Erwin, who includes a syllabus, contends that Pardo Bazán's novels offer opportunities to introduce masculinity studies to students. Finally, Javier Torre presents Pardo Bazán's series of travel accounts as fascinating and almost unexplored teaching material and situates the author within a wider framework of travel narratives by both Spanish and foreign authors.

This volume is designed for experienced nineteenth-century specialists and for instructors with less experience teaching Hispanic literature or the nineteenth century. It provides accessible essays on a wide array of topics for educators who seek guidance on effective teaching strategies and on course topics and design. By exploring historical and critical issues and by clarifying Pardo Bazán's place within the cultural context of the nineteenth and early twentieth centuries, this volume will be an essential tool for instructors to effectively teach the literary production of one of the cornerstones of Hispanic literature.

Many of the essays will be useful to instructors teaching Pardo Bazán in Spanish or English. Several essays, including those by Denise DuPont and Susan M. McKenna, address the intersections between Pardo Bazán's literary production and that of her English-speaking contemporaries and therefore will be especially useful for teaching Pardo Bazán in world literature and interdisciplinary courses. Similarly, Jennifer Smith's essay, on translating Pardo Bazán with students, underscores the many pedagogical opportunities associated with literary translation. Pardo Bazán's works engage with many themes that are currently in vogue in the academy—such as the construction of space and questions of gender, nation, and empire—and hence there are countless ways to incorporate her writings into a comparative literature curriculum.

The Conceptual Frame of This Volume

Pardo Bazán situated herself within the realist tradition practiced by male novelists. She was part of an educated minority—the Generation of 1868, named after the 1868 revolution that dethroned the Bourbon monarchs—that sought to create a cultural nationalism to compensate for the Spanish state's lackluster nationalizing policies. In an effort to create an imagined national community, the writers of the Generation of 1868 used Spanish history (albeit selectively), drafted representations of the country's present and past, and offered their readership a series of stories and values with which they could identify.

Although Pardo Bazán was an ardent defender of the realist novel, she struggled to negotiate the masculine perspective from which these texts envision the ideal Spanish nation. The realist novel presented a supposedly natural division of private and public spheres and confined middle-class women to the home, despite the post-Enlightenment liberal doctrine of human rights. Nineteenth-century medical experts considered women to be radically different from men because women's reproductive organs defined them entirely. As so-called angels of the house, women had no place in the public sphere, which served as a civic forum for the modern nation. While immersing herself in the nationalist mission of her literary cohort, Pardo Bazán advocated relentlessly for the inclusion of women in Spanish public life, arguing that Spain could not truly modernize if half its population was excluded from contributing to the nation's progress.

The Krausists—followers of the German philosopher Karl Christian Friedrich Krause (1781–1832), a disciple of Hegel's, whose ideas were introduced to Spain by Julián Sanz del Río (1814–69), an academic based in Madrid—supported secular reform and women's education through the creation of two entities, the Escuela de Institutrices (1869) and the Asociación para la Enseñanza de la Mujer (1870). The Krausists championed individual freedom, which they saw as a key to modernizing traditional Spanish society, in contrast to the corrupting influences of church and state. Pardo Bazán, who considered the Krausists a men's club from which she was excluded (DuPont, *Writing* 99), set an example for women's intellectual advancement in Spain by participating actively in the literary circles of her time. Her intellectual openness, extensive (autodidactic) study of literature and the arts, and travels abroad made her a key connection in national and international literary networks. As one of the principal critical voices of her time, she addressed Spain's regeneration after its loss of empire and was instrumental in the promotion of literary modernism and decadentism. Yet despite her entry into the almost exclusively male literary canon, her gender led her contemporaries to diminish the value of her writings by construing them as excessive both in volume of production and in foreign influences.

Pardo Bazán was a declared nationalist but also played a role in the regionalist movement of her native Galicia. She was president of the Society for Galician Folklore, which she founded, wrote articles on Galician literature and culture, and represented the region and its people in her novels. However, because she transgressed gender roles by pursuing literary achievements on the national level, Pardo Bazán was excluded from the Galician literary canon. According to the fathers of Galician nationalism, Pardo Bazán's writing lacked the feminine, emotive, and lyrical characteristics that they found exemplary in her literary predecessor, the Galician poet Rosalía de Castro.

Pardo Bazán considered issues of cultural nationalism inseparable from those of gender. In a 1915 interview she presented herself as a radical feminist and considered women the key to Spain's regeneration: "España se explica por la situación de sus mujeres, por el sarracenismo de sus hombres" ("Spain is explained by the status of its women and by Spanish men behaving like Arabs"; "Conversación").[1] The author, as a women's rights advocate, focuses on patriarchal conditions of subjugation, the sexual double standard, the effects of inadequate education for women, domestic violence, and the struggle for social equality between men and women. Her discussions of gender roles explore issues of masculinity as well. Her work marks an important contribution to the development of Spanish feminist thought, going far beyond the defense of her own individual right to work in the public sphere as a writer and intellectual.

The apparent incompatibility between Pardo Bazán's adoption of the dominant discourses of her time and her feminism is one reason for her appeal to
instructors and students alike. Other incompatibilities in her writings are just
as striking. Her conscious choice to stand apart from the community of female
authors seems inconsistent with her staunch feminism. In reference to her isolation from this group and her lack of popularity among Spanish women in general, the author notes, "[T]engo la evidencia de que si se hiciese un plebiscito
para decidir ahorcarme o no, la mayoría de las mujeres españolas votarían que
sí!" ("I have evidence that if a vote were taken to decide whether or not to hang
me the majority of Spanish women would vote yes!"; Bravo-Villasante 287).
Pardo Bazán was a Catholic naturalist who defended the concept of free will, in
contrast to Émile Zola, who adhered to pure determinism. She had progressive
ideas about women yet was politically conservative. She participated in nationalist and imperialist projects while regularly neglecting the importance of class
and race in her otherwise "radically revisionary imagined landscapes" (Hooper,
Stranger 20). These and other apparent incongruities that make the author's
work both attractive and challenging are the focus of this volume.

Theoretical Approaches

Pardo Bazán's oeuvre is remarkably broad, and the various geographic and historical contexts in which her texts have been received and presented are also notable. A search for Pardo Bazán's name in the *MLA International Bibliography*
yields, at the time of this writing, no fewer than 857 titles; only the most important scholarly contributions will be highlighted here. For an overview of studies
published until 2003, primarily those by European critics, one can consult José
Manuel González Herrán's essay "Ediciones y estudios sobre la obra literaria de
Emilia Pardo Bazán: Estado de la cuestión, 1921–2003" ("Editions and Studies
on the Literary Work of Emilia Pardo Bazán: The Current State of Criticism,
1921–2003") González Herrán demonstrates that the approaches to Pardo Bazán's work in Spain and France and earlier in the Anglo-American academy are
distinct from the cultural studies and gendered analyses that have become the
mainstay of Anglo-American criticism during the last twenty-five years.

Pardo Bazán's acceptance into the literary canon was often complicated by her
gender. Julio Cejador y Frauca, for instance, bluntly wrote in 1918 that it was
without a doubt that "Valera, Palacio Valdés y Blasco Ibáñez ganan a la Pardo
Bazán y que ni comparación admite con Galdós y Pereda" ("Valera, Palacio
Valdés, and Blasco Ibáñez surpass Pardo Bazán, and there is no comparison between her and Galdós and Pereda"; 283). As recently as 1993 Hazel Gold, in
The Reframing of Realism, wrote that modern readers still prefer "Galdós and
Clarín over Pereda, Pardo Bazán, and Valera" (185). The first studies to dedicate serious attention to Pardo Bazán's work from a feminist perspective, those
by Mary E. Giles and Teresa A. Cook in the 1970s and 1980s, came from the

Anglo-American academy; these were followed by many others in the subsequent three decades. In Spain, research groups created by the university professors José Manuel González Herrán, Ermitas Penas Varela, Cristina Patiño Eirín, Ana María Freire López, Marisa Sotelo Vázquez, and others have resulted in an important revival in Pardo Bazán studies. Based on original archival research, their rich philological studies tend to focus on close readings of Pardo Bazán's works; uncover unedited or undiscovered texts, journalism, and correspondence; and highlight relationships between Pardo Bazán and her contemporaries.

In this volume we present a variety of frameworks through which Pardo Bazán's works can be explored. We will categorize the scholarship on Pardo Bazán as pertaining to four major, overlapping critical fields: realism, naturalism, and literary connections; gender studies approaches; nation, empire, and geopolitics; and interdisciplinary approaches.

Realism, Naturalism, and Literary Connections

Maurice Hemingway, in *Emilia Pardo Bazán: The Making of a Novelist*, suggests that Pardo Bazán engages with many aspects of literary realism in her works while also mocking some of its tenets, such as its pretensions of documentary-style precision when describing social milieu (160). For many years Pardo Bazán was read and taught primarily for her literary naturalism, and generations of scholars focused almost exclusively on this aspect of her fiction. The strong link between Pardo Bazán and naturalism is due to her description and critique of the theories of the French naturalistic writer Émile Zola in her 1882–83 collection of essays, *La cuestión palpitante* ("The Burning Question"), which caused a scandal at the time of publication and even led to the writer's separation from her husband. Naturalist criticism of Pardo Bazán's oeuvre centers mainly on her two novels that engage most directly with this literary movement, *Los pazos de Ulloa* and *La madre naturaleza*. A handful of stories commonly anthologized, such as "Las medias rojas," are also frequently offered as examples of the author's naturalism.

Pardo Bazán's engagement with literary naturalism was much debated in the mid-twentieth century, starting with Baquero Goyanes's *La novela naturalista española* ("The Spanish Naturalist Novel"). Fernando Barroso, in *El naturalismo en la Pardo Bazán* ("Naturalism in Pardo Bazán"), foregrounded Pardo Bazán's rejection of the strict determinism inherent in the French school's engagement with naturalism (172). Likewise, in their recent study, *Au natural: (Re)reading Hispanic Naturalism*, J. P. Spicer-Escalante and Lara Anderson note that Spanish naturalism is "initially influenced, but not enslaved, by the tenets of French naturalism, led by Émile Zola" (8). Indeed, Pardo Bazán rejected graphic portrayals of society's ills as well as determinism, hallmarks of the French school. Critics have analyzed her unique brand of Catholic naturalism, which lessens the importance of external factors on the fates of her characters while developing their psychological complexity and preserving their free will. Hemingway assigns *Los pazos de Ulloa* a pivotal place in Pardo Bazán's oeuvre because the author shifts from experimentations with naturalism to a heightened focus on human psychology and more nuanced narrative techniques (*Emilia* 160). Nelly Clémessy's monumental two-volume study, *Emilia Pardo Bazán como novelista* ("Emilia Pardo Bazán as a Novelist"), also treats Pardo Bazán's literary naturalism. Clémessy believes that it was not the content of *La cuestión palpitante* that made the work so polemical but rather three important aspects of its publication: that it was serialized, that it appeared in a popular journal, and that it was written by a woman (1: 97–98). More recently, Jo Labanyi attributed the vehement criticism directed at *La cuestión palpitante* to the way the essay underscored "the uncomfortable fact that the Spanish realist novel was dependent on foreign models" (*Gender* 12). Pardo Bazán herself often deplores the influence of foreign fashions in her novels and journalism but never argues outright that Spanish literature should reject foreign models. In *Los pazos de Ulloa* and in several short stories, for instance, she incorporates conventions of the gothic tradition, which was imported from England (Labanyi, "Relocating" 181). Finally, a recent work that contributes to our understanding of her naturalism is Travis Landry's *Subversive Seduction*, which investigates the intersections between Darwinian sexual selection and the marriage plots of nineteenth-century realist novels, including *Doña Milagros* and *Memorias de un solterón*.

Scholars have explored Pardo Bazán's other literary connections as well. Denise DuPont ("Decadence") has looked at the author's periodic antagonism with other authors, such as Miguel de Unamuno and Leopoldo Alas (Clarín), and at her engagement with Saint Teresa of Ávila (*Writing*). Maryellen Bieder has studied the tensions and ambivalence that Pardo Bazán provoked in other Spanish literary women in the early decades of her career ("Emilia Pardo Bazán and Literary Women"). In addition, Íñigo Sánchez-Llama, in the extensive introduction to his 2010 edition of Pardo Bazán's critical writings, discusses her contemporaries' critical assessments of her works (Pardo Bazán, *Obra crítica* 9–139).

Gender Studies Approaches

In analyzing the work of Pardo Bazán through the prism of gender, critics have produced a remarkable number of engaging, thought-provoking studies that employ various theoretical models and include Lacanian analyses, detailed narratological readings, and gendered cultural studies. Teresa A. Cook's *El feminismo en las novelas de la Condesa de Pardo Bazán* ("Feminism in the Novels of the Countess of Pardo Bazán") was the first book-length study to offer feminist readings of many of Pardo Bazán's novels. Other important contributions to our understanding of the nuanced representations of gender in Pardo Bazán's novels are Bieder's "Between Genre and Gender: Emilia Pardo Bazán and *Los pazos de Ulloa*"; *Narratives of Desire*, by Lou Charnon-Deutsch; and "Confession and the Body in Emilia Pardo Bazán's *Insolación*," in which Noël Valis asserts,

"In *Insolación*, what is confessed to is not, in reality, sin but the body itself" (256). Likewise, the last two decades have seen many pages devoted to gendered readings of Pardo Bazán's short fiction. Bieder led the entry into this field with a 1993 essay that employs feminist narratological approaches to reveal "the contestatory nature of these texts and how they reposition the reader against conventional patterns" ("Plotting" 138). Joyce Tolliver's 1998 monograph *Cigar Smoke and Violet Water* follows some of these same lines of inquiry and ultimately asserts that Pardo Bazán's stories "become the site of tension between 'masculine' and 'feminine' discourse—between 'violet water' and 'cigar smoke,' if you will—a tension that is essential to the narrative complexity of these texts" (36). Following Tolliver's and Bieder's leads, Susan M. McKenna's monograph *Crafting the Female Subject* and Susan Walter's study *From the Outside Looking In* offer significant insights into narrative structure and gender in Pardo Bazán's short fiction. Recent studies by Erwin, Tolliver ("Framing"), Harpring, Tsuchiya ("Género"; *Marginal Subjects*), and others follow a current trend of examining representations of masculinity in Pardo Bazán's novels, journalism, and short fiction. The analysis of *Dulce dueño* in Eilene Jamie Powell's recent dissertation that looks at sadomasochism in Spanish novels forges new ground. The newest trend in gendered approaches to Pardo Bazán's work is ecofeminism, which underscores the ways in which patriarchal society has marginalized and subjugated both women and nature and posits a revised, more holistic worldview that gives a higher regard to both.

Nation, Empire, and Geopolitics

A burgeoning new area of focus in cultural studies approaches to Pardo Bazán analyzes how her representations of gender intersect with her connections to Galician and Spanish literatures and their links to national identity. In her monograph *Género, nación y literatura: Emilia Pardo Bazán en la literatura gallega y española* ("Gender, Nation, and Literature: Emilia Pardo Bazán in Galician and Spanish Literature"), Pereira-Muro suggests that Pardo Bazán's adoption of masculine cultural models helped the author gain acceptance into the Spanish realist canon. Pardo Bazán had a rather tense relationship with Galicia's national poet, Rosalía de Castro, and with Castro's husband, Manuel Murguía, a leading proponent of Galician nationalism. Pardo Bazán wrote prose instead of poetry and chose realism instead of Romanticism (Romanticism was associated with the *literatas* [female writers of sentimental fiction] of her generation). Educated as a member of the privileged elite, Pardo Bazán did not know the Galician language well enough to write in it (in this regard, Rosalía de Castro was an exception), yet the Galician settings of several of her novels offer "unexpected alternatives to the monolithically masculine Castile-focused version of Spanish culture" that informed the production of her male contemporaries (Hooper, *Stranger* 22). Joseba Gabilondo proposes a postnationalist feminist approach that "requires that, rather than enforce a nationalist understanding of literary history, we problematize this very concept in order to reveal the different geopolitical and bio-political articulations that nationalism disavows in order to uphold its hegemony" ("Towards" 266). Looking at how imperialism and gender intersect in Pardo Bazán's works, Tolliver also has made significant contributions to this field of inquiry ("Over"; "Framing"), and Margot Versteeg's forthcoming work looks into the connection between Pardo Bazán's drama and notions of nation-building and imperial loss (*Propuestas*).

Interdisciplinary Approaches

Interdisciplinary approaches to Pardo Bazán's works have opened new critical avenues. Recently, the author's cookbooks, travel narratives, drama, and journalism have received greater attention than before. One of the first important interdisciplinary studies is Labanyi's *Gender and Modernization in the Spanish Realist Novel*, which employs histories of urban planning, medicine, social thought, finance, economics, and fashion to reexamine the representations of public and private spheres in realist novels, including *Los pazos de Ulloa* and *La madre naturaleza*. In her study of Spanish culinary texts and their relation to nation building, Lara Anderson notes the tensions between French culinary models and an autochthonous Spanish cuisine and concludes that "Pardo Bazán's construct of a refined modern cuisine for Spain was related not only to cuisine but also to contemporary discourse on national difference, which greatly concerned intellectuals who were aware of Spain's need to integrate into Europe as a modern nation state" (149). In her 2013 monograph *Urbanism and Urbanity* Leigh Mercer lucidly examines representations of space and behavior in *La Tribuna* and *La sirena negra*, along with several other Spanish novels of the nineteenth and early twentieth centuries, to show how these novels "explored how specific people formulated a class through spatial territorialization and practices of inclusion and exclusion" (4).

The Structure of This Volume

The essays in this volume are clustered around five topics: "Gendered Perspectives," "Science and Medicine," "Nature, Empire, and Geopolitics," "Realism, Naturalism, and Literary Connections," and "Interdisciplinary Approaches." The essays offer a broad range of fresh and original suggestions for familiarizing students with different aspects of Pardo Bazán's extensive oeuvre. Because of the challenge of introducing students to the sociohistorical and cultural contexts that influence literature, survey respondents almost unanimously expressed a need for resources for teaching students the circumstances surrounding the production of Pardo Bazán's texts. Likewise, respondents noted that they often find it challenging to fully explain the author's complex body of work. The essays are therefore intended to offer detailed information and suggestions for further reading regarding Pardo Bazán's place in the cultural milieu of the late nineteenth and early twentieth centuries. They also aim to identify aspects of the author's work that can seem to be in conflict with other aspects, such as Catholicism versus naturalism and her progressiveness on gender versus her myopia on issues of class and race. The survey results point to a critical pluralism in the pedagogical approaches to the author's oeuvre. The essays address this pluralism by showing the various theoretical and interpretive lenses through which Pardo Bazán's work can be understood.

A rich array of themes is addressed in "Gendered Perspectives," such as Bieder's essay on Pardo Bazán's place in the women's intellectual circles of her time, both in Spain and abroad, and Lisa Nalbone's on the status of Spanish women at the turn of the century, specifically the paradigm of the angel of the house. Isabel Clúa shows instructors who are not specialists in gender studies how reading Pardo Bazán's work from a gendered perspective can be a useful mode of interpretation, and Erwin demonstrates that the author's novels are ideal for introducing students to masculinity studies.

"Science and Medicine" contains essays that shed light on the author's often conflicted treatment of modern science (Dale J. Pratt), her involvement with contemporary medicine (Sutherland), and her often inconsistent stance on race (Charnon-Deutsch). Pratt, who portrays Pardo Bazán as an avid follower of developments in technology, builds a framework for analyzing this compelling aspect of her work. Charnon-Deutsch explores what race means to Spain's most polemical woman writer, and Sutherland offers a project-based approach to the medical discourse in *Un viaje de novios*.

The essays in "Nation, Empire, and Geopolitics" offer guidance for teaching Pardo Bazán's work within transatlantic, global, and geopolitical frameworks. Helena Miguélez-Carballeira explores Pardo Bazán's texts from a postcolonial and transatlantic perspective, while Tolliver analyzes an aspect of the author's work that has gone largely unexplored: the role she played in the development of an ideology of Spanish colonialism. Rebecca Ingram's essay presents ways to foster classroom discussions of national identity through teaching Pardo Bazán's cookbooks, and Francisca González Arias offers ideas for approaching the author's conflicted relation with her native Galicia.

"Realism, Naturalism, and Literary Connections" groups essays that explore the dynamics of realism as a historically and culturally bound system of writing (Hazel Gold) and situate Pardo Bazán within the intellectual circles of her time, both national and foreign and as an author and a critic (Sánchez-Llama; DuPont; McKenna). DuPont's essay approaches the question of what Spanish literature is as it relates to Pardo Bazán and also examines the role of literature written in the other Peninsular languages with respect to Spanish identity. Harriet Turner productively reads Pardo Bazán's short stories alongside her journalism, while Versteeg shows the rich possibilities that Pardo Bazán's drama open up in the classroom.

The essays in the last section, "Interdisciplinary Approaches," offer effective teaching strategies designed to aid students' understanding of Pardo Bazán's texts in relation to visual culture (Alicia Cerezo), spatial theory (María

Luisa Guardiola and Susan Walter), the arts (Pereira-Muro), film (Willem), and travel writing (Torre). Smith discusses the benefits of teaching Pardo Bazán in translation.

Translations and Linguistic Considerations

The challenge of teaching Pardo Bazán is often exacerbated by the linguistic difficulties faced by nonnative speakers of Spanish. The author's choice in some novels to transcribe phonetically the speech of certain characters—to emphasize their particular dialects as a marker of regional origin or of social class—can be difficult for native and nonnative speakers alike. From a linguistic standpoint, Pardo Bazán's short fiction is more accessible. Because of their brevity and refined use of narratology, the author's short stories are ideal for courses that offer an introduction to literary analysis and in nineteenth-century literature courses for undergraduate students of Spanish. The short stories also work well in nineteenth-century European or world literature courses and in any number of interdisciplinary courses. Pardo Bazán's most accessible novels, such as *Memorias de un solterón* and *Insolación*, could very well be taught to undergraduate students at the intermediate-advanced level, while the most advanced students and graduate students will enjoy the more complex works, such as *Los pazos de Ulloa*, *La madre naturaleza*, and *Dulce dueño*. Because of their narrative complexity, most of Pardo Bazán's texts allow for readings against the grain, which make close literary analysis exciting and rewarding. Essays by McKenna, Turner, Cerezo, and González Arias offer fresh suggestions for approaching the author's stories. Essays by Ingram, Torre, and Versteeg encourage instructors to explore some lesser-known dimensions of Pardo Bazán's work, such as her cookbooks, travel narratives, and plays.

This volume highlights how instructors can take advantage of teaching Pardo Bazán in translation, which requires placing her work in a new linguistic and cultural context. Her fiction has generated a considerable number of English translations: nine titles were translated shortly after their publication in Spanish and five new translations have been published in the last two decades. Instructors teaching *The House of Ulloa* can choose between no fewer than three English texts. For instructors teaching Pardo Bazán in English, the selection of an appropriate translation will depend on the purpose of the course and on their sense of the students' needs. The selection, however, is not without consequences. We understand translation as an interpretive act; translators make choices that may diverge from those of other translators, and the resulting translated texts can reveal certain criteria through their linguistic choices as well as in their textual apparatuses. Smith's essay takes a practical approach to translation, showing how instructors can use translations to emphasize linguistic, literary, and cultural issues that influence a translator's interpretive choices and discussing how the reception of a work can vary from one historical period to another.

Sequence of Reading

While this volume is divided into five primary themes, there are other ways in which the various topics covered in the volume can be clustered, based on theoretical approaches, genre, particular novels, or types of courses. The interpretive intersections among various essays in the volume will help readers address the challenging complexities in Pardo Bazán's writings. Many survey respondents noted a need for guidance on approaching the many intellectual and cultural strands entwined in Pardo Bazán's oeuvre.

Instructors interested in Pardo Bazán and gender should first read the essay by Clúa, which offers an overview of gendered approaches to the author's works. Tolliver and González Arias explore how the author's ideas on gender intersect with her vision of Spanish and Galician identities. Nalbone, Ingram, Cerezo, and Erwin discuss the differences between the author's often progressive ideas about gender and her more traditional stance on topics related to class and other social hierarchies. Charnon-Deutsch, Pratt, Erwin, and Sutherland address Pardo Bazán's signature brand of Catholic naturalism and shed light on the author's treatment of thorny issues in science, medicine, and race. Instructors interested in empire, Galician studies, and postcolonial approaches could consult Miguélez-Carballeira, González Arias, and Tolliver.

McKenna, Turner, Cerezo, Gold, Nalbone, Pratt, and González Arias offer original insights on teaching Pardo Bazán's short stories, often in conjunction with journalism or visual culture. Suggestions for teaching another favorite in the undergraduate classroom, the short novel *Insolación*, are provided by González Arias and by Smith. Guardiola and Walter, Gold, and Miguélez-Carballeira offer ideas for teaching *La Tribuna*. Instructors who are looking for a fresh take on *Los pazos de Ulloa* and *La madre naturaleza* will be aided by the essays by Willem and by Erwin.

For instructors teaching Pardo Bazán's essays, the essays by Charnon-Deutsch, Tolliver, Nalbone, DuPont, and Sánchez-Llama are key. Essays by Torre, Bieder, Ingram, and Versteeg are essential on Pardo Bazán's lesser-known works, offering insights into her travel writing, correspondence, cookbooks, and plays, respectively. Many instructors will also benefit from Pereira-Muro's essay on the complex modernist novel *Dulce dueño*.

Instructors teaching Pardo Bazán in a world literature classroom should read the essays by DuPont, McKenna, and Bieder. These contributors place the author within the wider, international literary community by focusing on Pardo Bazán's essays that analyze literary movements outside Spain and by exploring foreign authors' influences on her work. Smith's essay will be of particular interest to instructors who teach Pardo Bazán in translation.

NOTE

[1] All translations are by the authors.

Pardo Bazán:
Family, Feminism, and Friendships

Maryellen Bieder

It would probably strike students today as odd if a literature or culture course did not include at least one woman author on the syllabus. In the 1960s, Emilia Pardo Bazán's *Los pazos de Ulloa* (1886; "The House of Ulloa") was the only novel by a modern Spanish woman author that was firmly entrenched in the literary canon. While the career trajectories and public activities of male authors generated respect, women's private lives inspired only limited interest. The prevailing New Criticism model of reading rejected the author's biography, giving close scrutiny instead to the work's structural and linguistic features. By the 1970s the feminist revolution in literary criticism had brought genealogical and archaeological approaches to texts by women, as women critics recovered overlooked or undervalued women authors and tracked the history of women's writing across the centuries in each literary culture. The criterion that a female author's work must exhibit equal value to that of a male author evaporated, leaving the opportunity to study women's writings regardless of their audience, market success, or the degree of recognition they had previously received. Feminist criticism made the entire span of Pardo Bazán's cultural production—novels, essays, short stories, and drama—its subject of inquiry and also explored the author's forays into male spheres of cultural activity and her attainment of intellectual prestige. Lou Charnon-Deutsch's landmark *Narratives of Desire: Nineteenth-Century Spanish Fiction by Women* (1994), which situates Pardo Bazán's fiction alongside that of other women authors, contributed to the miniboom in Pardo Bazán studies.

At the same time, feminist readings looked beyond the text to the circumstances of the life of the woman author, the way she dealt with obstacles, and how she created opportunities and opened a space for herself in the male world of publication and intellectual exchange. The women characters in Pardo Bazán's fiction, previously relegated to the background of literary study, now received serious attention. The construction of gender, first female and later male, gained ground as the focus of analysis, as subsequently did the construction of sexuality and the interface of sexuality and gender. Critics no longer treated gender as a given but as a process requiring scrutiny in each work to lay bare the author's underlying assumptions. With *Fictions of the Feminine in the Nineteenth-Century Spanish Press* (2000), Charnon-Deutsch introduced popular culture into feminist criticism by studying mass-produced representations of the female body. Since genealogical feminism brought biography to the fore, a woman author's performance of gender and sexuality led not only to a consideration of her relationships with men but likewise her friendships or tensions with other women. Meanwhile, Pardo Bazán's finely delineated distinctions of social strata—characteristic of realism and naturalism in general—attracted Marxist criticism, which had always insisted on the importance of class considerations. Thus, while feminist literary criticism brought new approaches to reading Pardo Bazán's works, other scholars, informed by Marxist thought and the politics of social equality, emphasized class and religion. Most recently, gender, class, and race have coalesced as primary concerns in studying the author's fiction and essays.

With the rise of feminist literary criticism, Pardo Bazán's vast repertoire of short stories, with their varied class and geographic settings, began to fascinate readers. The author moved confidently among the nobility and in Madrid's high society and intellectual spheres. She likewise knew the urban and rural working classes as well as the many gradations of Spain's middle classes, representing them all in her novels and short stories. *Los pazos de Ulloa* treats both rural and urban Galician life; *Insolación* (1889; "Sunstroke"), a novel set in Madrid, has as its female protagonist a widowed countess born, like Pardo Bazán herself, into an untitled but wealthy upper-middle-class family. Pardo Bazán depicts the middle classes in many stories, such as "La culpable" ("The Guilty Woman"), "Paracaídas" ("Parachute"), and "Feminista" ("Feminist"), and treats the plight of the impoverished middle class in others, including "Náufragas" ("Castaways") and "Las cutres" ("The Miserly Women"). Her public enjoyed stories of the aristocratic lifestyle, such as "Las vistas" ("The Wedding Gift Display") and "El encaje roto" ("Torn Lace"), but she wrote as well about poverty, ignorance, spousal abuse, and violence against women, as in "En tranvía" ("On the Streetcar") and "El indulto" ("The Pardon").[1] One of the grounding theories of realist fiction is that it presents its middle-class readers with a mirror of their own lives. Stories of the nobility or the very rich did not reflect her readers' lives—nor, of course, did stories of the working classes or rural laborers—and hence did not offer readers a replication of their lives in the characters' circumstances. Nevertheless, stories of the upper classes may produce envy or escapism in readers. Their distance from the realities of women readers may also allow meditation on the strictures placed on female characters or the challenge to social norms the characters enact. Many of Pardo Bazán's stories, as well as scenes in her novels, also convey the religious practices of Spanish society and speak in this way to her readers' lives.

Critical analyses of Pardo Bazán's stories proliferated, from my article "Plotting Gender / Replotting the Reader: Strategies of Subversion in Short Stories by Emilia Pardo Bazán" to Joyce Tolliver's insightful *Cigar Smoke and Violet Water: Gendered Discourse in the Stories of Emilia Pardo Bazán* and Susan M. McKenna's perceptive *Crafting the Female Subject: Narrative Innovation in the Short Fiction of Emilia Pardo Bazán*. Both books offer valuable introductions to Pardo Bazán's stories and readings of *cuentos* suitable for advanced undergraduate or graduate courses. Two anthologies of Pardo Bazán stories, *"El encaje roto" y otros cuentos*, edited by Joyce Tolliver, and, more recently, Linda Willem's *"Náufragas" y otros cuentos*, which includes an appended glossary, provide excellent selections.

Students can gain awareness of Pardo Bazán's cultural milieu by learning about the author's life in her native Galicia, her early marriage, her balancing of family with writing, her public renown in Spain and abroad, and her attempt to provide a basic library of contemporary issues for women with her book series, La biblioteca de la mujer. An emphasis on Pardo Bazán's life and achievements in isolation from the cultural practices of her day may leave students with the impression that the author was a free spirit, independent of constraints on her activities and opinions. Such is not the case, for normative gender constructs and the mores of her social class unavoidably shaped her persona and her writing, whether she embraced or challenged them. Pardo Bazán was an extraordinarily active, well-traveled woman whose publications appeared in all the leading periodicals in Spain and Spanish America and who participated in the major cultural events of her lifetime. These activities led her detractors to give her the nickname "La inevitable"—the Inevitable Pardo Bazán, always present and ready to express her view.[2] The problem she raises for some readers today resides in whether they appreciate, decry, or reject as insufficiently radical her groundbreaking actions, ideas, and fiction. Some critics lament her depiction of undemocratic class structures (democracy was not a concept with appeal for her or many of her compatriots) and her strong ties to the conservative Spanish aristocracy, which gave implicit obedience to male authority, in paradoxical contravention of her intellectual independence and stated belief in the equality of the sexes. Friends and relatives with noble titles provided her with respite from public condemnation of her visibility and granted her great satisfaction and enhanced self-esteem.[3] She was not the only woman author of her generation who enjoyed hobnobbing with Spanish royalty.

Pardo Bazán's attraction to the nobility began with her family's aristocratic connectons in A Coruña during her childhood. With only one year of formal education in a French-language finishing school in Madrid, she may have seemed provincial when she was presented to Madrid's high society, but she had received more schooling than was available to most women except select members of the urban elite. Although she was not born into the aristocracy, in 1871, when she was twenty years old and already married, Pope Pius IX bestowed the title of conde de Pardo Bazán ("Count of Pardo Bazán") on her father, a liberal politician who defended Galicia in politics and the interests of the Catholic Church in Spain and the pope in Rome. A papal title did not carry the prestige of a Spanish one and required permission for its use in Spain. The author's growing literary reputation as well as aristocratic friends and relatives "la introducen en esferas aristocráticas y políticas más altas" ("introduce[d] her to the highest aristocratic and political circles"; Faus Sevilla 1: 37) when she established herself in Madrid.[4] After her father died in 1890, Pardo Bazán, as his only descendent, had the right to reactivate the papal title but did not, undoubtedly in part because her mother retained the title condesa viuda de Pardo Bazán ("widowed Countess of Pardo Bazán"). Nevertheless the daughter's use of personal stationery with an embossed crown, signifying the rank of countess, manifests the appeal an aristocratic identity held for her. In 1908, at age fifty-six, she joined Spain's nobility in her own right when she received the title of countess from the king in recognition of her literary and intellectual career, an uncommon honor for an author. Biographies and criticism of Pardo Bazán frequently refer to her as the countess, especially those written by people who knew her or studied with professors who did; it is not an uncommon usage today in Spain.[5]

Pardo Bazán also emphasized her adherence to the Catholic Church: "Yo soy católica, de arraigada catolicismo" ("I am a Catholic, with a deeply rooted Catholicism"; "Discurso" 320), signaling herself as a conventional Spanish woman, surely in part to ward off accusations of feminist or antisocial leanings. Some scholars today criticize her aristocratic aspirations and allegiance to Spain's national religion as antithetical to the positions she expressed in her writings. Without directly questioning the sincerity of her religious faith, some critics opine that her attachment to the church's rich artistic tradition motivated her continued embrace of the religious practices expected of women, especially middle-class women. Public conformity to Catholicism provided a layer of protection from the barbs and arrows slung at rebellious women who did not meet social expectations of passivity and submissiveness.

It is important to emphasize to students that feminism was a fraught social issue in Pardo Bazán's time throughout Europe and North and South America and that women linked to it, including Pardo Bazán, were subject to condemnation and virulent verbal attacks. Geraldine M. Scanlon has detailed feminist initiatives for this period in her invaluable study, *La polémica feminista en la España contemporánea* ("The Feminist Polemic in Contemporary Spain"). In Spain, feminist thought and actions were considered an affront to the proper role of women as mothers and (subservient) wives and received scant approbation. Well aware of this disapproval, in a 1914 newspaper interview, when she was in her early sixties, Pardo Bazán self-deprecatingly acknowledged that, if given the option to have her hanged, the majority of Spanish women would vote in favor (qtd. in Acosta 525).[6] Whatever students today think of feminism, it may come as a surprise for them that any association with the international feminist movement provoked an uproar in Spain from men and women who rejected changes to prevailing social norms. Among leading male intellectuals there was more tolerance of feminism than among women. Any defense by a woman of women's education, even "para su propia dignificación" ("to enhance her self-respect") and to fulfill her role of wife and mother, was still considered in 1900 "una subversión del orden social" ("an act that subverted the social order"; Núñez Rey 84). Several women writers, principally Concepción Gimeno de Flaquer, Pardo Bazán's contemporary, publicly allied themselves with feminism at times—in part as self-advertisement, always with caution, and often softening the new feminist demands by interweaving them with adherence to conventional roles for women.[7] When Pardo Bazán aligned herself in print with absolute equality for women and men, she did so openly, in forthright declarations and without reservation.

In an 1890 letter associating herself with the goals of the Women's Franchise League in London—which she had joined on the invitation of the Englishwoman Gabriela Cunninghame Graham, her friend and a fellow author—Pardo Bazán makes common cause with British women in a compelling statement of her commitment to women's rights and of the origins of her support for feminism. The letter includes one of her boldest pronouncements on women's opportunities and equality with men. Such values were unexpected in a woman raised in a peripheral, conservative province and society. However, her father was an educated and cultured man who had inculcated in his only child "la convicción de que las diferencias injustas y arbitrarias entre la condición social y política del varón y de la hembra tenían que desaparecer al advenimiento de tiempos más racionales y más cristianos de lo que son los presentes, y de lo que fueron los pasados ya" ("the conviction that the unjust and arbitrary differences between the social and political position of men and that of women would disappear when more rational and more Christian times arrived than exist at present or existed in the past"). She recommends patience in the face of women's current state, which she calls slavery: "Armémonos de paciencia y energía para apresurar el fin de nuestra esclavitud" ("Let us arm ourselves with patience and energy to hasten the end of our slavery"). She looks forward to "la mujer futura, más libre, más feliz y más digna de la humanidad" ("the woman of the future, freer, happier and a more worthy exemplar of humanity"; Bieder, "Emilia Pardo Bazán and Gabriela" 734). Around the same time, she praised and identified herself with the values expected of men in contemporary Spanish society in a missive to Spain's leading author, Benito Pérez Galdós: "De los dos órdenes de virtudes que se exigen al género humano, elijo las del hombre . . . y en paz" ("Of the two types of virtues that are required of the human race, I choose the virtues required of men . . . and enough said"; Pardo Bazán, *"Miquiño mío"* 114). Pardo Bazán admired and desired to emulate the masculine ideal, not the feminine ideal of the pretty, passive, silent, homebound, devout woman.

In turn-of-the-century fiction the female protagonist often finds herself trapped without money or resources and at the mercy of scheming men. When reading such Pardo Bazán novels as *Insolación*, whose classroom edition prepared by Jennifer Smith makes it accessible to upper-level undergraduates, students frequently demand, Why doesn't the female character get a job? Or, in the case of one of the four sisters in *Los pazos de Ulloa*, why doesn't she leave home and rent an apartment? Pardo Bazán's own life raises similar questions. A woman of her upper bourgeois socioeconomic position would never consider having a job (not to mention that the only jobs for women consisted of the manual labor performed by the lower classes). Only those women without inherited money or family to support them worked to obtain the basic needs of food and shelter. Spanish society centered on the family. No woman, rich or poor, lived alone if she had family, although such strictures rarely applied to the very rich or those in abject poverty. Nevertheless, Pardo Bazán did create a position for herself that produced income, although there is little doubt that breaking into the world of letters and gaining recognition as an author initially mattered more to her than making money did. In a sense she did have a job, in the modern model of self-employment. She turned the writing of novels and short stories, as well as newspaper articles, biographies, and literary criticism, into a career, in an era in which a woman from her social background did not earn money or appear in public except on religious, family, or special social occasions involving her own class. Charitable work on behalf of lower-class women was an approved exception to this pattern.

Pardo Bazán made her name as a writer and even wrote about herself in an autobiographical essay, "Apuntes autobiográficos" ("Autobiographical Notes"),[8] at a time when some women published only under a male pseudonym to protect their anonymity or appended their husband's last name to their own (for example, Concepción Gimeno de Flaquer, married to Francisco Flaquer) to signal their respectability as married women. Pardo Bazán neither used a pseudonym nor added her husband's last name to her own. In fact, she opted to sign with only her father's two last names, Pardo Bazán, eliminating her mother's. In part this shorter last name was a practical choice, but it also pointedly tied her identity exclusively to her father. She signed both her publications and her personal letters as Emilia Pardo Bazán until, with her new title, she became the condesa de Pardo Bazán.

Pardo Bazán not only created a career for herself as an author but also shaped her own public identity. Middle-class women who attempted to achieve a similar public presence as authors needed the income to sustain themselves; they principally did so by publishing women's magazines, self-help books, and edifying tomes designed for women. Pardo Bazán's publications doubtless produced more income for her than that earned by other contemporary women writers, called *literatas* (the English termed such women "scribblers"), although it is difficult to compare subscription income from long-running periodical series with the royalties from fiction or the more substantial pay for short stories and articles published in leading newspapers and journals. Pardo Bazán wrote well over six hundred stories, an important source of income. In 1889, at age forty-seven, she wrote a personal letter to Galdós, in which she proposed the unthinkable: "Me he propuesto vivir exclusivamente del trabajo literario, sin recibir nada de mis padres" ("I have resolved to live exclusively from my literary work, without accepting anything from my parents"; *"Miquiño mío"* 114). This sounds like a resolution a college student today might make, but in fact it was quite an exceptional aspiration for the only daughter of a well-to-do, land-owning provincial family who had never lacked money. Men like Galdós earned a living from producing a constant flow of journalism and fiction. Pardo Bazán's goal of financial independence meant increasing her writing output to meet her expenses, including international travel and extended stays in Paris. Later in the same year, she expressed an even more far-reaching desire: "Yo necesito mi propia estimación, perdida desde hace año y medio. . . . [Q]ue murmure de mí el universo entero, pero que yo me juzgue bien" ("I need my own self-esteem, which I lost a year and a half ago. . . . [L]et the whole universe gossip about me, but let me judge myself right"; 164). In a strikingly modern sentiment, she puts self-respect above public opinion and social standing.

As a married woman separated from her husband and with three children, Pardo Bazán lived permanently in her parents' home.[9] Without her parents' economic and emotional support in raising the children, she could not have survived independent of the man who remained her legal husband (Acosta 217). De facto marital separation was an unadmitted reality in Catholic Spain, although the bourgeoisie denied its existence while even the aristocracy preferred to keep up appearances (217–18). This dependence on her family surprises most students today because it clashes with the image of Pardo Bazán as a woman who enjoyed the freedom of movement not sanctioned for other middle-class women. During her writing years she invariably spent the winter months at her family's home in Madrid and from three to six months of the warmer seasons either in the family's city home in A Coruña, Galicia, or at one of their country farm estates in rural Galicia. Following the death of her father, she began to have the old farmhouse transformed into the elegant, imposing Towers of Meirás, where she and her mother, an unpretentious hostess, entertained friends.[10] Her parents' stable home and loving care freed her for literary and social activities and afforded her the privacy of the long morning hours to write. However, her movements were inevitably constrained, and escaping parental surveillance required careful organization. Before her father died in 1890, she stayed in a hotel or rented an apartment in Madrid if her parents remained in Galicia. In a letter to Galdós in 1887 she writes of plans to acquire a pied-à-terre in Madrid for private rendezvous with him (*"Miquiño mío"* 79). After her father's death, her mother continued to run the almost exclusively female households in Madrid and Galicia in which Pardo Bazán, her mother, her unmarried aunt, and her children lived. Spain's traditional, family-oriented household arrangements applied equally to men as well as to women: the lifelong bachelor Galdós moved to Madrid as a student and after age twenty-seven lived with family members, including sisters and a nephew.

The exchange of letters between a married woman and a bachelor was a fraught matter if a woman's reputation were to remain intact, as Pardo Bazán reminds Galdós in 1889: "Esta te la enviaré por mano. Pero irá disimulada para que aunque la abras delante de tu familia no vean más que una cosa interesante" ("I will send this letter by hand. But it will be disguised so that even if you open it in front of your family they will only see something interesting"; *"Miquiño mío"* 94). In order to protect her good name, on another occasion she followed his wishes and altered her envelope so it would not appear to be from her (101). Even in less public exchanges she felt parental disapproval. In an era in which few middle-class women smoked cigarettes, Pardo Bazán enjoyed the habit "en privado y clandestinamente" ("in private and clandestinely"; Thion Soriano-Mollá, "Amistades" 135). When inviting a friend from Paris to visit her in Galicia, she requested that he bring her two boxes of cigarettes because she had already smoked all those she had brought back from Paris (132). In earlier correspondence from A Coruña to the same friend, she confessed: "Falta me hace que V. venga, para fumar. . . . [A]quí la sola idea de que yo acerque a mis labios ese confite, produce estremecimientos de horror, sobre todo en mamá" ("I need you to come for a visit in order to smoke. . . . [H]ere the very idea of my putting this treat to my lips produces spasms of horror, especially in Mama"; 130). Thus Pardo Bazán found satisfying ways to achieve independence and literary productivity within the domestic social conventions of her class, despite parental disapprobation and her responsibilities as a mother. Ultimately she approximated her goal of supporting herself—although not her children—on the income she earned. Nevertheless it was only in Paris that she experienced true independence, commenting that she moved "sola y libre" ("alone and free") through the city, feeling herself respected as a woman "porque aquél es un país culto" ("because that is a cultured country"; *Al pie* 15).[11]

Despite the outrage against her unleashed by her most hidebound compatriots, Pardo Bazán had many admirers among contemporary intellectuals, writers, and politicians. She also developed lasting friendships with many men and women and mentored or encouraged male and female authors younger than herself. Her celebrity and outspokenness on women's issues did not bring her general popularity among women, but she maintained a steadfast circle of women friends. Pardo Bazán and Blanca de los Ríos became members of Madrid's premier cultural institution, the Ateneo Científico, Literario y Artístico (Scientific, Literary, and Artistic Atheneum), when it first granted to women admittance with equal status to men. Pardo Bazán and de los Ríos collaborated on cultural projects in the Ateneo's literature section. Writing from Galicia, Pardo Bazán relied on de los Ríos in Madrid to further her ultimately successful candidacy for president of the literature section, casting her friend as her "muñidora electoral" ("election agent"; Letter [1905]). She also endeavored to advance de los Ríos's literary goals, and each woman enhanced the other's social network of women friends. Pardo Bazán, accompanied by her mother and daughters, enjoyed joining intimate friends at Galicia's elite spas, a setting she used in stories such as "Feminista" and "El encaje roto." From the spa at La Toja she enthuses to de los Ríos, "Aquí nos tiene a Blanca y á mi remojándonos en barro medicinal. Estamos muy contentas porque esto es la salud misma, pero el viaje es terrible" ("Here you have [my daughter] Blanca and me steeping in medicinal mud. We are very content because this is health itself, but the trip is awful"; Letter [1902]).

Pardo Bazán corresponded with some of the best-known writers of the generation after hers: Miguel de Unamuno, Azorín (José Martínez Ruiz), and others, as well as Cunninghame Graham, de los Ríos, and a leading voice among women activists, Carmen de Burgos[12] (Bieder, "Emilia Pardo Bazán: Veintiuna cartas"). Despite the destruction after her death of most of the correspondence she had received, some letters she wrote to other authors fortunately survive, allowing her voice to comment on her friendships, her aspirations, and her personal, cultural, and literary activities.[13] From the remaining side of the exchange of letters, we can still witness her generosity, professional support, and the mutual esteem between friends both in and outside Spain.

Pardo Bazán's letters to Cunninghame Graham reveal some of the author's feelings and opinions about Madrid society and about her critics. In a letter of 1895, she apprised her friend of her time-consuming social obligations: "La sociedad me roba mucho tiempo, y no veo camino de prescindir de ella, ahora que mis hijas van á ser grandes y tendré que presentarlas en el mundo" ("Society steals much of my time, and I see no way to do without it, now that my daughters are going to be grown up and I will have to present them in society"; Bieder, "Emilia Pardo Bazán: Veintiuna cartas" 60).[14] Of course, she also greatly enjoyed mingling in society. A prolific author, she compared books to children, especially when her books came under attack: "Lo unico que me obliga á recordarlos es cuando los atacan: entonces, el natural cariño del padre me hace sentir los dolores de mi progenitura" ("The only thing that forces me to remember them is when someone attacks them: then, an author's natural affection makes me feel the pain of my offspring"; 60). Outraged that critics had accused her of publishing a blasphemous story, she countered by resetting the priorities: "Un cuentecillo de 6 páginas! Yo que creía que hoy por hoy en España lo único de que debía hablarse es de la guerra de Cuba!" ("A little six-page story! I thought that at this time in Spain the only thing that one should talk about is the war in Cuba!"; 60). In facing the accusations of critics, she found consolation in Oscar Wilde's trial in Gabriela's native country: "también en Inglaterra dan más importancia á una aberración sexual, que á mi juicio no debiera ser cosa del pais, sinó á lo sumo del médico, que á las cuestiones sociales graves y serias. ¿Qué importan las aficiones de Oscar Wilde? Menos que nada para la marcha de la sociedad" ("in England as well they grant more importance to a sexual aberration, which to my mind should not be a matter for the state but at most for the doctor, than grave and serious social questions. What do Oscar Wilde's preferences matter? Less than nothing for the functioning of society"; 60–61). Finally, she looked forward to shifting into summer mode in Galicia: "donde respiraré aire puro, no trasnocharé, leeré mucho y tendré tiempo para escribir más despacio" ("where I will breathe clean air, I won't stay up late, I will read a lot and I will have time to write more slowly"; 61).

Generosity and professional support are also evident in Pardo Bazán's letters to women authors. She helped Cunninghame Graham make contacts and obtain books for her study of Santa Teresa de Jesús, and she forwarded money, changing pounds to pesetas, when her friend traveled to retrace Teresa's route across Spain. Pardo Bazán even stored and attempted to sell furniture for her (Bieder, "Emilia Pardo Bazán: Veintiuna cartas"). When de los Ríos wanted to have her play staged, Pardo Bazán interceded on her behalf with Spain's leading theater actor-manager, Fernando Díaz de Mendoza, and his wife, the actress María Guerrero. Pardo Bazán's concern for her friend's recurring bouts of ill health seem almost maternal (ironically, de los Ríos lived for almost a century). When Pardo Bazán vied for the presidency of the Ateneo literature section, she mused to de los Ríos about the advantages and disadvantages of the election for herself and for others: "Me vá á robar mucho tiempo si lo logro . . . pero ¿y la mujer? Este será un paso, una conquista . . . " ("It will steal a great deal of my time if I succeed . . . but, and [the cause of] women? This will be a step forward, a conquest . . . "; Letter [1905]). By 1905 she recognized herself as a feminist pioneer, breaking new ground—which she emphatically was and did. She was an exceptional woman in her day, and she probably would have been in ours as well.

NOTES

[1] McKenna's book studies "El indulto" (43–47, 52, 157), "En tranvía" (79–83), "La culpable" (87–91), "Las cutres" (113–17), and "Paracaídas" (134–40). Tolliver discusses "El encaje roto" (66–79, 84, 88–89, 172–73) and "Náufragas" (152–70) in *Cigar Smoke and Violet Water*. "Paracaídas" and "Feminista" (148–53) are treated in Bieder, "Plotting." Tolliver includes "El encaje roto" (58–65), "Náufragas" (101–09), "Los escarmentados" (93–100), and "Feminista" (110–17) in her edition of Pardo Bazán, *"El encaje roto" y otros cuentos*. In Pardo Bazán, *"Náufragas" y otros cuentos*, Willem anthologizes "El indulto" (25–34), "En tranvía" (35–42), "El encaje roto" (79–83), and "Náufragas" (123–29).

[2] The cover illustration of the humor magazine *Gedeón* depicts the author—improbably—bicycling around Paris as she covers the 1900 Universal Exposition for a Madrid newspaper. The caption reads, "La Inevitable en París" (Sileno).

[3] Her relatives included two prominent statesmen, the marqués de Figueroa, who was also a minor author, and the conde de Romanones.

[4] All translations are my own.

[5] On the eve of her son's marriage in 1916 to a woman from a titled family and heir to the title, Pardo Bazán requested the king to convert her Spanish title from condesa de Pardo Bazán to conde de Cela de Torres (a name of an ancestor) and subsequently to transfer it to her son, who would have inherited it anyway on her death. Now without a title from Spain, she activated her father's papal title and continued as before as condesa de Pardo Bazán. Although this information is available on specialized Web sites, accompanied by the requisite documentation, it frequently appears distorted and erroneous in scholarly studies. See Vales Vía.

[6] See El Caballero Audaz for the original publication of the interview.

[7] In 1903 Gimeno gave a lecture titled "El problema feminista" ("The Feminist Problem") at Madrid's Ateneo, whose membership was open only to men until 1905. The title of her lecture gives evidence of her ambivalence, as well as that of her audience, about her subject.

[8] "Apuntes autobiográficos" prefaces the first edition of *Los pazos de Ulloa*.

[9] After her mother's death in 1915, Pardo Bazán continued to make a home for her aunt and her unmarried daughter, both of whom outlived her.

[10] Both the house in A Coruña, now the Real Academia Galega and Casa-Museo Emilia Pardo Bazán, and the more rural Towers of Meirás are currently open to the public, the Towers on a limited basis.

[11] This essay quotes from the España Editorial version of *Al pie de la torre Eiffel* ("At the Foot of the Eiffel Tower").

[12] Carmen de Burgos was, like Pardo Bazán, one of the first women members of the Ateneo.

[13] When dictator Francisco Franco received the title to Pardo Bazán's Galician estate, the Towers of Meirás, he and his wife destroyed most of the author's books, papers, and letters left in the house by her surviving heir.

[14] In addition to the Pardo Bazán letter published in Bieder, "Emilia Pardo Bazán and Gabriela" (734), the following letters to Cunninghame Graham in Bieder, "Emilia Pardo Bazán: Veintiuna cartas" will hold interest for students: letter 2 (46–47; 1 Apr. 1890), letter 4 (47; 20 June [1890]), and letter 16 (55–56; July 1891).

Gender and Female Subjectivity: Approaching Pardo Bazán's Writings from a Gender Studies Perspective

Isabel Clúa

The exceptionality of Emilia Pardo Bazán, one of the most studied writers in Spanish literature, in a canon dominated by male writers has always been a source of interest to feminist criticism. At the same time, many of her texts reflect and address the situation of women and explore different female subjectivities. As a result, gender has emerged as one of the most important and fruitful ways of analyzing her work. However, several challenges present themselves in teaching Pardo Bazán from the persepctive of gender. First, the nineteenth-century pioneers of feminist consciousness, including Pardo Bazán herself, had significant contradictions in their thoughts and actions with respect to women and feminism; therefore, a certain level of knowledge about feminism and the situation of women in Pardo Bazán's time is required.[1] Second, it is difficult to choose the appropriate theoretical tools with which to explain sophisticated, sometimes abstract concepts contained within a tremendously diverse critical corpus. Finally, the breadth and diversity of Pardo Bazán's oeuvre—which in turn has generated a considerable amount of secondary literature—makes the selection of a reading list particularly difficult.

In my teaching experience, a good way to get into this jungle of texts is to use theoretical concepts as a guiding thread. Pardo Bazán's narratives often offer perfect examples of complex theoretical ideas, so that a tour from the concept to the text and back is ideally suited both to reinforce the theoretical idea and to analyze the text from the perspective of gender.

Gender and Technology of Gender

Simone de Beauvoir's classic formulation "On ne naît pas femme: on le devient" ("One is not born, but rather becomes, a woman"; 247)[2] established the notion that femininity is not a natural or biological quality of a subject but has a cultural dimension; thus, gender is understood as a set of representations and cultural expectations that are assigned to men and women as if such expectations were derived naturally from biology. Normally, students have no problem understanding the distinction between sex as biological and gender as cultural. However, more recent and complex formulations, such as Teresa de Lauretis's "technologies of gender," are more difficult for students to grasp. According to de Lauretis, gender is understood as a regulatory fiction, a semiotic production articulated at different levels of culture, which sculpts bodies and subjects and ultimately naturalizes sexual binarism. Fashion and clothing make good examples of technologies of gender, because students easily understand fashion as a semiotic device linked to sexual binarism: it is evident that the clothes we wear are understood to accord with parameters of femininity and masculinity. Fashion and clothing also help us visualize the natural and cultural dimensions involved in ideas about gender. As Joan Hollows points out, "[W]e are used to thinking of the body as a 'natural' identity—and for this reason the differences between male and female bodies as biological." Hollows goes on to note, quoting Kaja Silverman, that "fashion and beauty practices are a key element through which 'the human body [is made] culturally visible'" (137; Silverman 145).[3]

Pardo Bazán's story "Feminista" (1909; "Feminist"; *Cuentos completos* 3: 106–09) reinforces this aspect of gender theory exceptionally well.[4] In "Feminista," clothing (pants and skirts) is revealed as a technology of gender that invests the subject with some attributes (power or powerlessness) that are associated with notions of masculinity or femininity. The double cross-dressing that is narrated in the story breaks the continuity between what is natural (sex) and what is cultural (gender) and shows how this apparent continuity is articulated through clothing (gender technology). The story also encourages students to deessentialize femininity and masculinity and to understand them more dynamically.

Performativity and Empowerment

Following the technology of gender, students can tackle another key concept: Judith Butler's gender performativity. In Butler's theory, subjects are not natural, ontological essences but the product of the repetition of rules. Subjects are constituted through these rules and, in turn, the constant repetition of the rules naturalizes the norms, the subject, and his or her sexual and gendered behaviors. In its most extreme aspect—in which gender is understood as a discursive, cultural device by which "natural sex" is produced and established as "prediscursive" (7)—Butler's proposal is challenging for students. However, the idea that identity and gender are inextricably linked because "persons only become intelligible through becoming gendered in conformity with recognizable standards of gender intelligibility" is useful for the analysis of certain texts by Pardo Bazán (16).

The example of drag helps students understand the complex idea of performativity. Butler devotes much attention to drag as a phenomenon that destabilizes the "reality" of gender, since "[i]f one thinks that one sees a man dressed as a woman or a woman dressed as a man . . . we think we know what the reality is, and take the secondary appearance of gender to be mere artifice, play, falsehood, and illusion. But what is the sense of 'gender reality' that founds this perception in this way?" (xxiii). That perception, Butler argues, is based on the person's anatomy or clothes, which denote a form of naturalized knowledge, even though the perception is based on a series of cultural inferences. Drag generates a moment of doubt and hesitation, in which "one is no longer sure whether the body encountered is that of a man or a woman. . . . [I]t becomes un-clear how to distinguish the real from the unreal. And this is the occasion in which we come to understand that what we take to be 'real,' what we invoke as the naturalized knowledge of gender is, in fact, a changeable and revisable reality" (xxiv).

Butler's ideas are interesting and relatively simple to apply to Pardo Bazán's story "La mayorazga de Bouzas" (1886; "The Mayorazga of Bouzas"; 2: 21–27), whose main character does not embody a stable gender and calls into question gender categories. The Mayorazga first appears as masculine—a tomboy who rides on horseback, drinks wine at the tavern with other men, carries out farm work, and asks young men at village festivals to dance. However, the protago-nist's marriage to a young man from the city, Santiago, leads to a radical change: the Mayorazga becomes a caring wife consumed by the desire to be a mother.

The story does not resolve the tension between masculinity and femininity: the maternal, feminine Mayorazga is no more real or true than the violent, mas-culine one. At the conclusion of the story, the Mayorazga seems to reconcile both facets when, as a desperate, scorned wife she seeks revenge on her hus-band's lover with a violence incompatible with femininity. The Mayorazga acts both like a woman and like a man, which reveals that femininity and masculinity exist only through acting. The character of the Mayorazga also problematizes the notion that conceptions of male and female emerge naturally from sexed bodies. The narrator's reflection on the married couple is meaningful in this re-gard: "Físicamente los novios ofrecían extraño contraste, cual si la naturaleza al formarlos hubiera trastocado las cualidades propias de cada sexo" ("Physically, the couple offered a strange contrast, as if, when shaping them, nature had al-tered the qualities proper to each sex"; 22). Thus, the manly Mayorazga and her effeminate husband can disarticulate the correlations between body, sex, and gender and illustrate for students how gender performance creates the illusion of femininity and masculinity as natural and unchanging.

Applying Butler's idea of performativity to *Dulce dueño* (1911; "Sweet Mas-ter"), one of Pardo Bazán's most controversial novels from a gender perspective, is especially revealing.[5] The novel presents the story of Natalia/Lina Mascareñas, who, after receiving an inheritance from her aunt (who is actually her mother), undertakes an extreme reconstruction of her identity that involves a meaningful negotiation with normative gender models. The character's decision to establish a new identity narrative, detached from values such as truth or authenticity,[6] allows students to easily understand the discursive dimension of identity: the change of name from Natalia to Lina makes it plain. Moreover, the famous mirror scene in which Lina is invested with her new identity, stripping off her mourn-ing clothes and dressing in fine fabrics and luxurious jewels, can be connected to the notion of technology of gender, as clothing and jewelry are external de-vices that construct gender identity and make the subject intelligible.[7]

The notion of technology of gender is also useful for understanding the ar-ray of normative discourses that attempt to model Lina in a certain pattern of femininity as well as the resistance and disruptions to those discourses. The novel opens with Lina's confessor offering the story of the life of Saint Catherine of Alexandria as a Christian model of femininity. Hagiography, as well as the narratives about marriage offered by other male characters in the novel, is a discursive practice that aspires to inscribe itself on Lina as a body and a subject. But the inscription proves problematic because Lina welcomes the model of Christian virginity as a means to control her own desire and reject marriage. The moment Lina assumes the hagiographic ideal, she develops an identitarian performance, constructing herself as a subject acting and enacting the model and embodying the normative ideal that she has been offered.

Butler insists that performativity cannot be articulated freely: rules are not taken or discarded at will, so the ideal to which we must conform is never fully achieved. Therefore, continues Butler, performativity is not a guarantee of the subversion of the rule but a framework of possibility. The lively discussions generated by *Dulce dueño* relate precisely to this last point: Lina adopts and embodies a normative ideal, but there is a disruptive element in her performance, which results in a conflictive femininity far from the ideal of docility and humility that the hagiographic model promotes. What is less obvious is that this disruption will result in Lina's empowerment, her ability to establish herself as an autonomous subject and to overcome vulnerability to power structures. Discussing this point in class, in addition to being an exciting exercise because Lina arouses passionate and diverse opinions, allows students to fully understand, on a theoretical level, the tensions between performativity and the subversion of gender norms.

Otherness

Otherness is another classic concept of feminist theory. Beauvoir defined woman as other in *Le deuxième sexe* (*The Second Sex*) and substantiated her argument with a revision of the central myths and stories of Western culture.[8] Beauvoir's argument is widely known: such stories deny woman her status as an autonomous subject and exclude her from the public sphere and from any possibility of transcendence and symbolization (Segarra 85). Thus, the imaginary on woman is subjected to a circular logic in which the ideal and its opposite are connected, so that it only offers, according to Julia Kristeva, an abstract, desexualized, and ideal femininity or a particular, contingent, and unessential one (295–327). These poles take several avatars: Eve and Mary, life and death, light and night, and so forth.

The fin de siècle period was especially given to the textual production of femininity by stereotypes linked to this polarity. As Bram Dijkstra has shown, the proliferation of angelic figures (angel in the house, *femme fragile*) and evil ones (femme fatale) is closely related to anxieties about the increasing occupation of the public sphere by women and their claims to equality. The artistic use of these stereotypes shows the discursive effort to deny women subjectivity (Kristeva 312).

Several Pardo Bazán texts explore how otherness is configured from the available stereotypes of the era.[9] "Afra" (1894; 1: 307–12) presents the story of a singular young woman whose appearance, as indicated by the male narrator,[10] is defined in terms of vehemence, passion, and unwavering will, which give her an "almost manly" air and violate the prevailing model of femininity (307). Afra's impressive image is even more pronounced in contrast with that of her friend Flora, a *femme fragile* who plays a key role in the central anecdote of the story (told by a second male narrator): the death of the shy, blonde Flora in an accident at sea with Afra raises suspicions, as Afra had been deeply in love with Flora's fiancé. The story presents the stereotypes of femininity that sustain the circular logic of female otherness, reflected superbly in the closing phrase: "El corazón del hombre . . . selva oscura. ¡Figúrate el de la mujer!" ("The heart of man . . . a dark jungle. Just imagine what a woman's heart is like!"; 309). The quotation perfectly expresses the idea of woman as an enigmatic, unyielding, and threatening other. But, above all, it is interesting to observe how the narrative device pays attention to the artificiality of these stereotypes: the story proposes not exactly the stereotypes of women but the stereotypes of women in the view of the male narrators. In that sense, the story deploys and then sabotages the types of the *femme fragile* and the femme fatale: the polarity between Flora and Afra depends ultimately on the point of view of the male characters, who are, in turn, the narrators of Afra's story.[11]

The notion of otherness within feminist theory has been revised from other perspectives. Rosi Braidotti, for example, connects otherness and difference, pointing out how the devaluation of sexual difference is "not a hazard but rather the necessity of a structural system that can only represent 'otherness' as negativity" (64). Braidotti's observation develops the insight of Hélène Cixous, who connects otherness with the structure of Western thought, which is organized around binaries originating with the male/female binary. According to Cixous, the patriarchal logic appropriates the *étrangereté* (foreignness) embodied in the woman for fear of expropriation, separation, and castration; thus, she becomes a terrifying mystery — remember Freud's famous definition of woman as the dark continent (*Question* 212) — which Cixous explores through the myth of Medusa, in which death and femininity are closely linked because they are both unrepresentable. This line of thought has led to an extensive exploration of images of female monstrosity as a manifestation of female otherness.

The works of Pardo Bazán offer interesting material for reflection on this aspect of otherness. I propose reading two stories, "Mi suicidio" ("My Suicide"; 1894; 1: 250–53) and "La resucitada" (1908; "The Resurrected"; 3: 143–45), which present one of the classic figurations of the female other: the woman who returns from the grave, the *revenante*. To analyze how Pardo Bazán addresses this figure and its implications, I usually work through a comparative analysis with other stories, such as Edgar Allan Poe's "Ligeia" (1838) and Auguste Villiers de l'Isle-Adam's "Véra" (1874). As I have noted elsewhere, "Mi suicidio" can be understood as an ironic rewriting of "Véra" (Clúa). Both stories begin with a male subject, despondent after the death of his beloved, lost in the nostalgic exploration of her possessions and tempted by the idea of following her to the grave. While in "Véra" the dead woman's spectral presence is embodied and the narrative evolves into a ghost story, in Pardo Bazán's story a few letters that reveal to the protagonist his beloved's infidelity constitute the presence of the dead lover, and the narrative drifts into a story of betrayal. "Mi suicidio" rewrites ironically the model of female otherness in "Véra": instead of a female ghost, the dead female is in possession of an individual subjectivity hidden to her lover and, unlike the ghost of Véra, doesn't need to return from the grave to ignore the male subject's desire to possess her. "La resucitada" is a twist on the classic model that stories like "Ligeia" propose. In place of the terrified male subject who observes the beloved's true nature when she returns from the grave, "La resucitada" dismantles this rhetoric by telling the story from the point of view of the resurrected woman. Pardo Bazán, using the metaphors and traditional elements of the story's model, reveals in an obvious way that female otherness vanishes the moment a woman takes the word and becomes the subject of discourse.

NOTES

[1] *La mujer en los discursos de género* (Jagoe et al.) provides a comprehensive overview of nineteenth-century discourses on gender, combining primary sources with explanatory essays.

[2] All translations are my own.

[3] Other useful references on fashion are Wilson; Entwistle.

[4] I cite Pardo Bazán's stories in Paredes Núñez's four-volume edition, *Cuentos completos*.

[5] Bieder connects *Dulce dueño*'s Lina with the decadent hero and understands her mysticism as "el triunfo de una experiencia radicalmente transformadora del individuo" ("the triumph of a radically transformative experience of the individual"; "Divina" 16); Kirkpatrick, *Mujer*; and Charnon-Deutsch, "Tenía," consider Lina's mysticism an obstacle to the process of liberation; and Medina even considers the novel an "alegato moralista" ("moralist plea"; 302).

[6] Lina's reflection when considering her new life is more than clear: "La mentira no es antiestética. Me conviene. Dueña de la verdad, encierro esta espada desnuda en un armario de hierro y arrojo la llave al pozo" ("Lying is not unartistic. It suits me. Owner of the truth, I enclose this naked sword in an iron cabinet and throw the key into the well"; *Dulce dueño* 147).

[7] Valis links identity, modernity, and exteriority: "ser moderno significa construir una identidad, no desde dentro, sino desde fuera hacia dentro" ("to be modern means to construct an identity, not from within, but from the outside"; "Figura" 103). Kirkpatrick points out that the novel destabilizes the binaries inner/outer, soul/body, signified/signifier (*Mujer* 108–28).

[8] Beauvoir (163–242) includes all types of texts: biblical stories that provide archetypal images of woman (Eve, Mary, Salome), folk tales (Sleeping Beauty), classics of Western

literature (courtly poetry, Boccaccio's *Decameron*, Balzac's *Le père Goriot*, Shakespeare's *Hamlet*, Lorca's *La casa de Bernarda Alba*, and so on), and reflections of the philosophers Nietzsche and Bataille, among others.

[9] Pardo Bazán explores, among others, the figure of the adulteress ("La careta rosa" [1918; "The Pink Mask"], "La flor seca" [1893; "The Withered Flower"], "La perla rosa" [1895; "The Pink Pearl"]); the madwoman ("Aire" [1909; "Air"]); the murderess ("Los buenos tiempos" [1894; "Good Times"]); the femme fatale ("La bicha" [1897; "The Snake"], "Saletita" [1898; "Saletita"]); and the *revenante* ("La resucitada" [1908; "The Resurrected"], "Mi suicidio" [1894; "My Suicide"]).

[10] On the implications of narrative technique in Pardo Bazán, see Bieder, "Plotting"; Tolliver, *Cigar Smoke*; and Walter, *From*.

[11] One can approach Pardo Bazán's novel *La quimera* ("The Chimera") similarly: Clara Ayamonte and Espina Porcel are configured as the two extremes of feminine polarity. As Kirkpatrick has pointed out, the novel propagates these standardized images of the feminine while "dota a ambas mujeres de una subjetividad paralela a la del artista/protagonista masculino" ("endowing both women with a subjectivity that is parallel to that of the male artist/protagonist"; *Mujer* 108).

The Legal, Medical, and Social Contexts of the Angel in the House

Lisa Nalbone

This essay discusses the teaching of Pardo Bazán's ideas about women and motherhood in the undergraduate classroom. The texts referenced here work well in an upper-level literature class that covers women's writing. Students could explore the topic of the angel in the house through the lens of family composition, medical discourse, women's education, or women's rights.

Spain's fin de siècle society positioned the ideal woman as a domestic subject excluded from the power hierarchies associated with public life. Women's roles in society were shaped by philosophical currents, legal mandates, medical discourse, and economic trends that codified a rigid structure to determine what was considered desirable or transgressive in feminine subjects.

Women in Nineteenth-Century Spanish Society

Pardo Bazán's texts constitute a rich terrain for examining women's subordinate place in nineteenth-century Spanish society. Mary Nash asserts that women's citizenship and rights—for example, the right to vote, to an education, to property ownership—were not taken into account in the creation of Spain's 1812 constitution ("Rise" 246). This legal sidestepping of women's rights continued through the 1868–74 period known as the Sexenio Democrático (248–49). Despite the revision of legal codes during the First Republic (1873–74) that deemed marriage a civil rather than a religious union, wives were subjected to the authority of their husbands. Through the marriage contract, women voluntarily renounced their civil rights and gave their spouses all rights to their property. Wives had the "obligation to obtain their husbands' permission for such activities as the administration of their own personal belongings, legal transactions, and the publication of scientific or literary works" and were considered subordinate to their husbands in all senses (249).[1] The lack of educational opportunities and voting rights, as well as the supposition that women were not to work in order to gain financial autonomy or access to power hierarchies, created vast inequalities and proved to be solid barriers for women. Women were also treated differently in the penal system, often receiving harsher punishments, particularly for crimes of passion and adultery (252). In sum, aspirations for equality between men and women were met with resistance at the institutional level and in society as a whole. Two of Pardo Bazán's short stories that dialogue well with each other in this context are "¿Justicia?" ("Justice?"; *Obras completas* 8: 481–86) and "El indulto" ("The Pardon"; 7: 125–35).[2] Students may read these stories to identify and analyze the subordinate position of women and the consequences they suffer when they transgress their marriage contracts.

The Catholic Model of Womanhood and the Angel in the House

The Catholic model of womanhood, based on the portrayal of the virtuous woman that evolved from the writings of Juan Luis Vives (*Instrucción de la mujer cristiana* [1524; "The Education of a Christian Woman"]) and of Fray Luis de León (*La perfecta casada* [1583; "The Perfect Wife"]), to a large degree determined the lives of women during the time Pardo Bazán lived and wrote. Women were expected to marry, have children, and dedicate their lives to raising their children and instructing them in the teachings of the Catholic Church. This idealized yet restrictive portrayal of the perfect wife highlighted an essential feminine quality that defined women as nurturers. More important, it lent credence to medical and scientific discourses of the time that claimed the biological inferiority of women, who relied on their emotions to guide their actions, as opposed to men, who relied on their ability to think and reason.[3] The maternal figure as an archetypal representation of women's experience arose from these ideas. Students may read the introductory chapter in Bridget Aldaraca's foundational study *El ángel del hogar: Galdós and the Ideology of Domesticity in Spain* and learn how this archetype developed from the sixteenth-century Counter-Reformation through the nineteenth century (25–54). Aldaraca shows from a sociohistorical and socioreligious perspective how this ideal feminine figure exists both in isolation and in conjunction with the men in her life, but Aldaraca is careful to point out that the angel in the house, who is entrusted with her children's moral education, operates within the familial structure rather than as an independent entity. The relation between family and society is "more often depicted as antagonistic and mutually exclusive" inasmuch as their separation prevents society from contaminating the moral integrity of the family (55).

In literature, the type of the angel in the house originated in Victorian England. Coventry Patmore's narrative poem "The Angel in the House" first appeared in 1854 at the height of English realism and responded to the cultural shift that saw marriage as a contractual agreement rather than an arrangement between two families. Women were supposed to be selfless caregivers and models of virtue and purity necessary for marital happiness. According to Catherine Jagoe, the term *angel in the house* in the Spanish context referred to the middle-class woman's primary mission to uphold moral and religious values in her home; compared with a man, she possessed superior, innate qualities that equipped her for this work (*Ambiguous Angels* 22–23). Jesús Cruz notes that the "idealized image of femininity incorporated all the components of the traditional Christian wife resituated in a modern bourgeois family" (*Rise* 49). The term *angel* became a synecdoche for woman, specifically with reference to the middle class.

The idea prevailed that marriage transformed man and woman into husband and wife, each with a specific role. Whereas the husband negotiated the public sphere, the wife found herself confined to the private, domestic sphere. Beginning in the mid-nineteenth century, she was guided by conduct manuals and numerous journals dedicated to the smooth operation of the home, such as María del Pilar Sinués's weekly periodical *El ángel del hogar* (1864–69). Pardo Bazán often points to limitations inherent in the paradigm of the angel in the house by creating characters that face adversarial relationships that threaten or jeopardize their well-being. In "Subversion of Victorian Values and Ideal Types," Janet Pérez shows how several of Pardo Bazán's short stories "expose women's discontent with 'angelic' confinement to domestic space, and indict the power of public opinion and gossip to destroy a woman's reputation . . . [while they also] ridicule masculine claims to ownership of women" (41–42). In class, visual materials can be used to bridge the temporal and spatial gaps between the contexts in Pardo Bazán's writing and those that are familiar to students today. To engage students and to demonstrate how this model of ideal female behavior was propagated in the nineteenth century, instructors could incorporate a *PowerPoint* presentation with images of women in the nineteenth-century Spanish press and have students analyze them in the light of the paradigm of the angel in the house.[4]

Medical and Hygienist Writing

Pardo Bazán's writings often engage with medical discourses, which offer opportunities for teaching the medical and hygienist ideas of the time. The medical conditions that appear in the author's texts tend to have origins that can be traced to the female reproductive system.[5] To gain an understanding of the shift in scientific thought during the Enlightenment from the one-sex to the two-sex theory of human anatomy, students may read Thomas Laqueur's essay "Orgasm, Generation, and the Politics of Reproductive Biology." As Laqueur notes, this shift occupied mid-nineteenth-century medical discourse and "emerged at precisely the time when the foundations of the old social order were irremediably shaken" (16). In the nineteenth century the medical discourse that began to privilege the two-sex theory became "the means by which such differences could be authoritatively represented" (35). For the Spanish context, both the introduction (Jagoe and Enríquez de Salamanca) of the volume *La mujer en los discursos de género: Textos y contextos en el siglo XIX* ("Women in Gender Discourses: Texts and Contexts in the Nineteenth Century" and Catherine Jagoe's chapter "Sexo y género en la medicina del siglo XIX" ("Sex and Gender in Nineteenth-Century Medicine") in the same volume provide excellent overviews of the prevailing medical discourse of this era. Also useful in this regard is Lou Charnon-Deutsch's outline of Pedro Felipe Monlau's 1865 study *Higiene del matrimonio* ("Marital Hygiene"), which explains in detail the prescribed gender roles that were dominant at the end of the nineteenth century ("Discurso" 179–81). Reading Pardo Bazán against Monlau sparks interesting observations about the ways in which Pardo Bazán questions or challenges the discourses of women's reproductive health. Consulting Monlau's original essay gives students an opportunity to evaluate his statements aimed at dictating women's behavior and explaining biological processes, such as the following reference to pregnancy: "La profunda revolución que se opera en el organismo de la mujer fecundada, trasciende alguna vez a su parte intelectual y la constituye maníaca o en una verdadera locura" ("The profound revolution that operates in the pregnant woman's organism at times transcends her intellectual state and renders it maniacal or truly insane"; 330).[6]

With Monlau's statement in mind, students could read Pardo Bazán's short story "Un diplomático" (1883; "A Diplomat"), in which the lower-class wet nurse of the baby of a diplomat suffers the loss of her own son (*Cuentos completos* 4: 62–66).[7] The transmission of the wet nurse's malaise to the diplomat's baby after the loss of her child is the suspected cause of the diplomat's baby's subsequent death. Pardo Bazán's story explores how the shift of responsibility from the child's biological mother to the wet nurse places the baby in jeopardy. Reacting to the social convention that an upper-class mother should not nurse her child, Pardo Bazán encourages her readers to understand wet nursing's life-threatening consequences. In "Un diplomático," Jennifer Smith asserts, both women "suffer the loss of a child because society insists on limiting the purposes and capabilities of the female body: it must be either untouched and decorative or sturdy and functional" ("Wet Nurse" 47).

Representations of the female body in Pardo Bazán's texts reveal the shortcomings of the medical discourses that prescribe certain capabilities to women on the basis of their social class. The wealthy family's employment of a wet nurse from the lower classes may be viewed as more than a commentary on social class and on the medical discourse that dictated the utility of the woman's body for childbearing and mothering. As working women, wet nurses exercise a financial agency that subverts the domestic model of the angel in the house. Women who use the financial means of their husbands to employ wet nurses do so as a "symbol of financial prosperity" (Baumslag and Michels 40), while wet nurses gain a certain level of financial freedom from their husbands by commodifying their bodies. The commodification of the female body through wet nursing may be compared with other representations of working women in Pardo Bazán's oeuvre, particularly the prostitute, and with the ways female subjects appropriate a sense of financial autonomy.

Krausism and the Education of Women

Pardo Bazán's writings on women's education need to be evaluated in the context of Krausism. Julián Sanz del Río introduced the ideas of the German philosopher Karl Christian Friedrich Krause to Spain. Krausism was a liberal reform movement that proposed that the key to Spain's regeneration was comprehensive educational and cultural reform. According to Juan López-Morillas, "Kraus-ist ethics invites man to develop more fully his moral potential and this potential is synonymous, according to Krause, with a more or less conscious aspiration to the fullness of life that springs from rational knowledge of God" (15). Intro-duced in Spain in the mid-nineteenth century, Krausism gradually gained vis-ibility in Spanish society after the Glorious Revolution of 1868. According to Jo Labanyi, Krausism posited that society represented a "harmonious conjunction" and considered the family as the primary human community and the basis of all other communities. Krausism was "above all a school of political philosophy, concerned with creating an active civil society based not on competition but on cooperation" (*Gender* 58). The Krausists attached great importance to the edu-cation of women because they saw the deficient education of Spanish women as an obstacle to the nation's progress. According to the Krausists, women, excep-tionally suited to instill moral values in their children, needed to be educated to fulfill their roles as wives and mothers. While the Krausists stressed the great im-portance of women's domestic role, they did not confine women to the home and were instrumental in founding several institutions for the education of women, such as the Escuela de Institutrices (1869) and the Asociación para la Enseñanza de la Mujer (1870) (Rowold 155–80).[8]

The Krausists focused on the middle class in particular, which, according to Pardo Bazán, prepared its daughters to aspire only to matrimony, despite the sacrifices they would need to make, in Pardo Bazán's words, "para la pesca con-yugal" ("for husband hunting"; "La mujer española" 101). She criticizes the education that middle-class women received, which by and large was merely a varnish to make them desirable as wives. Certain subjects were deemed more suitable for women, such as geography, drawing, music, French, and English, while others were seen as inappropriate, such as history, rhetoric, astronomy, and Latin. Despite reforms in the educational system during the nineteenth century, the illiteracy rate among women in Spain was 81.2 percent in 1887 (Rowold 164). Pardo Bazán followed the Krausists in the belief that many changes were needed to truly improve women's access to quality education.[9]

Social Class and the Maternal: "La mujer española"

The representation of femininity beyond the domestic sphere constitutes another area of study, one that can be elucidated by a close analysis of Pardo Bazán's es-say "La mujer española," which first appeared in the London-based *Fortnightly Review* as "The Women of Spain" (1889) and contextualizes women's perceived submissiveness within patriarchal society. The essay expresses her dissatisfac-tion with the inequality between men and women in educational freedom, re-ligious freedom, the right to free association, suffrage, and participation in the parliamentary system (89). Students may be guided to explore the connections and implications of these inequalities as they pertain to motherhood, specifically discussing Pardo Bazán's references to the role of woman as educator of her children within the framework of Catholicism and Krausism. An effective way to flesh out these points is to identify the expectations of women's contributions to society, as presented in "La mujer española," and the many instances in which Pardo Bazán's characters fail to meet these expectations. The author's journalistic and narrative writings highlight these paradoxes experienced by women in her society. Students may also gain insight into the weight given to the mother figure's morality and religious fervor by considering Pardo Bazán's remarks: "No haber recibido de su madre enseñanza religiosa, se juzga casi tan humillante como no tener padre conocido; y decirle a un hombre que su madre carecía de principios religiosos es ultraje poco menos que si la acusásemos de libertinaje" ("Not to have received from one's mother religious instruction is deemed almost as great a humiliation as not knowing who one's father is, and to tell a man that his mother lacked religious ideals is to insult him scarcely less than if one were to accuse her of lasciviousness"; 90). Here, Pardo Bazán underscores society's double standard that mothers must be devout Catholics who instruct their children in the church's teachings while fathers are permitted lax morals and freedom from even the most basic parental responsibility, paternity. In "La mujer española," Pardo Bazán dishes swift criticism of the influence men have over women: "la mujer es tal cual la hace y quiere el hombre" ("the woman is as the man makes her and wants her to be"; 103). Tasking students with finding other examples of representations of women in "La mujer española" that seem to contradict the way women are represented in Pardo Bazán's narrative production, specifically related to women's lack of equal legal protection, yields material for meaningful discussion of Pardo Bazán's stance on women's rights and gender equality.[10]

In "La mujer española" Pardo Bazán discusses women of different classes, noting that middle-class women are more dependent than women from the lower and upper classes on their husbands to determine their place in society. Sections of the essay that deal with the middle class can be read fruitfully in conjunction with several short stories. In "Náufragas" (1909; "Castaways" [Pardo Bazán, *Torn Lace* 108–17]) Pardo Bazán pits a widowed mother and her two daughters, having lost the small-town, middle-class comfort they enjoyed while the family's father was still alive, against the threat of poverty in the unforgiving urban setting of Madrid. The story establishes a link between the shift in geographic locales and social-class standing and presents the problem of women's lack of access to education. As Joyce Tolliver asserts in her edition of Pardo Bazán stories, *"Torn Lace" and Other Stories*, in "Náufragas" the author captures in literary form essential ideas from her essays "La mujer española" and "La educación del hombre y de la mujer" to criticize "the traditional lack of formal education and job training provided to Spanish women" (108). Pardo Bazán shows the ineffectiveness of both secular and religious education in preparing women for anything but domesticity as well as the dire financial straits to which this poor preparation can lead.

Textual Dialogue: Maternal Figures and the Modern Reader

Maternal figures of varying types abound in Pardo Bazán's novels and short stories. *Los pazos de Ulloa* (1886) refracts maternity on many levels. While traditionally studied within the paradigm of naturalism, the novel probes gender construction and motherhood through the binary opposition of the characters Sabel and Nucha. Sabel, "the unfit mother" (Charnon-Deutsch, *Narratives* 128), provides the contrast with the idealized Nucha, whose positioning as the angel in the house is never fully realized because of her early death. Guiomar Fages points to the contrast between socially prescribed motherhood in an urban setting (Nucha) and imposed motherhood in a rural environment (Sabel) while also signaling the priest Julián's transgression of gender roles relating to maternity in his interactions with Nucha's daughter, Manolita (44–47). Asking students to explore the representations of these two women—through the lenses of gender and class, for example—creates a natural segue into the novel's many thematic threads. Discussion of the interplay between the women and other key elements of the novel, such as representations of masculinity, politics, religion, science, nature, gothic elements, and decadence, affords instructors the flexibility to analyze the novel in ways that best suit curricular objectives.[11]

Students could also explore the theme of motherhood in Pardo Bazán's short stories. With "En tranvía" (1890; "On the Tram") students can compare the hapless mother's treatment by her husband with the narrator's description of how the streetcar passengers react to her (*Cuentos completos* 2: 97–101). Paramount to the discussion is the attention Pardo Bazán pays to the middle and lower classes as distinct and separate groups in society. For example, the story indirectly criticizes the charity offered to the poor woman by the bourgeois narrator and by other passengers. The woman herself is indifferent to the charity, and the implication is that it is a temporary fix. The inherent irony of the narrator's advice to the poor mother at the end of the story further underscores the division between mothers of different social classes. The visible signs of the mother's physical abuse coupled with her son's blindness point to the story's determinism and the improbability that she will rise above her circumstances. Nevertheless, to some degree this character represents a normative portrayal of the mother figure: students may take note of how she cradles her son and how his tidy appearance contrasts with hers.

But the figure of the mother as a biological nurturer is not the only version of motherhood presented in Pardo Bazán's fiction. In *Doña Milagros* (1894) and *La sirena negra* (1908; "The Black Siren") the author explores the idea that good mothering is not exclusively attributed to biological motherhood. Infertility and alternatives to biological motherhood are explored in several short stories, such as "La estéril" (1892; "The Barren Woman"), "Sara y Agar" (1894; "Sarah and Hagar"), "El belén" (1898; "Nativity"), and "Aventura" (1899; "Adventure") (Versteeg, "'Una mujer'"). In "Leliña" (1903) a poor, unmarried, intellectually challenged woman gives birth to and skillfully nurtures a healthy baby, while, in contrast, a wealthy, married woman's marriage yields no children (*Cuentos completos* 2: 322–30). The married couple's infertility is considered to be entirely the woman's fault. This story may be read as a protest against the medical discourse of the period that suggests that infertility always rests with the woman, even if accurate knowledge of the female reproductive system was not available until early in the twentieth century.[12] Furthermore, the story exemplifies how, according to Margot Versteeg, Pardo Bazán "intentó combatir prejuicios sociales basados en . . . cierto tipo de unión conyugal caracterizada por la incomunicación entre los esposos" ("tried to combat social prejudices based on . . . a certain type of conjugal union characterized by the lack of communication between the spouses"; "'Una mujer'" 49).

The topics of maternity and science (or the lack of scientific knowledge) also appear in "La adopción" (1901; "The Adoption"), set in India and narrated by a doctor, in which a noble woman, Kandrya, cedes her last living son to a sorceress figure to save him from a fatal curse the mother believes this pariah cast on him (*Cuentos completos* 4: 41–45). In this story, as in "Un diplomático," gender intersects with social class and medical discourse. Because the incurable illnesses that ended her two elder sons' lives are believed to be the result of the curse, Kandyra forgoes medical advice and relinquishes her son to the sorceress (who serves as wet nurse) in the hope of preserving his life. While her son flourishes to ultimately become a powerful rajah, Kandyra soon dies from anguish. The recasting of maternity across social class and in this exotic location invites analysis of how these factors play into the story's outcome.[13]

Students may work with "Los escarmentados" (1909; "The Forewarned") as an example of the repercussions of childbearing outside marriage (*Cuentos completos* 3: 111–14), even when the pregnancy is the result of a "desliz" ("mistake"; 112) or perhaps of something more sinister: "¡Quién volvería a sorprenderla, a engañarla!" ("Who would surprise or deceive her again!"; 113). Pardo Bazán situates the unmarried expectant mother, Agustina, on the road to Madrid, shrouded by inclement weather. Agustina vows to leave the social confines of her hometown, where a woman in a similar predicament was found dead at the bottom of a well (112). Pardo Bazán problematizes the inevitable social stigma associated with becoming pregnant outside marriage by suggesting that Agustina may have been raped.

Few mothers in Pardo Bazán's writings fit the mold of the angel of the house. Yet, as Charnon-Deutsch asserts, "there are no terrible mothers in Pardo Bazán's works" (*Narratives* 123). Meaningful class activities and assignments that examine the role of maternity give students the opportunity to analyze the primary sources and to situate these writings within the context of the prevailing medical, social, and religious discourses of the time. In presenting mother figures in a variety of economic and geographical contexts, Pardo Bazán's novels and short stories highlight the multiplicity of maternal experience while also interrogating the hegemonic view of femininity as synonymous with motherhood.

NOTES

[1] For a discussion of the marriage contract in the light of liberal reforms in the nineteenth century and Rousseau's ideas on "natural sexual difference," see Labanyi, *Gender* 39–51.

[2] I cite "¿Justicia?" and "El indulto" in the twelve-volume *Obras completas* edited by Darío Villanueva and José Manuel González Herrán.

[3] Christina Dupláa presents a succinct overview of the ideal female subject as defined by androcentric thought, which was shaped by bourgeois liberalism (190–92).

[4] A valuable resource for nineteenth-century images of women is Charnon-Deutsch's *Fictions of the Feminine in the Nineteenth-Century Spanish Press*; instructors can also search the Biblioteca Nacional de España's *Hemeroteca Digital* Web site for nineteenth-century periodicals aimed at a female audience, such as *El correo de la moda*, *La guirnalda*, and *La ilustración de la mujer*.

[5] The root of women's illness or injury not related to reproduction, however, was often attributed to social ills such as domestic violence and other crimes.

[6] All translations are my own.

[7] Unless otherwise noted, I cite Pardo Bazán's short stories in Paredes Núñez's four-volume edition, *Cuentos completos*.

[8] On Pardo Bazán's thoughts about Krausism and Rousseau, see Labanyi, "El diálogo."

[9] For detailed studies of the education system in nineteenth-century Spain, see Jagoe, "La enseñanza"; and, more recently, Rowold 155–80.

[10] For a detailed discussion of Pardo Bazán and John Stuart Mill, see Bretz, "Emilia Pardo Bazán on John Stuart Mill."

[11] Representations of motherhood have also been discussed critically with respect to other Pardo Bazán novels, such as *El cisne de Vilamorta* (1885; "The Swan of Vilamorta"), *La madre naturaleza* (1887; "Mother Nature"), *La quimera* (1905; "The Chimera"), and *La sirena negra* (1908). Likewise, the theme of failed maternity in Benito Pérez Galdós's *Doña Perfecta* (1876) and in Leopoldo Alas's *La Regenta* (1884 and 1885; "The Regent's Wife") has also received critical attention.

[12] For a discussion of the scientific knowledge of the reproductive system before the twentieth century, see Laqueur, "Orgasm." Laqueur explains that nineteenth-century scientific discourse suggests that "a sovereign organ, the ovary, ruled over the reproductive processes that made women what they were" (20). As Labanyi writes, this shows that men and women were identified by anatomical differences in the reproductive organs "that supposedly determined their entire being" (*Spanish* 90).

[13] Instructors may choose to have students read "La adopción" in *Blanco y negro* (a digital version is available), which includes illustrations along with the text. Exploring visual representations of the stories allows for a deeper understanding of them within the print contexts in which they were first read. For more on this connection between Pardo Bazán's texts and their nineteenth-century contexts, see Turner's essay in this volume.

Teaching Masculinity in Pardo Bazán's Novels

Zachary Erwin

A striking number of male characters in late-nineteenth-century Spanish realist novels are explicitly unmanly, often due to physical weakness, effeminacy, ineffectuality, infantilization, or impotence. Just a few examples in novels by Benito Pérez Galdós and Leopoldo Alas (also known as Clarín) include the good-for-nothing Juanito Santa Cruz and the fragile Maxi Rubín in Galdós's *Fortunata y Jacinta* (1886–87; "Fortunata and Jacinta") and the sexually inadequate Víctor Quintanar in Alas's *La Regenta* (1884–85; "The Regent's Wife"). In Emilia Pardo Bazán's oeuvre, we find the feminized priest, Julián Álvarez, in *Los pazos de Ulloa* (1886; "The House of Ulloa") and the immature law student, Rogelio Pardiñas, in *Morriña* (1889; "Homesickness"). Comparing characters like these with the model—or models—that defined manliness in nineteenth-century Spain reveals the Spanish realist novel to be a fertile ground for introducing students to the study of masculinity.

An exploration of masculinity in Spanish realism also offers the opportunity to examine Spain's complicated process of modernization, which affected representations of manliness (or the lack of it) in the realist canon. As I have argued elsewhere, nineteenth-century Spain was influenced by a post-Enlightenment, bourgeois ideal of masculinity that arose in more industrialized countries, such as England and France. But because Spain was slower to industrialize than these other countries, this modern ideal often clashed with the ancien régime model of manliness, which was based on feudal hierarchies, inherited wealth, and aristocratic leisure. Consequently, in Pardo Bazán's *Memorias de un solterón* (1896; "Memoirs of a Confirmed Bachelor"), both Mauro Pareja and Benicio Neira are caught between these competing models of masculinity yet fail to embody either model successfully (Erwin 549–50).

Within the Spanish realist canon, Pardo Bazán's body of work is uniquely well suited to the study of masculinity, particularly as it relates to uneven modernization in Spain. While Galdós wrote mainly about Madrid in his contemporary novels, Alas about provincial capitals, and José María de Pereda about the countryside, Pardo Bazán's male characters move within and between all these spaces, offering a more subtle and complete picture of the masculinities of the author's era than any other realist novelist. For example, *La madre naturaleza* (1887; "Mother Nature") details the citified Gabriel Pardo's sojourn from Madrid to the Galician countryside, but in *Insolación* (1889; "Sunstroke"), we find him living once again in the capital. Similarly, *Morriña*'s Rogelio Pardiñas and *Insolación*'s Diego Pacheco plan trips to the country from Madrid at the ends of their respective stories, while *La Tribuna*'s Chinto and *Memorias*'s Benicio Neira move to Marineda (Pardo Bazán's fictionalized stand-in for her native A Coruña) from more rural locales. These characters' migrations put differing standards of masculinity as well as differing degrees of modernization in contact—and frequently in conflict—with one another. In *Los pazos*, for example, Julián Álvarez, an educated city dweller of slight build from Santiago de Compostela, moves to the isolated Ulloa estate, while Pedro Moscoso, the stout, rural-born lord of the Ulloa manor, spends significant time in the polite society of Santiago. Both men struggle to fit into their new surroundings.

I have taught Pardo Bazán's novels in several undergraduate Spanish courses on masculinity and also in an introductory masculinity studies course in English, which used Paul O'Prey and Lucía Graves's *The House of Ulloa*, a translation of *Los pazos de Ulloa*. Here, however, I focus on a graduate-level seminar I taught a few years ago, the syllabus of which appears in the appendix to this essay.[1] The course focused on the link between masculinity and modernization in the Spanish realist novel—mostly in texts by Pardo Bazán but also in two novels by Galdós. I grouped the novels by the setting in which most of their action occurs: from the Galician countryside in Pardo Bazán's *Los pazos* and *La madre naturaleza*, to the provincial capital of Marineda in *La Tribuna* and *Memorias*, and, finally, to Madrid in the remaining Pardo Bazán works and the two Galdós novels.

The first two weeks of the seminar gave students the theoretical and historical framework for thinking critically about masculinity and modernization. In the first class session, we discussed scenes from an early episode of the British television series *Downton Abbey* (Fellowes). In the series, a distantly related, middle-class lawyer becomes the heir to a landed estate in 1912 England after a sudden death in the family, putting his bourgeois values at odds with those of his new, aristocratic way of life. While *Downton Abbey* is set neither in Spain nor in the nineteenth century, I found it to be an accessible and enjoyable way to introduce certain themes students would encounter in the course. Specifically, I asked students to think about how the episode depicts class status, attitudes toward work, and masculinity, as well as the conflicts that arise when male characters representing disparate worldviews and models of masculinity come into contact with one another.

I began the second class session with a lecture on modernization in Spain in the late nineteenth century, starting with a working definition of modernization as the rise of capitalism, industrialization, urbanization, and representative government; a general increase in literacy rates; the implantation of a dominant bourgeois ideology; and the related decline of an agriculture-based economy and of feudal social hierarchies. I then traced some aspects of modernization in England, which represents, according to Jordi Nadal, "el modelo clásico" ("the classic model") of industrial development (9).[2] I compared nineteenth-century Spain's economic, social, and political history with that of Victorian England in order to illustrate Spain's uneven modernization in the period.[3]

Next, I introduced students to the concept of the crisis of masculinity. There is some debate about the validity of this concept among masculinity studies scholars

(Segal 239; Tosh 20–21; Connell 84), but I find it useful in thinking about Spanish masculinities, particularly as defined by José Cartagena Calderón. For Cartagena Calderón, a crisis of masculinity is

> una situación histórica en la que las formas tradicionalmente dominantes de la masculinidad se han vuelto tan imprecisas, modificadas o contestadas que los hombres (y las mujeres) debatan entre sí o tratan de redefinir que es lo que significa ser un "verdadero hombre," ya sea en respuesta a cambios sociales, políticos y económicos y/o por nuevos modelos desafiantes de masculinidad (y feminidad) que emergen a partir de dichos cambios.   (9–10n1)

> a historical situation in which traditionally dominant forms of masculinity have become so imprecise, modified, or contested that men (and women) debate among themselves or try to redefine what it means to be a "real man," either in response to social, political, and economic changes and/or new, challenging models of masculinity (and femininity) that emerge from said changes.   (my trans.)

Finally, I posed the following overarching questions for students to consider throughout the semester:

> How can a man embody modern, bourgeois norms of masculinity in a country still strongly tied—both economically and ideologically—to the ancien régime?
> How do aristocratic and bourgeois models of manhood interact with one another in the Spanish realist novel?
> How are working-class men depicted in Spanish realism? How do the rural peasant and the urban proletarian fit within the continuum of late-nineteenth-century Spanish masculinities?
> How can we apply Cartagena Calderón's definition of the crisis of masculinity to the late-nineteenth-century Spanish context? How is manliness debated or redefined in the Spanish realist novel?

After the lecture, we discussed readings on the history of masculinity studies (Campbell et al.), on the development of post-Enlightenment notions of gender and masculine norms (Laqueur, *Making*; Connell; Mosse; Tosh), and on manifestations of—or challenges to—those standards in eighteenth- and nineteenth-century Spain (Haidt; Encinas). We also talked about Galdós's "Observaciones sobre la novela contemporánea en España" ("Observations on the Contemporary Novel in Spain"), focusing on the author's discussion of Spain's modernization (Pérez Galdós, "Observaciones"). Students gave ten- to twenty-minute presentations on these texts, for which they summarized the article, essay, or book chapter; critically evaluated its arguments; drew connections between the text and other assigned readings; and posed questions for further class discussion.

Each subsequent week was dedicated to a particular novel (long novels were divided over two weeks). Student presenters again led discussions of additional historical, theoretical, critical, or primary texts to accompany each novel. If there was no critical article or book chapter explicitly addressing masculinity for a given novel, I assigned a critical text on some other aspect of gender in the novel. To keep our conversations as student-centered as possible, I also asked students to choose a particularly interesting or relevant passage from the week's novel to discuss in class. As we began to talk about the week's assigned novel, I polled the students in order to group their chosen passages by theme. We then proceeded from theme to theme, and I added relevant passages of my own choosing.

Our discussion of *Los pazos de Ulloa*, for example, took place over two weeks. For the first week, in addition to the first half of the novel and a relevant excerpt from Donald Fowler Brown's *The Catholic Naturalism of Pardo Bazán*, we discussed a selection by the sociologist R. W. Connell detailing the theory of hegemonic masculinity. Connell states that hegemonic masculinity "is not a fixed character type, always and everywhere the same," but rather "the masculinity that occupies the hegemonic position in a given pattern of gender relations" (76). Connell's theory emphasizes the submission of women by men but also "specific gender relations of dominance and subordination between groups of men" (78). The theory thus recognizes hegemony not only of men with respect to women but also of men with respect to other men. In *Los pazos de Ulloa*, my students and I analyzed the particular masculinity represented by male characters of varying social classes, physical characteristics, and personality traits, including Primitivo, Pedro Moscoso, and Julián Álvarez. We then examined how these characters negotiate and renegotiate their relationships to one another—and the power dynamics inherent in those relationships—as the novel progresses.

Throughout the semester, I encouraged students to pay attention to the narrators' descriptions of male characters; how those characters view and interact with one another (and with female characters); and how politics, cross-class relations, and geographical space affect their perceived manliness. I have found that love triangles can be particularly useful in helping students focus on how male characters view and compare themselves with one another. For example, how does Mauro Pareja, the middle-class, first-person narrator of *Memorias de un solterón*, describe his own appearance, activities, and personality? By contrast, how does he describe Ramón Sobrado, the working-class man whom he sees as his rival for the affections of Feíta Neira? Or how does the omniscient narrator of *La madre naturaleza* describe Gabriel Pardo, the bookish, cosmopolitan aristocrat, and Perucho, the strong, handsome son of a maid, who was raised in the country and who competes with Gabriel for the love of Manuela Moscoso? How do Gabriel and Perucho describe each other—either through dialogue or through free indirect discourse? What do all these descriptions tell us about the masculinity each character embodies? And how are these masculinities illustrative of or affected by late-nineteenth-century Spain's complicated process of modernization?

As the course progressed, our focus on masculinity led naturally to discussions of ideal feminine roles in the nineteenth century, such as the angel of the house, and to Pardo Bazán's avowed feminism. Descriptions of male characters allowed us to examine the influence of literary naturalism on Pardo Bazán's writing, in which physical attributes often give clues to personality traits. In other words, just as Pardo Bazán's novels served as a fruitful introduction to the study of masculinities, the focus on masculinity in those novels also gave students a deeper understanding of the texts themselves and of the broader literary landscape in Spain at the end of the nineteenth century.

It was important to me that students see how a masculinity studies approach could also enrich their readings of texts outside the Spanish realist canon, especially because there was a wide range of literary interests and proposed specialties among the seminar participants. At the same time, I wanted students to feel comfortable applying other theoretical approaches to the realist novels we had read. For that reason, I gave two options for their final essay: to analyze any cultural product within the student's proposed area of specialization through the lens of masculinity studies or to write on any aspect of one or more novels covered during the semester. While many students wrote their papers on novels from the course, others produced interesting analyses of masculinity in Latino literature, in the contemporary Spanish novel, and in popular magazines in post–Civil War Spain.

NOTES

[1] All works referenced in the appendix appear in this volume's works-cited list.

[2] My remarks on Victorian England are based primarily on the work of François Bédarida and that of Sally Mitchell.

[3] For my discussion of nineteenth-century Spain's social and economic history in general, I rely mainly on Shubert; Ringrose, *Madrid* and *Spain*; Tuñón de Lara; Cruz, *Gentlemen* and *Rise*. Gemie's study is useful for a brief yet specific treatment of Galicia.

APPENDIX
Syllabus for Masculinity and Modernization
in the Spanish Realist Novel

WEEK 1: Introduction
Downton Abbey (Fellowes)

WEEK 2: Masculinities: Theory and History
Campbell et al.; Laqueur, *Making* 1–24; Connell 185–99; Mosse 3–39; Tosh 29–58; Encinas; Haidt, 107–20; Pérez Galdós, "Observaciones"

WEEK 3: Rural Spain as a Problem
Pardo Bazán, *Los pazos de Ulloa*, chs. 1–15; Brown 2–29, 83–99; Connell 67–86

WEEK 4: Rural Spain as a Problem
Pardo Bazán, *Los pazos de Ulloa*, chs. 16–30; Charnon-Deutsch, *Narratives* 114–39

WEEK 5: Rural Spain as a Solution?
Pardo Bazán, *La madre naturaleza*, chs. 1–18; Forth 1–18; Amago

WEEK 6: Rural Spain as a Solution?
Pardo Bazán, *La madre naturaleza*, chs. 19–36; Pardo Bazán, "Confesión"

WEEK 7: Social Class and the Provincial Capital
Pardo Bazán, *La Tribuna*; Scanlon, "Class"

WEEK 8: Resistance to Gender Norms
Pardo Bazán, *Memorias de un solterón*; Pardo Bazán, "Marineda"; Aldaraca, "El ángel"; Harpring; Erwin

WEEK 9: The Metropolis and the Periphery
Pardo Bazán, *Insolación*; Tsuchiya, *Marginal Subjects* 136–61

WEEK 10: The Mother, the Motherland, and the Son in Madrid
Pardo Bazán, "La mujer española"; Pardo Bazán, *Morriña*; Feal

WEEK 11: Gender and Class in Madrid
Pérez Galdós, *La desheredada*, part 1; Labanyi, *Gender* 91–92, 103–26

WEEK 12: Gender and Class in Madrid
Pérez Galdós, *La desheredada*, part 2

WEEK 13: Gender, Genre, and the *Indiano*
Pérez Galdós, *Tormento*, chs. 1–18; Sieburth 100–36

WEEK 14: Gender, Genre, and the *Indiano*
Pérez Galdós, *Tormento*, chs. 19–41; Ferrer del Río, "El indiano"; Copeland

WEEK 15: Final paper presentations

Evolutionary Logic and the Concept of Race in Pardo Bazán's Short Fiction

Lou Charnon-Deutsch

The writing career of Emilia Pardo Bazán spanned nearly half a century, during which she engaged with the most controversial intellectual debates of the day regarding human origins and ways of being. Advanced undergraduate and graduate students can approach her theories on evolution, race, agency, and determinism by examining her *Reflexiones científicas contra el darwinismo* (1877; "Scientific Reflections against Darwinism"), the article "Progreso: Cuestión de razas" (1900; "Progress: The Question of Races"), and the volume *De siglo a siglo, 1896–1901* (1902; "From Century to Century") and by familiarizing themselves with recent studies that broach the question of evolution and race in the Spanish context, especially Travis Landry's *Subversive Seduction: Darwin, Sexual Selection, and the Spanish Novel* (2012) and Joshua Goode's *Impurity of Blood, Defining Race in Spain, 1870–1930* (2009). Hasty conclusions about her stand on these issues can be avoided by surveying stories in which she challenged readers to contemplate alternative, sometimes contradictory, ways of understanding the human condition. The inconclusiveness regarding questions of agency and choice that Landry identifies in Darwin's theories (18) characterizes Pardo Bazán's fiction. Her zealous defense of individual agency was consistent with her Catholic beliefs, but her recognition of both social and biological pressures shows she also understood and embraced the paradoxes of Darwin's "ethical indeterminism of choice" (Landry 37).

In *Reflexiones* Pardo Bazán comments on physiological influences on human character, acknowledging that "el cuerpo influye en los movimientos del alma, que los estados totales o parciales del sueño, de enfermedad, de embriaguez, de pasión, de cólera o de locura, motivan resoluciones inexplicables en ánimos equilibrados, que las circunstancias empujan de un modo eficaz, aunque no irresistible, al hombre" ("the body influences the movements of the soul; that total or partial states of dream, sickness, inebriation, passion, anger, or madness result in inexplicable resolutions in balanced spirits, and that circumstances effectively drive, although not irresistibly, mankind"; 658).[1] Her stories show a tug-of-war with questions of perfectibility, nature, Providence, and determinism, but they never reach a definitive stand on these questions precisely because she understood, as did many sociologists of her day, that what determines how human beings act and look was scientifically irresolvable. In some of her most naturalist stories, like "Las medias rojas" ("The Red Stockings"), Pardo Bazán emphasized the grim, inescapable materiality of human nature, while in others the idea of individual agency, the exercise of free will to overcome all obstacles, was sacrosanct, as in "Los padres del Santo" ("The Parents of the Saint"). In still others, like "Fraternidad" ("Brotherhood"), she left the question open for readers to decide.[2] Author of over six hundred stories, she explored all alternatives; yet some critics mistakenly conscript her thinking on these subjects on the basis of a narrow selection of texts.

The paradoxical contest between free will and physiological determinism is reflected as well in Pardo Bazán's thinking on heredity and race. In *Reflexiones* the author soundly rejected natural selection and the theory of evolution as explanations for the common origins of all living things. She described Darwinism as a "novela" (567) and insisted that its sterility and phantasmagorias only reinforced the "claridad de la concepción filosófico-cristiana del Universo" ("truth of the philosophical-Christian concept of the universe"; 569). Yet she accepted the notion of atavism and organic memory, that is, the idea that we remember our ancestors in our bodies and may even inherit their mental and emotional proclivities. In explaining variations among human beings she acknowledged the innate "lucha por la existencia" ("struggle for existence"; 545) and ability to adapt to environmental pressures but insisted, in the absence of fossil evidence, that natural selection could not produce a new species. If natural selection perfected existing species or produced new ones, she reasoned, there would be no low creatures that had not yet evolved into higher forms. Any individual aberration in a family was merely an atavistic inheritance from a distant relative or poor education and acculturation, not a regression to a previous moment on the evolutionary scale or an inexorable degeneration of the species. Group deficiencies were also signs of deficient education or cultural disadvantages. An eloquent precursor of the notion of intelligent design, Pardo Bazán insisted that the divine artist "coronó su obra con la más noble de las criaturas" ("crowned his work with the most noble of creatures"; 564), endowing man simultaneously with language and reason; all human beings were alike in this sense.

The idea of race in Pardo Bazán's short fiction is inconsistent—as it is in the work of many of her European contemporaries—and it is best to approach this issue in the classroom with circumspection. Her use of the racialized term *children of Ham* to refer to Africans in some stories signals her acceptance of monogenism, or monophyletism, the popular division of races according to a biblical genealogy that held that all men descended from one of Noah's sons, Japheth, Shem, or Ham, as outlined in the book of Genesis.[3] Scientists in Pardo Bazán's time were beginning to float the idea of polygenesis, the notion that human beings appeared simultaneously in several parts of the globe. Rejecting this, Pardo Bazán makes reference to the book of Genesis in a number of stories to help her mark off Africans from the white races, as if races were stable categories. Collectively, however, the use of the term *raza* in her fiction is so diverse that it comes to signify less a genetic category and more the notion of social group, as sociologists were beginning to use it.

It should be stressed in the classroom that this vagueness does not reflect some unusual imprecision in Pardo Bazán's lexicon but points to the general ambiguity of the term and concept of race among social scientists of the time. Ludwig Gumplowicz, a sociologist who influenced Pardo Bazán's thinking on group identity, complained in his 1883 *Der Rassenkampf* ("The Struggle of the Races"; translated to Spanish as *La lucha de razas*) that the meaning of a people, race, tribe, population, nation, or nationality was arbitrary: "todo es opiniones y apariencias subjectivas: en ninguna parte se encuentra terreno sólido" ("all is opinion and subjective appearances: nowhere can one find solid ground"; 204–05). For both Gumplowicz and Pardo Bazán, race was an unstable concept and did not necessarily imply consanguinity or ethnicity. Rather, it designated groups with homologous characteristics, shared interests that drew them together, or antipathy that pitted one against the other. Despite accepting the biblical notion of descendants of Ham as a cursed race and the "obra misteriosa de las afinidades étnicas" ("mysterious work of ethnic affinities"; *De siglo* [Administración] 205), Pardo Bazán believed there were no naturally superior races, only ones to which civilization had yet to arrive. Racial superiority was not a question of virtue; if a race was superior, like the Anglo-Saxon she singled out in "Progreso," it was because it was "*superior*-dominadora" at the time, not because it was morally or permanently superior: "la *superioridad* no consiste en el ejercicio de esta o de aquella virtud: consiste en la fuerza, consiste en la salud, el vigor, la energía, la actividad" ("*superiority* does not consist of the exercise of this or that virtue: it consists of strength, it consists of health, vigor, energy, activity").

The following sampling of stories illustrates variant usages of race in Pardo Bazán's short fiction. In the broadest sense, *race* refers to all human beings ("Los años rojos" ["The Red Years"]; "El conde llora" ["The Count Weeps"]) and bears no moral connotations. The author occasionally employed the term, following the lead of anthropologists, to categorize races according to skin color or facial characteristics, like the aristocratic Aryan dandy in "Drago" or the slanted-eyed Asian bearing the "sello de la raza" ("sign of his race"; *Cuentos completos* 3: 38) in "Deber" ("Duty"). Especially in moral comparisons between groups the term acquired pejorative connotations popular at the time, as when she characterized Slavic races as crude and irrational in "La turquesa" ("The Turkish Woman") or Arabs as prone to jealousy and violence in "Apólogo" ("Apologue").

Pardo Bazán invested considerable energy contemplating Spain in its idealized relation to other nations. Students will find that she frequently ascribed negative or positive racial characteristics to deficiency or strength in acculturation on a national scale, using race as a shorthand term to refer to a nation's identity not as a political organization but as something that, as Carmen Pereira-Muro has shown, is natural or instinctive even though it is transmitted through acculturation (*Género* 126).

Numerous stories use race to mark national temperament as an instinctive characteristic—for example, Russian capriciousness in "El cerdo-hombre" ("The Pig-Man"), Spanish innate religiosity in "La risa" ("The Laugh"), Malaysian ferocity in "Página suelta" ("Loose Page"), and British ambition in "Dos cenas" ("Two Suppers"). Even a region of a country could be classified as a race with defining characteristics, as Galicia is in "La lumbarada" ("The Bonfire"), "La capitana" ("The Captain"), and "El voto" ("The Vote"). Students could read these stories to examine Pardo Bazán's conception of race as a sort of innate collective identity.

The vaguest use of the term designates a quality shared by a group of individuals of similar talent or profession or simply a group with homologous characteristics unrelated to national or ethnic identity, as in the suggestion in "El frac" ("The Dress Coat") that a historian's stoicism demonstrates the "paciencia, el estoicismo resignado de la raza" ("patience, the resigned stoicism of his race"; *Cuentos completos* 4: 82) where "raza" distinguishes a group of dogged researchers. Finally, she used the term to distinguish the remote past from the present, or civilized groups versus those to whom civilization had yet to reach: the "razas inferiores" of non-Western groups whose lax morality or barbarism show they have not yet been civilized, as in the story "El sino" ("Fate"). Similarly, in "De vieja raza" ("From an Ancient Race"), in which an aristocrat preserves the dignity and virtue of her daughter even in the face of the guillotine, race connotes a moral category, here applied to women who have preserved moral values from a bygone era.

Forty years ago Brian Dendle suggested that Pardo Bazán held entrenched racist views, especially about Jews, a conviction shared by Isidro González, who called her a "decidida antisemita" ("decided anti-Semite"; 172). Students might easily reach this conclusion on reading some of her longer fictions (especially the novel *La prueba* ["The Test"]) or a story like "El buen judío" ("The Good Jew") in which the "good" Jew is seen as a glaring exception and his Jewish killers the ancestors of modern Jews of Paris or Vienna. Yet in her journalistic articles Pardo Bazán often praised Jews like the Rothschilds for their philanthropy and protection of the arts,[4] and she signed the manifesto in support of Ángel Pulido's campaign for Spanish reconciliation with Sephardic Jews (González 186).

Pardo Bazán was frequently led by nationalism to racialize groups in order to contrast them with Spanish humanitarianism, especially after the Spanish-American War of 1898. "Entre razas" ("Between Races") is an ideal story to measure her defense of Spaniards' brotherly attitude toward peoples of African descent against her characterization of Americans' racist attitudes and abuse.[5] The narrator is a gentlemanly Spanish count who accompanies an arrogant Yankee around Madrid shortly after the war. The two men find themselves in a disreputable bar one night, when a "negrazo" ("large Negro"; *Obras completas* 1: 1534) passes by their table. When the Spaniard comments admiringly that the man is a great "ejemplar" ("specimen"; *Obras completas* 1: 1534), the coarse American replies that such a Negro would make a great slave. The American is later found stabbed to death in a dark alley. The question students should discuss is whether the implied message of the story is about the exaggeration of the African-Cuban's vengeance or simply about Spanish equanimity compared with American barbarity and racism.

According to Dendle, Pardo Bazán also treated Asians and Africans with "scant respect" (23); however, it should be pointed out that she often insisted on deficient acculturation to explain aberrant behavior. The drunk African in "Benito de Palermo" is truly despicable, possessing an offensive "olorcillo de la Raza de Cam" ("vague scent of the race of Ham"; *Cuentos completos* 2: 151), but the narrator insists that Benito is laboring under the legacy of slavery that explains if not excuses criminality. In contrast, the Ethiopian Melchor of "La visión de los reyes Magos" ("The Vision of the Magi") projects a positive beacon of hope. He alone of the three kings is able to see the Star of David and hear the celestial music that guides the trio to the nativity scene. Pardo Bazán uses Melchor to establish a point of Christian doctrine regarding the equality of the "raza de Cam" with other races. Melchor rejoices in the conviction that the infant Christ recognizes the equality of all races: "Mi progenie, la oscura raza de Cam, ya no se diferencia de los blancos hijos de Jafet. Las antiguas maldiciones las ha borrado el sacro dedo del Niño" ("My progeny, the dark race of Ham, is no longer different than that of Japheth. The ancient curses have been erased by the sacred finger of the Child"; *Cuentos completos* 2: 248).

While race in some stories implied ineluctable ethnic destiny, frequently Pardo Bazán insisted racial identity was constructed and impermanent. In "La adopción" ("The Adoption") the narrator looks critically at the tendency of British colonizers to foster the notion of naturally superior and inferior races and castes. The result is predictable: "cuando se condena a una raza o a un ser a la ignominia, involuntariamente se teme que esa raza o ese ser desarrollen una especie de fuerza maléfica. . . . Así se ha supuesto de las brujas y aun de los judíos" ("when a race or a person is condemned to ignominy, involuntarily it is feared that that race or person develops a type of malefic force. . . .That is what presumably was the case with witches and Jews"; *Cuentos completos* 4: 42). A child removed from his upper-caste family and raised by untouchables will change races, not just families: "Aquella criatura había dejado de pertenecer a la raza superior" ("That creature no longer belonged to a superior race"; 4: 43). The idea that environment and education trump race and atavism is reinforced in several essays in which Pardo Bazán framed her opposition to evolution. In her essays in *De siglo a siglo*, she put the idea to the service of the monotheistic claim that while a chain connects all men past and present there are yet ways for them to overcome any inherited instinctual drives: "Los instintos del hombre son los mismos, de seguro, en todas partes; eran probablemente en las épocas más obscuras de la prehistoria muy poco diferentes de lo actual: lo que modifica, diversifica y reprime esos instintos, son las circunstancias, la educación (en el sentido social de la palabra), el ambiente, etc." ("The instincts of man are the same, surely, in all parts; it was probably in the darkest eras of prehistory very little different than today: what modifies, diversifies and represses those instincts, are circumstances, education [in the social sense of the word], environment, etc.."; 234).

The notion of adaptation is one of the core issues of Pardo Bazán's fiction and essays. Across the four decades of her literary career she returned repeatedly to the question of what determines human beings' physical and psychological attributes and how those attributes can be improved, though she avoided ascribing potential change to evolution or natural selection as these concepts were popularly understood. Although the issue of racial history and destiny surfaces in dozens of comments about characters' features and traits, Laura Otis suggests that in Pardo Bazán's fiction nature records the past haphazardly and the pull of race is partial and arbitrary (*Organic Memory* 156). Even if characters "represent their races and absorb their environments . . . appearances can be deceiving" (157). This deception of appearances is something that time and again informs Pardo Bazán's short fiction. Her ambiguity was a product of both her voracious reading and the social matrices of the time. All the contradictions in Spanish thought on perfectibility, progress, degeneration, and race found shelter in her probing mind. And, despite her moralizing, she allowed issues to emerge in her work that sometimes challenged her own, and her readers' belief systems and logic.

This commonplace ambiguity is obvious in one of Pardo Bazán's last stories, which students should be encouraged to discuss. Toward the end of her life, when her fiction gravitated to modernism and decadentism, questions of race and evolution in relation to collective identity continued to occupy her thoughts. In 1910 she planted the question squarely in the center of "Fraternidad" ("Fraternity"), in which a paleontologist obsessed with the notion of race goes to Tangiers in search of cranial evidence to support the prehistoric similarity of Spaniards and Africans. His research project stems from his conviction that all men are descended from a single source, a theory that Pardo Bazán subscribed to in some of her stories and essays, including the *De siglo a siglo* articles. The paleontologist denies the existence of inferior races, speculating that, having descended from a single pair, all human beings belong to the same race: "esas supuestas inferioridades no son sino diferencias debidas a las condiciones de la vida y del ambiente" ("those supposed inferiorities are but differences owing to the conditions of life and environment"; *Cuentos completos* 4: 83). This belief echoes Pardo Bazán's frequently voiced notion that differences in racial types were determined by culture or environment.

The paleontologist's plan to prove "la ley de fraternidad universal y omní-moda" ("the universal and absolute law of fraternity"; 83) through the study of skulls fails miserably. His "efusiones de fraternidad" ("fraternal effusions") with the locals in Tangiers are rejected, and his camp is robbed. His opinions changed, the paleontologist describes the thief who is later apprehended as a perfect specimen of a primitive caveman, a "gorila apenas perfeccionado" ("barely perfected gorilla"), suggesting indirectly man's possible evolution from animal species or at least the idea that some men have not evolved as far as others. When the thief is killed and his skull presented to the paleontologist as a gift, he weeps for his lost "ensueño fraternal" ("fraternal dream"). His ideas about "la cadena humana" ("the human chain"), he concludes, were "precipi-tadas"("precipitous"), implying that no such chain links Africans and Spaniards and that the notion of universal brotherhood (and possibly even Pardo Bazán's cherished notion of monophyletism) was a dream. Did Pardo Bazán reverse her opinion that there could be no low creatures that had not yet evolved into higher forms? The only clue, inconclusive, comes in the last sentence: "Y yo lloré mi ensueño fraternal. . . . Como lloraría un ensueño de amor" ("And I wept for my lost fraternal dream. . . . As I would for a lost dream of love"; 84).

NOTES

[1] All translations are my own.

[2] Most of Pardo Bazán's stories are available on the Web site *Biblioteca Virtual Miguel de Cervantes*, but students will find definitive versions in Paredes Núñez's edition of *Cuentos completos*, which I cite unless otherwise noted.

[3] For the curse on the children of Ham, students can consult the King James version of the Old Testament (Gen. 9.20–27). See Hannaford for a general discussion of the concept of race.

[4] See two untitled articles she published in her column, La vida contemporánea: *La ilustración artística*, 8 Sept. 1902, p. 586; *La ilustración artística*, 11 Dec. 1916, p. 794.

[5] I cite "Entre razas" in Pardo Bazán, *Obras completas* [Sainz de Robles and Kirby] 1: 1533–35.

From "Fundamental Truths" to "Playthings of Science": Science, Technology, and Modernity in Pardo Bazán

Dale J. Pratt

Twenty-first-century students of Emilia Pardo Bazán often do not appreciate the astonishing pace of scientific and technological developments during the nineteenth century. Pardo Bazán was an avid observer of those changes and filled her essays with references to contemporary science and applied technology. Additionally, much of her fiction makes specific mention of scientists and their ideas, and virtually all her writing is informed by a critical worldview she would have considered scientific. To help students understand her engagement with science, I have them consider the roles technology and science play in their own lives and what Pardo Bazán might think of today's technology if she were alive today: Would she have a smartphone, a *Facebook* page, an avatar in *Second Life*? Would she look forward to the latest discoveries of science or dread the implications they might hold for humanity? Would she side with evolutionists or with creationists? Though we cannot be certain of the answers to these questions, her writing provides clues. I then ask students to imagine how they would negotiate an ordinary day in the 1880s in the light of the scientific knowledge and technological applications of the era. This exercise underscores the importance of context to sophisticated reading and can inspire interest not only in Pardo Bazán's fiction but even in her most recondite essays.

In her justly famous *La cuestión palpitante* (1882; "The Burning Question"), Pardo Bazán employs the scientific method in her criticism of Émile Zola's efforts to mimic in fiction the praxis of French physiologist Claude Bernard. Frequently misread and overinterpreted, *La cuestión palpitante* criticizes "la ciencia mal digerida de Zola" ("Zola's half-digested science"; 151).[1] Pardo Bazán argues that Zola "tomó las hipótesis por leyes, y sobre el frágil cimiento de dos o tres hechos aislados erigió un enorme edificio" ("took hypotheses for laws, and erected an enormous edifice upon the fragile foundation of two or three isolated facts"; 151), an accusation she had previously leveled against proponents of Darwinism, as I discuss below. A student can understand that Zola's notion that a novel should be an experiment bears little relation to actual experimental science. The methods of observation employed by the realist and naturalist writers—visits to cigarette factories, hospitals, slums, asylums, prisons, and so on—to garner material for their novels certainly were more grounded in the direct observation of life than the process a writer such as Enrique Gil y Carrasco used to create his Romantic novel *El señor de Bembibre* (1844). However, the literary experiment is equally the product of the writer's imagination, and whatever conclusions were drawn from the experiment were givens from the beginning. Maurice Hemingway justly criticizes *Los pazos de Ulloa* ("The House of Ulloa") as a failed experimental novel, given that Julián's and Nucha's weaknesses rig the negative outcome for religion and civilization (*Emilia* 28). Of course, if we believe Pardo Bazán is not wedded to novelistic experimentation, then we need not second-guess the novel's tragic emplotment. Hemingway indeed praises *Los pazos* as "a study of the mental life of Nucha and Julián" (29). Unfortunately, much scholarship has zealously scoured Pardo Bazán's writings for naturalistic tendencies or judged them for how well they conform to Zola's ideal experimental paradigm. Recognizing the place of science in Pardo Bazán's thinking nuances our understanding of her complicated approach to naturalism.

Although some of Pardo Bazán's earliest texts deal extensively with theories, inventions, and what she called "la ciencia amena" ("delightful science"), in her later work modernity's technological accoutrements did not always engage her imagination, and her focus shifted to the "verdades fundamentales" ("fundamental truths") she could extract from the science she harmonized with religious faith (Faus Sevilla 2: 203). In her fiction she depicts science as a (mostly untapped) resource for progress, a set of rational explanations about the world and a (different, and perhaps dubious) set of speculations about the origins and nature of human beings. Technology in her fiction is often symbolic of the progress she understood to be a promise for improving the lives of the laboring classes yet also a tool for exploiting them.

Students from humanities, premed, and STEM programs typically show great interest in debating the meanings of science and technology. In traditional accounts of scientific practice, scientists seek to decipher nature's mysteries by careful observation, conducting experiments according to the scientific method (sometimes using highly complex instruments and machinery) and communicating their findings through respected channels. Natural science deals with plants and animals, rocks, gases, stars, bodies, brains, and the like. Technology is seen both as applied science (engineering, navigation, and medicine, for instance) and the useful products arising from such application, such as bridges, city planning, medical treatments, and, more recently, airplanes, computers, and cell phones. José Ortega y Gasset viewed the use of technology as an inextricable part of human identity; science, or knowledge about the world, follows our always already technologized engagement with the world. Foucault expanded the definition of *technology* to include the process and fruits of instrumental reason (as in "technologies of the self").[2] Technology, under this broad view, includes not only gadgets but also the mental techniques used to create them—the thinking that underwrites theory and praxis. Assignments to read Pardo Bazán under these various definitions of technology provoke deep critical thinking. This essay hews to Pardo Bazán's more traditional conception of science and technology, examining her early engagement with popularization and critique, with an emphasis on her take on Darwinism; her fiction's often ironic stance regarding the self-assured representatives of science; and her self-deprecating detachment concerning her own relation to modern inventions.

As a popularizer of science in "La ciencia amena" (1876–77; "Delightful Science") and as a semiobjective Christian apologist in *Reflexiones científicas con-*

tra el darwinismo (1877; "Scientific Reflections against Darwinism"), Pardo Bazán frequently cites others' ideas without attribution. José Manuel González Herrán asserts in the introduction to his edition of *La cuestión palpitante* that "'refritos' o resúmenes de obras poco conocidas de sus lectores" ("'rehashes' or summaries of relatively unknown works"; 56) constitute much of her writing about science. Far from discrediting her, this helps us understand her as a popularizer fascinated by cutting-edge science. In the classroom, we compare her glosses with early articles from *National Geographic*, a few pages from Darwin's *Origin of Species*, and the French biologist Jean Louis Armand de Quatrefages de Bréau's (1810–92) critique to guide our discussion of summation, popularization, and questions of originality and plagiarism. In "La ciencia amena," Pardo Bazán glosses the ideas of the Italian scientist Fra (Pietro) Angelo Secchi (1818–78) into popular idioms—dressing science in "bello ropaje" ("fine robes"; 17). For example, she describes caloric (a hypothetical substance alleged to cause all heat) as "la respiración de los grandes pulmones de la maquinaria toda movida por el vapor y de la gigantesca serpiente del ferrocarril" ("the breathing of all vapor-powered machinery and of that gigantic serpent, the railroad"; 26). "La ciencia amena" also reveals her thinking about the future. She laments the possibility of coal running out by 2075 (41). She speculates that the earth once emitted sufficient caloric to heat the moon to life-sustaining temperatures and suggests that one day the sun will cool enough to support life (50).[3] She envisions electricity replacing steam (90) and imagines new uses for electrical current, such as instantaneous trains and accelerators for growing trees and hatching eggs. Throughout "La ciencia amena," science offers explanations of and potential uses for natural phenomena.[4]

Pardo Bazán published *Reflexiones científicas contra el darwinismo* in the journal *La ciencia cristiana* in 1877. She again cites Secchi and relies heavily on Quatrefages, quoting many passages from his *L'espèce humaine* ("The Human Species"), published earlier that year. In the 1870s, the terms *Darwinism* and *darwinismo* were diffuse and politically charged, even more so in Spain than in England.[5] Darwin's *Descent of Man* (1871) was new, but *The Origin of Species* had passed through six editions since 1859, as Darwin added lines of argument, new data, and responses to his critics. By the 1870s, two criticisms were particularly challenging to Darwinian theory: Kelvin's objection that the calculated ages of the sun and the earth did not provide sufficient time for natural selection and the Scottish engineer Fleeming Jenkins's assertion that there was no vehicle by which a new variety (we would call it a mutation) could be maintained over generations and selected for by competition.[6] Pardo Bazán indeed presents a valid scientific critique of Darwinian theory as it stood in the 1870s; however, many of her criticisms are leveled against elaborations of the theory propounded by Ernst Haeckel and not by Darwin himself. While *Reflexiones* captures a snapshot of the reception of Darwinian theory, twenty-five years later little of its criticism remained valid. To prime students for reading Pardo Bazán's novel *La madre naturaleza* (1887; "Mother Nature") and short stories broaching Darwinism, a good small-group exercise is to have them outline Pardo Bazán's arguments in *Reflexiones*. Though it is impossible to know how Pardo Bazán would have viewed Darwinism's relation to Catholicism after the scientific problems she presents were resolved by the discoveries of radiation, the sun's nuclear fusion, and genes, we can hear echoes of these discussions in her later stories about creation and the origins of culture.

La madre naturaleza, set in rural Galicia, interrogates evolution's and nature's roles in shaping and influencing humanity. Unaware they are siblings, Pedro and Manuela seem predestined to become lovers. In chapter 1, they seek shelter from a rainstorm, first under a tree and then in a grotto, each site allegorically representing a different possible origin for human nature, the Genesis story and Darwin's evolutionary model. The tree — "árbol patriarcal" ("patriarchal tree"; 84) — is Eden's tree of life; the cave (really an abandoned quarry) does not hold the thorns and weeds of a fallen world but recalls the teeming life of Darwin's "tangled bank" (*Origin* 408). After the storm, the couple sees a rainbow promising God's grace; they have not yet fallen. However, they soon encounter la Sabia, whose grotesque goiter presents a "lustrosa y horrible segunda cara sin facciones" ("shiny and horrible second face without features"; 99) and underscores the Janus-faced struggle that pits religion and culture against the forces of environment and nature that incite their sexual desire. Pedro and Manuela make love late in the novel, partaking of the forbidden fruit and suffering the fall upon learning the identity of Perucho's father. At the novel's close, Manuela's uncle, Gabriel, hails Mother Nature not with "Ave María" but as "madrastra" ("stepmother"), announcing the monstrous birth of incest (405). Earlier, Gabriel ruminates at length on evolution and its interference in human relationships, concluding that "la lucha misma, el combate de todos contra todos, es la única clave del misterio. Lo dice muy bien Darwin" ("the struggle itself, the combat of all against all, is the only key to the mystery. Darwin says it well"; 304). Not an unequivocally didactic experimental novel, *La madre naturaleza* refuses to judge between the natural forces that foster authentic romantic love between Pedro and Manuela and the incest taboo that will forever separate them.

Pardo Bazán later supplements these allegories of Eden and the "tangled bank" with literary representations of prehistory. As in *La madre naturaleza*, these fictions involve couples estranged from their tribe. Students can compare the brief "Progreso" (1907; "Progress"; *Cuentos completos* 4: 213–15) — in which a Paleolithic couple discovers fire and flees their tribe to found their own civilization — with the lengthier *novela breve* ("short novel") *En las cavernas* (1912; "In the Caves").[7] For this unit, students also read Genesis 1–4, Pardo Bazán's account of her visit to the Altamira cave ("Las cuevas"), and the last sixteen paragraphs of Darwin's *Origin* — from "I see no good reason why the views given in this volume should shock the religious feelings of anyone" (401). In *En las cavernas*, the prehistoric Napal's inventions and his partner Damara's innovative expression of female sexuality and fashion transform their group. Damara's refusal to participate in forced promiscuity creates the conditions for genealogy and inheritance; incites prehistory's first feelings of love, jealousy, and greed; and provokes murder. Issues of family relations, gender construction, cultural memories, secrecy, and revelation resonate between the assigned texts. Students enjoy discussing Damara as representing the missing link between female hominids and modern women and how she and Napal radically alter tribal culture to create a new human family (Pratt, "Sex" 43). They compare the contexts and choices made by Damara and Napal and by Manuela and Pedro and consider how Pedro's obscured paternity and Manuela's choosing him as a mate cause the destruction of the house of Ulloa. Although siblinghood does not preclude sexual love for Damara and Napal (nor for Adam and Eve), it irrevocably denies happiness to Pedro and Manuela.

Students also have the opportunity to analyze how representatives of science misread and are misread. After I stress to students Pardo Bazán's competence in accurately interpreting and representing science, we examine how she depicts how others — scientists, intellectuals, priests, superstitious peasants, and so on — fail to do so. Pardo Bazán frequently portrays scientists and doctors as arrogant, proud, pedantic, foolish, and selfish, even when they make discoveries or successfully manipulate nature.[8] These characters disdain unscientific explanations, which frequently leads to their own blindness about psychology and behavior. *La piedra angular* (1891; "The Cornerstone") sardonically depicts spokesmen for Cesare Lombroso's criminology. The narrator rejects the attribution of criminality exclusively to physiological characteristics, the reading of delinquency in a person's body. *La nueva cuestión palpitante* (1894; "The New Burning Question") similarly rebuts Lombroso's and Max Nordau's arguments about degenerate artistic geniuses: scientific criticism can only be prescriptive and reductive; it does not supply tools to sufficiently appreciate polysemic art. In "Un poco de ciencia" (1909; "A Little Science"; *Cuentos completos* 3: 197–99), Champollion deciphers Egyptian hieroglyphics with ease, even from a transcription cobbled from random figures by a desperate clerk. "Un destripador de antaño" (1890; "The Heart Lover"; 2: 5–21) contrasts peasants' superstitions with the new pharmacist's rationality and potent medicines. Pepona commits murder when she misreads Custodio as a magical *destripador* desirous of virginal cadavers; the scientist tragically underestimates the depths of Pepona's superstitious cruelty. "La santa de Karnar" (1891; "The Saint of Karnar"; 2: 77–85) depicts a similar interplay between superstition and medicine yet with opposite results. When a pubescent girl falls ill, her doctor recommends a trip to the country, despite its being January. The girl's family travels ever farther from Santiago, until in the tiny village of Karnar they meet "la Santa," an emaciated, semicomatose woman who supposedly consumes nothing but the consecrated Host. The experience heals the girl; hysteria's "wandering uterus" falls into place with a torrent of vitality as she passes menarche. Despite the girl's recovery, the doctor scoffs at the story. Even the girl, an old woman at the time of narration, questions her interpretation of the experience. Discussions of Pardo Bazán's representations of misreading lead students naturally to self-conscious reflection on their own habits of reading and their attitudes toward contemporary debates about science.

The class explores how medical and scientific equipment also lend themselves to misreading. In "Un destripador," labels in Custodio's pharmacy resemble alchemical formulae (13), what appear to be severed heads are really models of the nervous system (*La madre naturaleza* 146; *La piedra angular* 319), and medical instruments mimic devices of torture (*La piedra angular* 319). Pascual López likewise misreads Professor Onarro's lab—he compares its machinery to illegible Chinese characters (*Pascual López* 71). In "La operación" (1897; *Cuentos completos* 1: 450–53), a capitalist reveals the secret of his success: a complex surgical procedure that releases smoke from his skull. The operation allowed him to conduct business free from passions and heroics, but a skeptic calls the smoke "lo ideal" ("idealism")—whereupon the capitalist taps the skeptic's "wooden" head and pronounces him incurable. From "Un destripador de antaño" to *Pascual López* and "La operación," thematic misreadings of science serve both tragic and comic purposes.

Pardo Bazán's aristocratic status allowed her to be surrounded by the latest innovations. She frequently mentions applied technology and gadgetry in her long-lived column in *La ilustración artística*, La vida contemporánea (1895–1916), a splendid source of topics for undergraduate theme papers.[9] She was an early adopter (in 1915 her Madrid telephone number was 22) but not a techie; were she alive today, she would probably have the latest smartphone but be unable to program it. She confessed that "mi ineptitud para la mecánica pasa de los límites de la verosimilitud" ("my mechanical ineptitude passes the borders of verisimilitude"; Faus Sevilla 2: 454). She felt incapable of giving accurate scientific descriptions of lab work (2: 53). She enjoyed film and early on recognized it as art (Ruiz-Ocaña Dueñas 260). In 1896 she foresaw that the automobile—which she called "el artilugio trepidante" ("the frenetic contraption")—would bring a revolution in social customs and mores (qtd. in Ruiz-Ocaña Dueñas 359). Aviation, though, did not make the same impression: in 1910 she ridiculed the fantasy of convoys of airplanes transporting people and merchandise, and in 1911 she doubted aviation would ever have practical appeal (Ruiz-Ocaña Dueñas 361). Her intuition did not fail her, however, when she contemplated the "vastos horizontes" ("expansive horizons") for commerce promised by refrigerated transportation (Faus Sevilla 2: 463).

Pardo Bazán believed the "verdades fundamentales" of both science and her Catholic faith could be reconciled through reason and careful examination of scientific claims (Faus Sevilla 2: 203). In her fiction and essays, she depicts science as regularly misreading and misinterpreting reality, and thus as not truly scientific because it discounts the spiritual components of human existence. Science, too, is misread by some of her characters who are superstitious or skeptical. Yet for Pardo Bazán, far from being "meros juguetes de la ciencia" ("mere playthings of science"), scientific discovery, innovation, and invention "son agentes poderosos de la obra civilizadora" ("are powerful agents of civilizing work"; qtd. in Faus Sevilla 2: 461). Despite her unease with describing the inner workings of gadgets, such as a watch (Faus Sevilla 2: 454), she is the opposite of her character Pascual López, who glides through scientific lectures and demonstrations without comprehending them, deeming his limited understanding sufficient for survival in the modern world. Instead, Pardo Bazán exposes weaknesses and limits of scientific hypotheses, mocks scientific pedantry and arrogance, and touts the benefits to civilization of careful science and applied technology.

NOTES

[1] This essay quotes from José Manuel González Herrán's 1989 edition of *La cuestión palpitante*. All translations are my own.

[2] On the concept of technologies of the self and Pardo Bazán, see Smith, "Women."

[3] The supposed cooling of the sun justifies one of her objections to Darwinism in her later essay *Reflexiones científicas contra el darwinismo*.

[4] Otis ("Science") has meticulously analyzed "La ciencia amena" and its relation to Pardo Bazán's novel *Pascual López*.

[5] Landry describes the social dimension of *darwinismo* as "a nomenclature born from a need to describe Darwin as filtered through the popular imagination" (71).

[6] Pardo Bazán admired Kelvin's writings on heat (Otis, "Science" 78). Eiselely outlines major challenges to Darwin's theory. For a summary of Pardo Bazán's critical essay on Darwinism, see Kirby.

[7] I cite Pardo Bazán's short stories in Juan Paredes Núñez's four-volume edition, *Cuentos completos*.

[8] Elsewhere I discuss scientific spokespersons as mediating figures who reflect (sometimes distorted) images of scientific theories and praxis (Pratt, *Signs* 55–58).

[9] Study of Pardo Bazán's column, La vida contemporánea, must begin with the monumental work of Ruiz-Ocaña Dueñas. Faus Sevilla collates many of the essays with Pardo Bazán's biographical context. Students can be assigned different articles that deal with specific inventions or theories—selected from the detailed lists of themes provided by Ruiz-Ocaña Dueñas—and be asked to compare them with any of Pardo Bazán's fictional works.

Naturalism, Medicine, and
Un viaje de novios

Erika M. Sutherland

One of the challenges of teaching nineteenth-century Spanish literature is making it relevant to a student body ever more focused on credentialing and on the practical outcomes of their studies. At Muhlenberg College a significant percentage of advanced Spanish students combine their Spanish major or minor with studies in another discipline. This diversification mirrors national trends: in its 2013 survey of double majors, the Teagle report found that students were twenty times more likely to combine language studies with a second major than to study a language alone (Pitt and Tepper 56). At Muhlenberg, known for its excellent preparation for graduate studies in the health professions, neuroscience, and psychology, many students choose Spanish along with these prehealth majors.

The Teagle study noted the broad appeal of majoring in both a foreign language and a second discipline but found less evidence of integrative learning among those double majors. Language students who chose a double major were twice as likely as those who chose other kinds of double majors to see virtually no relevance of one major to the other (59). The pedagogy presented in this essay is designed to address this disconnect between disciplines. For students majoring in Spanish and a prehealth discipline I provide tools and opportunities to reach beyond their preconceived notions of literature and to engage with specific aspects of the texts likely to resonate with them.

The value of literature in medicine has been evident for many years now. In the nineteenth century medical journals published *novelas de folletín* (serial novels). For example, the newspaper *La España médica* (1855–56; "Medical Spain") offered readers a review of medical advances and contemporary issues along with serialized novels.[1] The opening chapter of Benito Pérez Galdós's first foray into naturalist literature, *La desheredada* ("The Disinherited"), appeared in the pages of *El diario médico* (1881–82; "The Medical Journal"). More recent evidence of these connections includes an MLA volume titled *Teaching Literature and Medicine* (Hawkins and Chandler McEntyre) and recent studies on the value of literary reading groups for health care professionals. Amy Levin and Phoebe Stein Davis observe that close reading of literature can enable clinicians to make or change diagnoses and to understand how their experiences or prejudices affect their ability to give care—for example, the assumption that a construction worker has a higher tolerance for pain than a white-collar executive. Even small textual details may lead to a change in practice that signals care and compassion (429). The most profound connections between literature and medicine grow out of the questions that texts can suggest—often questions with no set answer.

Emilia Pardo Bazán's *Un viaje de novios* (1881; "A Wedding Trip") connects medical science past and present in many ways and is a manageable length for undergraduates exploring literature in a second language. I have used this novel and the questions it inspires in my eighteenth- and nineteenth-century survey course and in my senior seminar, On Love and Other Diseases: The Body in Spanish Literature. Some of the questions this text raises include the following:

> How did medical tourism function in the nineteenth century? Does it still exist?
>
> Is the medical information in *Un viaje de novios* real or made up? How did Pardo Bazán learn about medicine? What access did women have to medical information? Were there women doctors?
>
> Are the disorders represented in *Un viaje de novios* real? What does the medical literature of the nineteenth century have to say about these disorders? Are they present in today's medical literature? If not, when did they disappear?[2]
>
> Are all the characters identified as doctors actually physicians? Do these doctors correspond to professional categories of the nineteenth century? Are the approaches to treatment portrayed in the novel realistic? traditional? cutting-edge? Do they respond to a specifically Hispanic perspective on healing?
>
> How do today's medical practices compare with those portrayed in the novel?

While some of these questions may remain unanswered, they all point to the value of teaching *Un viaje de novios* through the lens of naturalism and medicine.

When I teach this novel, I begin with a reading guide to help students focus on specific aspects of the text; the guide, which follows Bloom's taxonomy, includes questions, key quotations, and prompts for individual and group projects. First, students identify key points of information. Once the key vocabulary and topics have been established, students can master a series of tools that lead to higher orders of thinking. I use *PowerPoint* presentations to guide discussion, incorporating additional questions and images to stimulate quick discussion and to connect with the preparation done outside class. These presentations often serve as springboards to in-class writing assignments. The assignments, like the presentations, are made possible in large part by the availability of nineteenth-century primary materials in digitized formats, which facilitates easy access to huge stores of primary sources. The model that follows shows how these resources enrich students' reading of *Un viaje de novios*.

Knowledge

Students new to the study of literature confront new terminology; in a second-language literature class, even familiar terms may need to be relearned. Students need to familiarize themselves with the resources available to help them navigate technical terms and must determine which terms are key. In her preface to the novel, Pardo Bazán introduces two contrasting terms, *realismo* ("realism") and *naturalismo* ("naturalism") (53). In a traditional literature course, the debates that roiled around Zola's doctrine could provide a semester's worth of reading. Here, however, a summary of the movement's main content and ideological aspects suffices to establish a conceptual framework.

Medical terminology appears throughout the novel. While many terms are cognates—*asma* (asthma; 65), *anémicas* (anemic; 85), *alopecia* (alopecia [hair loss]; 165)—online dictionaries such as the *Diccionario de la lengua española* ("Dictionary of the Spanish Language"), published by the Real Academia Española, may provide definitions for less familiar terms like *materialista* (a follower of materialist theories; 77), *glóbulos rojos* (red blood cells; 85), and *ojeras* (dark circles under the eyes; 169).[3] Technical medical terms, along with their English translations, etymologies, and etiologies, are easily researched through the University of Salamanca's online *Diccionario médico-biológico, histórico y etimológico* ("Historico-Etymological Dictionary of Medicine and Biology"). Students are challenged to describe the new concepts using both words and graphics. Using key words in Spanish, images can be culled from *Google Images*, from the *Hemeroteca Digital* Web site of the Biblioteca Nacional, the *Sociedad Española para la Historia de Medicina* ("Spanish Society for the History of Medicine") Web site and its links, and from the History of Medicine Division of the *U. S. National Library of Medicine* Web site.

To introduce the idea that images are themselves complex texts, I present a Spanish painting that is contemporary to *Un viaje de novios* and have students consider its multiple interpretations. Enrique Simonet's 1890 *Anatomía del corazón o ¡Y tenía corazón!* ("Anatomy of the Heart; or, And she Had a Heart!") is on first glance unambiguous: the doctor is examining a human heart. For a student of literature, the heart is immediately understood to represent something more than mere valves and muscles. LaVera Crawley invites the medically minded reader to follow suit, pointing out

> the highly interpretive and subjective nature of what we might otherwise hold as purely objective. The goal of the humanities is not to dispute whether or not an object is a sickled red blood cell or a ruptured chorda tendineae, but in the interpretive process of assigning meaning to objects a curricular focus on semiotics and narrative representation may enhance the student's ability to reflect and think critically. . . . Such inquiry . . . can provide the thick descriptions that restore biomedicine to its place within the larger human context.   (320)[4]

I introduce Simonet's portrait of an anatomist early in the course, in part to model the use of relevant imagery and in part to show how Zola's notion of the experimental novel as a living document is an ideal difficult to achieve: the heart belongs to a woman lying dead on the autopsy table. Students must approach the naturalist text with care.

By focusing on specific words from the initial pages of the novel, students realize that not every word must be investigated (important especially for students new to reading long texts in a second language) and that exploring certain terms opens up new breadths of context and depths of meaning.

Comprehension

As students develop a level of comfort with the text and familiarity with the dictionaries and other knowledge-building tools, it is important to assess their comprehension of the novel. Close reading is a fundamental skill that both leads to and confirms understanding. Students write a formal analysis of a key passage fairly early in the novel; the section recounting Joaquín's inquiries regarding the suitability of the marriage of Aurelio de Miranda to Lucía offers rich possibilities for both analysis of the narrative and insight into contemporary medical concerns (84–86). A second textual analysis might focus on the passage describing the different reasons why Miranda and Pilar seek relief at the spa at Vichy (162–69) or the description of the curative role of the Jesuit Padre Arrigoitia (254–56).

Application

Working in small groups, students present how specific disorders or treatments are described in the novel, such as the nineteenth-century understanding of Miranda's liver ailment, hydrotherapy, and medical tourism. The presentations must include textual references, but they draw primarily on the contemporary sources and images available at the *Hemeroteca Digital* site. A review of medical journals and the back pages of mainstream newspapers yields advertisements for products promising cures for long lists of ailments, which students find entertaining. The names of ailments and products discovered in the newspapers can become search terms for students to investigate more serious medical journals, archived in *Google Books* and the *U. S. National Library of Medicine* site. Anthologies of primary documents are useful (Nash, *Mujer*; Jagoe et al.), but activities that require students to seek out primary sources in their original contexts afford opportunities for the students to stumble upon surprisingly frank descriptions of conditions considered taboo in contemporary American culture, unexpected bits of quackery, and clear evidence of evolving science.

Analysis

Armed with a deeper understanding of the novel and its context, students work in groups for a second project, an analysis of the authenticity of the novel's portrayal of Artegui's depression, Perico's verbal tic, or Pilar's anemia and eventual tuberculosis. The exceptional details marking Pilar's decline permit critical comparisons with period case histories. The *Colección Historicomédica de la Universitat de València* ("Historico-Medical Collection of the University of

Valencia") Web site has links to case studies, including an especially compelling clinical case history of a young woman with tuberculosis (Mangraner y Marinas). For this project, students once again work from medical and popular newspaper documents available through the *Hemeroteca Digital* (the Biblioteca Nacional's digital newspaper archives) and from period medical texts available on *Google Books*. They also consult critical essays to support their analyses. In addition to *SciELO* (*Scientific Electronic Library Online*), *Dynamis* ("Dynamics") and *Asclepio* ("Asclepius") are two Spanish journals dedicated to the history of science and medicine, both of whose Web sites have searchable content.

Synthesis

I ask students to write a longer essay that builds on their new skills and knowledge: they must offer a final prognosis for Lucia or Ignacio using evidence from the novel and from both period and current medical theories. Students can refer again to the *Diccionario médico-biológico, histórico y etimológico*, this time consulting its links to contemporary and historical studies related to each search term.

More advanced students might take on the reconstruction of a diagnosis left unarticulated. The frequent use of ellipses surrounding the medical background of Miranda points to the possibility of syphilis. Students able to connect the groom's physical description in chapter 1 (59–60), Miranda's half-silenced self-diagnosis of "una afección hepática complicada con otra de carácter . . . " ("a liver ailment compounded by another . . . ailment"; 77), and Dr. Vélez de Rada's "discreción profesional" ("professional discretion"; 85)—invoked as he refuses to recommend Miranda as a suitable husband for Lucía (85)—will find ample parallels between the novel and highly coded nineteenth-century medical and social discourses surrounding syphilis and marriage. Using the search terms *matrimonio* and *impedimento* or *sífilis* in *Google Books* will lead students to forensic medical texts that show the deep dismay felt by many doctors at contemporary laws that kept them from revealing medical reasons to refuse or dissolve a marriage. For example, Dr. Pedro Mata y Fontanet argued that women should be made aware of any deformity or disease, including syphilis, that could affect her or any offspring the marriage might produce: "Mezclad entre las flores y ramilletes de su boda los fórceps, los ganchos o el bisturí, a los que bien pronto habrá que recurrir para la salvación del engendro y de su madre, y ved si esa misma mal aconsejada hembra no arrojará horrorizada la corona nupcial en las aras del himeneo" ("Mix among the wedding flowers and bouquets the forceps, hooks, or scalpel that soon enough will be sought to save the child and his mother, and see if that poorly counseled woman doesn't cast away the wedding crown at the very altar"; 236). His vivid lament is one that students may encounter again in their own clinical experiences; students are reminded of the power they will hold and the dilemmas they will face as health care providers. Students interested in the broader social implications of syphilis can research the impact of the disease using the resources of the Museo Olavide. Located on the campus of the medical school of the Universidad Complutense in Madrid, the museum houses the Academia Española de Dermatología y Venereología's collection of nineteenth-century wax models of dermatological and venereal afflictions. Images of the collection and related medical documents are available on the museum's Web site.

Evaluation

In their final essays, students are challenged to make and defend judgments drawn from what they have learned, incorporating other texts read in the course and contextualizing *Un viaje de novios* within the students' broader experiences. Students might be asked to defend the medical use of spas today or to analyze the relevance of this novel for a contemporary doctor.

The American Association of Medical Colleges (AAMC), the organization responsible for setting the admissions standards for medical schools, recently redefined the competencies expected of incoming medical students to include social skills, cultural competence, teamwork, reliability and dependability, oral and written communication, resilience and adaptability, and capacity for improvement ("Core Competencies"). My approach to teaching Pardo Bazán's *Un viaje de novios* facilitates the development of many of these competencies—indeed, they are developed in any language and literature class. Additional AAMC competencies that my pedagogical approach to naturalist literature addresses are critical thinking, scientific inquiry, and an understanding of living systems and human behavior.

The new AAMC competencies are one reaction to the recent emphasis placed on increasing health care providers' ability to see and understand their patients holistically; my model for teaching naturalist literature shares this aim. I close with Ann Jurecic's challenge to contemporary readers who approach texts about disease and suffering from a critical distance. She argues that the "empathy gap" is of concern to practitioners of medicine and literature alike and fears that "those whose training and careers have steeped them in a hermeneutics of suspicion" are unable to connect the representation of illness with real disease and suffering (13–14). Teaching *Un viaje de novios* to students headed for careers in the health professions can help close that gap by embracing the ambiguity and complexity of Pardo Bazán's work and by connecting real medical issues to their literary representations in a way that is dynamic for students and new for instructors.

NOTES

[1] Digital copies of *La España médica* can be accessed at the Web site *Biblioteca Virtual de la Comunidad de Madrid*.

[2] In her study of the representation of hysteria in *Los pazos de Ulloa* (1886), Robin Ragan posed a series of similar questions: "How did Spanish women writers portray hysterical

women? How did they deal with symptoms, causes, and cures? What kind of answers, if any, were they providing to explain women's illnesses? What kind of relationship did their female characters have with their doctors? Were their female characters falling ill or being diagnosed as ill?" (144).

³ The appendix to this essay lists the online resources mentioned here.

⁴ Crawley advocates a reader-response approach for prehealth student readers, noting its potential for integrating a text's scientific content with the ambiguities and personal insight that can move the focus from disease to a more patient-centered viewpoint (323).

APPENDIX
Online Resources for Teaching Pardo Bazán
in Medical Contexts

Asclepio, asclepio.revistas.csic.es

The journal of the history of medicine published by Spain's National Research Council offers free access to all of their issues.

Colección Historicomédica de la Universitat de València, hicido.uv.es/Expo _medicina

The Web site of the University of Valencia's History of Medicine Collection offers well-curated links to exhibitions, including online images, texts, and clinical studies.

Diccionario de la Real Academia Española, www.rae.es

The Royal Academy's *Diccionario de la lengua española* is the essential starting point for exploring general vocabulary. It contains links to historical dictionaries as well.

Diccionario médico-biológico, histórico y etimológico, www.dicciomed.eusal.es

This online medical dictionary is a valuable resource for technical words and historical usages.

Dynamis, www.revistadynamis.es

Published by the University of Granada, *Dynamis* focuses on the history of medicine and science; its Web site offers free access to all its issues.

Hemeroteca Digital, Biblioteca Nacional de España, hemerotecadigital.bne.es /index.vm

The National Library of Spain has a large and growing digital collection of periodical publications. Texts can be searched by dates, keywords, and authors or browsed by publication category, including medical papers and journals.

Museo Olavide, museoolavide.aedv.es/obras-olavide

The Museo Olavide focuses on skin disorders, including, notably, syphilis; its Web site presents clinical studies, texts, print images, and images of their anatomical models as well as links to other museums and collections of anatomical models.

SciELO (Scientific Electronic Library Online), www.scielo.org/php/index.php ?lang=es

SciELO is a massive database of current research in the sciences, medicine, and the history of medicine from Latin American and Spanish sources. Some references link to full-text articles, while others must be accessed in print or through interlibrary loan.

Sociedad Española para la Historia de Medicina, www.sehm.es/pages/recursos -para-la-investigacion/museos

This portal has links to the Web sites of several Spanish medical museums, most of which have a variety of print and graphic resources.

U.S. National Library of Medicine, History of Medicine Division, www.nlm.nih .gov/hmd/index.html

The History of Medicine Division is home to one of the largest collections of Spanish medical texts and journals and to a collection of some seventy thousand digital images documenting the history of medicine.

Teaching Pardo Bazán from Postcolonial and Transatlantic Perspectives

Helena Miguélez-Carballeira

The postcolonial and transatlantic dimensions of the work of Emilia Pardo Bazán, a writer and intellectual who traditionally has been located in the Spanish-language literary canon, may not spring readily to mind. However, I propose in this essay that the postcolonial and transatlantic frameworks prove extremely helpful in contextualizing Pardo Bazán as a Galician (and therefore peripheral) figure trying to amass literary capital in the metropolitan literary system based in Madrid during a period when Spain's transatlantic status (its fall as a major colonial power in America; the subsequent reconfiguration of trade) was also undergoing a historical shift. Many facets of Pardo Bazán's work as a literary writer and a public intellectual come into relief when viewed through postcolonial and transatlantic prisms: the political and cultural tensions between Spain and Galicia and the problem of colonial representation that they raise; Pardo Bazán's literary idiom, a hybrid language whose full comprehension requires, ideally, knowledge of both Spanish and Galician; and the recurrent role that an Atlantic imaginary plays in her literature.

The work of Joseba Gabilondo on Pardo Bazán provides a good starting point for a postcolonial approach to her texts and ideally should be required reading for any teaching proposal aiming to foreground this aspect of her work ("Towards"). Referring to postnational methods for literary history and not to postcolonial theories proper, Gabilondo criticizes the failure to adequately integrate Pardo Bazán's work into the Spanish literary canon—because of her gender—and the Galician—because the author never used Galician as a literary language and had tense relations with some of the founding figures of late-nineteenth-century Galician nationalism, including the historian Manuel Murguía and the poets Rosalía de Castro and Curros Enríquez. The patriarchal and nationalist modes of traditional literary history in both Spain and Galicia have therefore diminished, rather than projected, the significance of Pardo Bazán's work. Gabilondo's article goes beyond the question of canonicity to point to the salient but seldom examined question of Pardo Bazán's literary language, particularly in her works on Galician themes, which comprise around one hundred short stories, some of her best-known novels—*Pascual López: Autobiografía de un estudiante de medicina* (1879; "Pascual López: Autobiography of a Medical Student"), *La Tribuna* (1882; "The Tribune"), *El cisne de Vilamorta* (1885; "The Swan of Vilamorta"), *Los pazos de Ulloa* (1886; "The House of Ulloa"), *La madre naturaleza* (1887; "Mother Nature"), *Morriña* (1889; "Homesickness"), and *Insolación* (1889; "Sunstroke")—and dramatic texts such as *La suerte* (1904; "Luck"). In essence, Gabilondo describes Pardo Bazán's literary language in these texts as marked by traces of the Galician language, almost as though the author writes from a (self-)translational perspective—that is, translating internally from Galician into Spanish—in "a failed attempt to other the non-modern Galicia that haunts her" ("Towards" 258). This idea has important implications for any teaching approach to Pardo Bazán that includes elements of close textual reading. Some of the most important tools in postcolonial theory can come in handy: Edward Said's orientalism—the system of patronizing cultural representations brought about by hegemonic cultures onto the colonized—and Homi Bhabha's concepts of the "third space" (53)—a site for identity construction that materializes through a hybrid language or enunciation position—and of "cultural hybridity" (3) provide theoretical prisms with which to explain the complex interplay of power, identity, and language at work in Pardo Bazán's texts about Galician themes. This interplay is intricately involved in the history of Spanish-Galician conflict, a conflict that I have described in *Galicia, a Sentimental Nation: Gender, Culture and Politics* as postcolonial. The teaching proposal that I present here seeks, therefore, to place Pardo Bazán firmly within this framework.

Toward a Postcolonial Pardo Bazán

Said's *Orientalism* taught us that empire is built as an edifice of representation. This means that the power of one culture over another is legitimized discursively as an act of imaging, whereby the colonial-postcolonial culture is looked upon condescendingly by the (post) imperial center as the curious object of a patronizing yet depreciative gaze. Often, as other postcolonial theorists such as Franz Fanon and Bhabha have concluded, orientalist discourses are predicated upon stereotypes that prefigure an exotic, uncivilized, feminine, or dangerous subject in order to legitimize subjugation of that subject. Although the theory of orientalism has not been frequently brought to bear on Spain's internal national conflicts, some of its existing applications concern Pardo Bazán's work. Akiko Tsuchiya's article "Género y orientalismo en *Insolación* de Pardo Bazán" ("Gender and Orientalism in *Insolación* by Pardo Bazán") interprets the novel *Insolación* as an allegory of the negotiated construction of a Spanish identity away from its southern other, embodied in the feminized character of the Andalusian Pacheco (773). However, any attempt to teach Pardo Bazán's texts through the theoretical lens of orientalism will find a much richer range of examples by focusing on the Spanish-Galician axis, and, specifically, on how Pardo Bazán depicts, largely for Spanish-speaking literary consumption, the Galician rural classes.

Pardo Bazán's short story "Eterna ley" (1922; "Eternal Law") stands out for the ease with which it lends itself to an orientalist reading. The story is only three pages long, so it can be read in class rather than prepared in advance. It tells a simple observational anecdote from the point of view of a first-person narrator on a leisurely walk around the Galician hill fort of Santa Tegra (on the border with Portugal), in the company of a female British tourist, a young journalist, and a local priest. The members of the group comment curiously on a passing young villager on his way to the local *romería* (village festivity), only to witness subsequently how he gets entangled in a violent fight with a young man from a rival village and is eventually killed. Although the story may seem far-fetched in its excessively violent outcome, the episode observed is described by the narrator as a "bravata de parroquia a parroquia" ("scuffle between parishes"; *Cuentos completos* 3: 271).[1] After students are given a historical introduction to the emergence of leisurely travel, modernity, and privilege in late-nineteenth-century Spain, which may include John Urry's influential concept of "the tourist gaze," they can be asked to identify passages in the story where the narrator—representing the group's collective voice, marked by privilege and leisure—distances herself and the group from the surrounding landscape, including the human landscape, as if these were purely objects of their amused observation. This distancing and objectifying become most obvious in how the narrative voice depicts the passing male villager, which students can fruitfully analyze through the critical tools of Said's orientalism. There is, first and foremost, how the object of their orientalist gaze, a Galician peasant seen from a bourgeois perspective, is explicitly feminized. Of his appearance, the narrator remarks that he seemed a "fornido labriego, que de veinte años no pasaría, pues era su cara lampiña y hermosa, como de mujer" ("robust peasant, no older than twenty, since his face was smooth and pretty like a woman's"; 270). The young man is also turned into a sexualized object by the tourists' gaze: "era una aparición en extremo típica, y todos dijimos a la vez: ¡Vaya un muchacho guapo!" ("he was a most typical example, and we all said in one voice: What a handsome young man!"; 270). But perhaps the most evident example of the orientalist dynamic is found in the passage where the young, rural Galician is described as an ethnic specimen, an authentic native suitable for museological admiration:

> Le mirábamos, admirando el ejemplar. La estatura, las formas eran atléticas; pero el semblante, apenas curtido por el sol, tenía la corrección y el

modelado de una estatua antigua. Un bozo rubio empezaba a sombrear los labios de cereza, y los ojos, de oscuro y profundo azul, eran grandes y candorosos. El pelo, rizado, color de miel, que se vió al quitarse el galán su fea boina, completaba la perfilación de la testa y su carácter de modelo artístico.   (270)

We observed him, admiring the exemplary specimen. His height and shape were athletic; but his face and skin, barely tarnished by the sun, had the precision and contours of an antique statue. Some blond stubble was beginning to shade his cherry lips, and his dark, deep blue eyes were big and innocent. His curly, honey-colored hair, which we saw when the young man took off his shabby cap, completed the profile of his head and his air of an artist's model.

Pardo Bazán's oeuvre is full of examples of this kind, where a narrative voice supposedly at a distance from the Galician rural classes depicts them in an orientalizing manner, as if they possess a mysterious ethnicity that would befit an ethnographic museum. Descriptions in this vein reinforce the postcolonial tension in Pardo Bazán's texts on Galicia, where the region's rural classes often remain as the voiceless subalterns (to evoke another key postcolonial notion, that of Gayatri Spivak) who are represented by the subject writing history — in this case, a female author aiming to build her literary career in the increasingly professionalized circuits of late-nineteenth-century Spain.

A more demanding seminar in terms of linguistic and stylistic analysis would look at hybridity in Pardo Bazán's literary language. My proposed teaching strategy here includes the reading of a particularly revealing literary review written by Pardo Bazán, "Vides y rosas" (1888; "Vines and Roses"). In this review of the Galician poet Benito Losada's work, Pardo Bazán digresses on the untranslatability of certain aspects of the Galician language. "El gallego," she writes, "con su jugueteo de modismos, diminutivos, giros familiares, palabras expresivas sin equivalencia exacta en el castellano, pierde toda la gracia en las traducciones" ("The Galician language, with its play of idiomatic phrases, diminutives, familiar turns, and expressive words with no direct equivalence in Castilian, loses all its gracefulness in translation"; 900). Taking the idea of untranslatablity as a starting point, a guided reading seminar could lead students through the many instances of untranslated words and expressions that pepper Pardo Bazán's novels. If students' knowledge of Galician is advanced, this task can be set as a critical writing assignment. If postcolonialism is the theoretical focus, students should be alerted to the different ways the author presents untranslated words: for example, terms that relate to the Galician popular culture of superstition and esoteric healing (*verme, cavilación, meigallo, serpe*) are left untranslated. Students may also note that untranslated words are either marked with various stylistic devices (italics, quotation marks) or none at all, thus suffusing the text with a Galician inflection not easily perceived by readers with no knowledge of the language.

The novel *La Tribuna* offers a rich range of examples of language hybridity. Pardo Bazán points out in her prologue that the question of language in the novel had been a matter of reflection. In dialogue with Benito Pérez Galdós and José María de Pereda, she announces that one of her aims in writing this novel was to "hacer hablar a mis personajes como realmente se habla en la región de donde los saqué" ("make my characters speak as they really speak in the region from which I have taken them"; 116). An analysis of the novel's language vis-à-vis the notion of postcolonial hybridity, however, reveals power imbalances between the narrative voice and those of the characters. The voices of the female proletarians in A Coruña's tobacco factory are ventriloquized by the narrative voice for a variety of purposes. Students could be asked to ponder, for example, why Pardo Bazán represents at various points in the narrative the female workers' path toward political awareness through their faulty grasp of the language of politics. Scenes where the increasingly politicized Amparo rallies her fellow workers, for example, are filled with the factory women's erroneous use of certain political terms: *espotismo* (for *despotismo*; 142), *descentraizar* (for *descentralizar*; 148), *josticia* (for *justicia*; 210), *borricadas* (for *barricadas*; 212). If we consider also that the Castilian that they are made to speak in Pardo Bazán's narrative is marked by a Galician inflection (*Madrí, perficionar la labor*; 148), the resulting hybrid idiom can be interpreted as infusing the text with humor that allays the hard political issues faced by the female workers (exploitation, insalubrious work conditions) while prefiguring the eventual failure of their struggle. Such an analysis of the interplay among language, gender, class, (Spanish) center, and (Galician) periphery reveals an important postcolonial tension underlying Pardo Bazán's vision for Spanish naturalism. How regional identities are represented or allowed a voice through a series of postcolonial tropes has been central to a power-oriented understanding of Spanish cultural and political history, and Pardo Bazán's narrative choices are intricately embedded—although not without some contradictions—in the transmission of these tropes.

Transatlantic Imaginaries in Pardo Bazán

Pardo Bazán's rise to public stature as a Spanish novelist, literary critic, and intellectual in the last third of the nineteenth century coincided with a period of intense decline in Spanish colonial rule overseas. Her personal investment in the Spanish colonial project in America is exemplified by her active participation in the 1892 commemorations of the quadricentennial of Spanish contact with America. By this time, Pardo Bazán had already set up her own cultural magazine, *Nuevo teatro crítico*, which she wrote and financed entirely by herself for three years (1891–93). In its pages, she advocated Spanish transatlantic imperialism in commentaries about the various exhibits, public conferences, and events organized under the auspices of the commemoration (Charques Gámez, "El descubrimiento"). Her role as a public intellectual who took on historical

and political issues related to the Spanish colonial program in America also underlies her short story collection *Cuentos de la patria* ("Patriotic Stories"), composed of stories published in periodicals between 1898 and 1901 and published
in 1902 as a reaction to the Spanish-American War (which led to Cuban independence and the Philippine Revolution). The heightened anti-American sentiment motivating these stories—see, for example, "Entre razas" (1898; "Between
Races")—could certainly provide a compelling theme for class discussion on
the historical context of Pardo Bazán's literary treatment of Spanish-American
transatlantic relations in a period when debates on the Spanish stance toward
modernity were inevitably positioned vis-à-vis the rise of North America to economic, political, and cultural hegemony.

Pardo Bazán's Galician-themed narratives further explore the transatlantic
imaginary, albeit in a richly ambivalent way. Some of the stories included in *Historias y cuentos de Galicia* ("Stories and Tales of Galicia"), for example, dwell
on the theme of the Galician exodus to America from an almost social-realist
perspective. The extradiegetic narrator of "De polizón" (1896; "Stowaway") confesses that she went to the seaport, in voyeuristic fashion, just to witness the
customary scene of poor Galician people embarking on a transatlantic ship to
America, "queriendo ver de cerca una escena triste" ("wanting to see a sad scene
close up"; *Cuentos completos* 2: 85). After relating the story of an old man who
tries to embark the ship with his stowaway grandson hiding in a chest but is left
behind when the port guards discover the grandson, the narrator makes a plea
to the government to do something about the population drain from the Galician rural regions. The theme of the young Galician girl pining for her migrant
lover, a recurrent trope in twentieth-century figurations of Galician sentimen-
tality, is also at the core of the more humorous "Esperanza y Ventura" (1903).
Class discussion on this short story can prove fruitful from both postcolonial and
transatlantic perspectives, as the text is rich with free indirect speech echoing
the Galician language of the young sisters. The sisters represent two extreme
poles of the Spanish colonial fantasy of the Galician female peasant: the boister-
ous and almost animalistic Ventura—who feigns being possessed by devils to
attract the attention of the community, including that of the priest—and the
subdued and virtuous Esperanza, doomed to mourn the absence of "aquel mozo
que marchó a América, a hacerse rico, y que ya no escribió más ni mandó otra
noticia de sí" ("that lad that went to America to make a fortune, and never wrote
again or sent any news"; *Cuentos completos* 4: 140).

In various other texts by Pardo Bazán, the transatlantic stands for a semantic
indeterminacy, an indecipherable tension, as well as a yearned-for escape route
from gender oppression. The short story "Las medias rojas" (1914; "The Red
Stockings"), which describes how a peasant girl's attempt to emigrate from Galicia
to America is frustrated by her father's brutal beatings, is a good example of
how the transatlantic imaginary often serves as the backdrop for feminist critique in Pardo Bazán's literature. On occasions, as with Esclavitud's mother in
Morriña—a character described by Maurice Hemingway as a "woman of easy

virtue" ("Emilia" 146–47)—who emigrated from Galicia to America and left her illegitimate daughter behind, the spaces of Galician transatlantic emigration stand connotatively for moral lassitude or, simply, the experience of having escaped the tight corset that Catholic morality kept on Spanish women. The novel *Insolación* could be discussed in this light, as the appearance of a transatlantic imaginary in the text signals the point of the female protagonist's momentary lapse into sexual temptation. Asis Taboada, a thirty-two-year-old widowed marchioness from Galicia living in Madrid, accepts an invitation by Pacheco, an Andalusian idler, to have lunch in a tavern in the lowly outskirts of Madrid. Inebriated and sunstruck, the protagonist experiences the beginning of sexual desire as a transatlantic longing (*Insolación* 146).

By dint of grappling with the range of Pardo Bazán's texts discussed above, students arrive at an understanding of how the author's literary texts are part of the wider cultural and political imaginaries of late-nineteenth-century Spain, particularly with regard to the country's national and international colonial tensions. The postcolonial and transatlantic frameworks afford students and instructors the opportunity to discuss historical contexts and literary texts in close relation to each other and to confront some of the pressing political questions with which Pardo Bazán directly or indirectly engaged.

NOTE

[1] Translations of quotations are my own. Citations to Pardo Bazán's short stories refer to Paredes Núñez's four-volume edition, *Cuentos completos*.

Pardo Bazán and Spain's Late Modern Empire

Joyce Tolliver

Students who know Pardo Bazán through novels such as *Insolación* ("Sunstroke") or *Memorias de un solterón* ("Memoirs of a Confirmed Bachelor") or through stories such as "Las medias rojas" ("The Red Stockings") or "El encaje roto" ("Torn Lace") may be surprised to find ideas that are unabashedly imperialist and sometimes disturbingly racist in some of her essays, such as "La España remota" ("Far-Off Spain"), "Novelas amarillas y leyendas negras" ("Yellow Novels and Black Legends"), and "Esperando" ("Waiting"). In essays like "Artículo-Excolonial" and "Siempre la guerra" ("Always the War"), in contrast, the author asserts that the economic and cultural impact of the colonial wars are firmly rooted in everyday material realities, thus offering present-day readers a more nuanced understanding of how the last colonial wars affected quotidian life in Spain.[1]

Studying a selection of Pardo Bazán's essays on the colonies expands students' understanding of this canonical figure of Spanish intellectual thought and literature while also providing an opportunity to question and to complicate assumptions about the intersections among ideologies of race, gender, and class. I suggest an approach that pairs Pardo Bazán's essays on the late Spanish empire with her stories dealing with the colonial wars. This approach encourages comparison of how Pardo Bazán employed the different rhetorical tools afforded by the two genres and also reveals the subtleties, and even the contradictions, of how the author dealt with this vital and painful subject. Echoing the arguments of Harriet Turner and of Alicia Cerezo in this volume, I also note the advantages of studying the versions of the texts that were originally published in journals.

Many of Pardo Bazán's essays on the late colonial wars appeared in her monthly column in *La ilustración artística*, La vida contemporánea, published between 1895 and 1916. Pardo Bazán gathered a selection of these and other essays in *De siglo a siglo, 1896–1901* (1902; "From Century to Century"), often revising them for publication in this volume.[2] The analyses sketched here are meant to suggest just one of the many productive classroom approaches to these texts.

In December of 1896, when the Cuban crisis was coming to a head and the Philippine Revolution had already begun, Pardo Bazán published "Días nublados" ("Cloudy Days") in her Vida contemporánea series. In contrast to the more formal essays she published in other venues or delivered as lectures,[3] the essay is an apparently rambling contemplation of the effects of the incipient war on everyday life in Spain. She comments on the atypically somber response to the crisis, which results in a dramatic drop in theater attendance and in the suspension of the festive dance parties of the holiday season. She finds this change of custom alarming because it indicates a national anxiety and paralysis (54).

This suggestion of an incipient social paralysis may align Pardo Bazán with the lamentations of the intellectuals associated with the Generation of 1898.⁴ But her analysis returns insistently to the everyday effects of the war—what is experienced and, above all, felt by Spaniards who have played no conscious part in the debates over the colonies, far removed from the men who wage faraway wars. She evokes the impact of the war through a personal reminiscence of a lawn party she held the summer before:

> . . . se reunió bastante gente joven debajo de los árboles . . . , y bailaron en el amplio hemicicio que sombrean acacias enormes. Pues bien: uno de aquellos muchachos, casi niños, Santiago Sangro, ya pagó su tributo a la muerte, bajo el firmamento de la Habana. Increíble nos parece a los que recordamos al jovencillo imberbe y rubio, que haya sido la guerra la que segó su vida cuando alboreaba; pero ¿quién no tendrá hoy en su familia, entre sus amigos, de estos dolores, de estas impresiones que son como una ducha glacial, algo que corta el aliento?   (55)

> . . . quite a few young people gathered beneath the trees . . . , and danced in the wide amphitheater shaded by enormous acacias. Well, one of those young men—they were practically children—Santiago Sangro, has already paid his tribute to death, under the Havana skies. It seems incredible to those of us who remember the little blond, smooth-faced youth that it was war that cut off his life just when it was beginning; but these days who doesn't have someone in their family, or among their friends, who has had those same sorrows, those shocks that are like a shower of ice-cold water, a thing that takes your breath away?⁵

In this passage, Pardo Bazán crystallizes a rhetorical strategy she uses regularly to reflect on the loss of the colonies: it is the strategy of a writer of realist fiction who understands the impact that a particular detail can have on the reader's imagination. We imagine the trees under which the young people dance and the face of the young man—a particular person—who died in the war. The news of such a death, or even the essayistic mention of it, is experienced not in the mind but in the body.

The young man is simultaneously a specific individual and a representative of all the men whose lives are taken by a distant war. Pardo Bazán both immortalizes him and generalizes the meaning of his death so that the force of his individual death serves as a synecdoche for the human toll of the war. This "tricking out [the] larger meaning through the interplay of part and whole" is an essential characteristic of Spanish realism, as Harriet Turner has observed (82). In "Días nublados," Pardo Bazán combines realist fiction's attention to detail with the ease of the apparent digressions allowed by the essay structure. The short story "Oscuramente" ("Darkly"), published four years later, could be read as a more extended meditation on the meaning of the death of the "smooth-faced youth" of the 1896 essay. Santiago, the young man of Pardo Bazán's acquaintance, may or may not have been the inspiration for Martín, the protagonist of "Oscuramente." The story develops the narrative that Pardo Bazán summarizes in a brushstroke or two in "Días nublados": a young provincial man who is far from virile, and hardly prepared for combat, is drafted into the army and sent to fight in Cuba, where he is killed shortly after his arrival. But, as I have argued elsewhere ("Framing"), in "Oscuramente," Pardo Bazán frames the story of a young soldier's death by questioning traditional concepts of manliness and of courage: the young soldier, whom the townspeople ridicule for his effeminacy, is reluctant to go to war because he is the sole guardian of his beloved younger sister. The narrator hears the story of Martín from the village priest, who repeats a version of Martín's story even as he questions its veracity:

> A Martín le saltaron a la cara dos negrotes. Lo particular es que aseguran que se defendió como una fiera. . . . Pues ¿no dice que Martín envió al otro barrio a uno de los mambises, que era un animal atroz? ¿Y no cuenta que casi podría con el segundo, y si no fuese porque tropezó y resbaló y el otro se le echó sobre el cuerpo y con todo el peso, lo acaba?
> (Pardo Bazán, *Cuentos completos* 2: 185)

> Two big blacks jumped out at Martín. The strange thing is, they swear he defended himself fiercely. . . . He even says Martín took down one of the *mambises*, an awful animal; and that he almost got the other one too, except that he tripped and fell and the other one threw himself on top of him and crushed him to death.

This account emphasizes that the war is a racial conflict: the *mambises*, guerrilla soldiers, are not Cubans but "big blacks," one of whom is "an awful animal," not a soldier. This concept of the Cuban war as a war between races is highlighted in "Días nublados" as well. In the essay, Pardo Bazán explains that, in the Galician countryside, "no pueden darse cuenta del por qué andamos a trastazos con los negros" ("they can't understand why we're having a row now with the blacks"), adding that many of her countrymen have never seen a black person in their lives, and that they imagine that "el negro será una especie de monstruo con garras, piel de oso y ojos de lumbre" ("a black person must be a kind of monster, with claws, bear skin, and glowing eyes"; 57). She represents the country person's bewildered lament that the threat to draft all men between the ages of eighteen and forty will leave working the land up to women:

> "¡Y todo por los negros!" añaden ellos con expresión de asombro. "¿Qué les hemos hecho a los negros?" preguntan. Sería tan penoso desengañarles, decirles que los negros no hubiesen danzado este horrible danzón del machete y de la tea a no ser por los blancos, nuestros hermanos, sangre

nuestra, mal que les pese, porque de los mansos indios de Cuba no queda
ni la memoria. . . .   (57)

"And all because of the blacks!" they add in amazement. "What did we
ever do to the blacks?" they ask. It would be a shame to set them straight,
to tell them that the blacks wouldn't have danced that terrible dance of
the machete and the torch were it not for the whites, our brothers, our
flesh and blood whether they like it or not, because not so much as a
memory is left of the gentle Indians of Cuba. . . .

A reading of "Oscuramente" in isolation may lead students to focus on the author's racism — particularly if they do not take into account that it is a fictional
character, within a framed narration, who presents the Cubans as savage animals. In "Días nublados," however, while Pardo Bazán confirms the racist basis
of popular discourse about the Cuban war, she also complicates it by reminding
her readers that the conflict is indeed a colonial war and by suggesting that the
men fighting on the Cuban side may have been as little to blame as the baby-
faced Santiago Sangro. The fuller, historical context of "Días nublados" can
be appreciated when the essay is read as originally published in *La ilustración
artística*. The issue, whose cover is almost entirely filled with a portrait of a
young Filipina girl ("Islas filipinas" 785), includes an article on the United States
president-elect, William McKinley, as well as several elaborate prints of locales in the Philippines, such as a reconstruction of the Eiffel Tower next to
the Cathedral of Jaro (800). Only two weeks after the publication of this issue,
President Grover Cleveland would warn of possible United States action against
Spain if Cuba's bid for independence was not recognized.

Around the time when Pardo Bazán must have been drafting "Días nublados,"
she was also reviewing a new American book that portrayed Spain as stolidly
traditional: H. Chatfield-Taylor's *The Land of the Castanet*. Pardo Bazán's review
characterizes the book as a tourist guide, a genre she considers superficial and
often ill-intentioned ("El país" 48). Again drawing on her personal experience in
order to reflect on a larger political issue, she relates that she met Mr. Chatfield-
Taylor during his brief visit to Spain, in which he was welcomed with a show of
hospitality (48). Despite this warm reception, Chatfield-Taylor, she complains,
views Spaniards with an air of superiority (48–49). She criticizes both the American author's boorish ingratitude and the arrogance of the United States, which
had officially supported the independence of Cuba: "¡*El país de las castañuelas*!
¿Sería amable que un español festejado en Norte América escribiese un libro
y lo titulase, v. gr.: *El país del rey dollar*?" ("*The Land of the Castanets*! Would
it be gracious for a Spaniard to be wined and dined in North America and then
write a book titled, for instance, *The Land of King Dollar*?"; 49).

Pardo Bazán again lampoons American arrogance in her short story "El viaje
de novios de Mr. Bigpig" ("Mr. Bigpig's Honeymoon"), published about a month
after "Días nublados" and just days before her review of *The Land of the Cas-*

tanet. Like "Días nublados" and "Oscuramente," the book review and the story seem made to be read together. Like H. C. Chatfield-Taylor, Mr. A. H. Sadler Bigpig is touring Spain with his wife; like Mr. Chatfield-Taylor, Mr. Bigpig is unimpressed by Spanish ways of life and by the Spanish nation. But while Mr. Bigpig consumes copious amounts of Tío Pepe—the only good thing about Spain, to his mind—his wife Gladys explores all of Seville, under whose spell she loses "el aire púdicamente amarimachado de su robusto cuerpo y la calma fría de su espíritu" ("the prim mannishness of her strong body and the cold calm of her spirit"; 1). Having traded her sporty American clothing for silk and lace, Gladys, who has a doctorate in law, now finds it charming when men on the street flirt with her, while her husband explodes in "invectivas contra la barbarie y el atraso de esta gente" ("rants against the barbarism and backwardness of these people"; 1). Just as Pardo Bazán assumes Chatfield-Taylor represents the entire United States in her book review, she presents Mr. Bigpig as a stand-in for American capitalist crudity. The synecdoche is emphasized when the jealous husband realizes that his wife has fallen in love—not with a Spaniard, but with "¡España toda!" ("all of Spain!"; 2). Finally, Gladys abandons her husband, leaving him a note explaining that she now thinks of herself as "española" (2). While Henn rightly notes the "patriotic propaganda" of this story (418–19), students might be encouraged to consider Pardo Bazán's gendering of this propaganda, which treats the education and independence of privileged American women more sympathetically than the vulgarity of American male industrialists.

When Pardo Bazán published this story in her self-compiled volume, *Sud-exprés* (1909), she revised it substantially, even changing the title to the more innocuous "Por España" ("Around Spain").[6] Students who compare the two versions might be asked to research the historical events that occurred during the fifteen years that elapsed between the publication of "Bigpig" and its revision as "Por España." There is a wealth of material for discussion if students consult the version published in *El liberal* on 27 December 1896: the headline of the issue, "Españoles y yankees," frames not only the story but all the news filling the issue, which includes a translation of the full text of President Cleveland's ultimatum to Spain (2). Students could do online archival research to discover how the same events were portrayed in the United States press, an exercise that may offer them additional insight into the inevitable ideological nature of journalism and perhaps even of realist fiction.

The study of Pardo Bazán's writings on the Spanish-American War allow students to better understand the complex—and sometimes troublesome—thinking of this writer. Productive questions may be raised, such as how her progressive gender politics square with her stridently colonialist stance. In researching this question, students would learn not only about the histories of feminism and colonialism but also about the historically conditioned relation, or lack thereof, among various liberal causes. Ultimately, students could be encouraged to situate their own assumptions about progressive ideologies. The following might be other questions to explore: Did Pardo Bazán's supposedly limited literary naturalism actually extend to a racial determinism—and if so, how do naturalism and the period's scientific discourses on race intersect? Why did the author champion modernity yet reject the United States' project of modernization through industry and territorial expansion? When students analyze these texts and research their historical contexts, they have the opportunity to learn about the discursive affordances of fiction, essays, and journalism; about a key moment in the shared history of Spain and the United States; and ultimately about their own assumptions. The study of Pardo Bazán's writings on the late Spanish empire thus encourages our students to bring unexpected perspectives to bear on their own thinking about the interactions of race, gender, and nation. They may also come to recognize the challenges and conflicts inherent in the quest for intellectual and artistic rigor.

NOTES

[1] "Novelas amarillas y leyendas negras," "Esperando," "Artículo Ex-colonial," and "Siempre la guerra" appear in Pardo Bazán's *De siglo a siglo, 1896–1901*.

[2] Sánchez-Llama's scholarly edition of Pardo Bazán's essays, *Obra crítica, 1888–1908*, and Ruiz-Ocaña Dueñas's voluminous study of all the La vida contemporánea essays, *La obra periodística de Emilia Pardo Bazán*, provide valuable guidance to these works.

[3] See, for example, "La España de ayer y la de hoy" ("Spain of Yesterday and Today"), which is a tightly constructed analysis of Spain's imperial legacy.

[4] For Pardo Bazán's relation to the Generation of 1898, see also González Herrán, "Emilia"; and Gómez-Ferrer Morant, "Emilia."

[5] All translations are my own.

[6] The version available on the Web site *Biblioteca Virtual Miguel de Cervantes* is "Por España," which is the revised version as it was published in *Sud-exprés*. The note preceding the text erroneously states that the text reproduced on the Web page is the story as it was published in *El liberal*.

National Identity and Class Conflict in Pardo Bazán's Cookbooks

Rebecca Ingram

In the last decade of her writing career, Emilia Pardo Bazán published *La cocina española antigua* (1913; "Traditional Spanish Cuisine") and *La cocina española moderna* (1914/17; "Modern Spanish Cuisine"), which concluded the Biblioteca de la mujer book series that she had established in 1892 to educate Spanish women about feminism. I teach these cookbooks in a cultural studies seminar focused on cuisine and in a course on gender and sexuality in modern Spain. Students take the cuisine class for various reasons: they studied in Madrid and either suffered uninspiring meals as part of their homestay experience or fell in love with *tortilla española* and sought out the best versions of it all around town; others come intrigued by the food studies focus but unaware of the international acclaim that has greeted Spanish cooking over the past fifteen years.

Pardo Bazán's cookbooks allow undergraduates to study the role of women and domestic arts in relation to the Spanish national project. They are among a number of twentieth-century culinary and gastronomical texts that debated the existence of a Spanish cuisine (Vázquez Montalbán 101). The cookbooks were published during a period when political, social, and economic factors—including uneven modernization exacerbated by a lack of infrastructure outside large cities, an inadequate communications system, and the absence of statewide internal markets—inhibited the formation of a Spanish national-liberal identity (Álvarez Junco, "Rural" 83). Significant rural immigration to cities expanded the industrial proletariat, but workers and peasantry remained largely outside the politics of "official Spain" (82–86). Literacy and access to education were also expanding rapidly (Botrel, *Libros* 309), but cooking from a book was a certain demarcator of social class.

Through study of a selection of articles or sections from a good history text, students acquire the sociohistorical context necessary for their analyses of the cookbooks. More specifically, since many have never read cookbooks critically, I remind students that their analyses of Pardo Bazán's writing must consider the relation of her texts to their audience (Grossberg 13) and the conventions of culinary writing and recipe giving (Leonardi 340). I also ask them to consider how these cookbooks, as they penetrate the intimate spaces of the household, influence the actions and attitudes of women.

Like other national discourses, cuisines arise from specific historical, economic, and social conditions that lead to cooking's codification in print. In the prologue to *La cocina española antigua* (*Cocina* 15–18), Pardo Bazán invokes tradition, culinary ethnography, the soul of the *pueblo* ("people"), Spanish literature, and the imperialist incorporation of dishes from Cuba to Chile, all of which suggest that cuisine is a field of cultural production as important as literature. *La cocina española moderna*, by contrast, represents the adaptation of foreign dishes to the Spanish table, principally by encouraging culinary aesthetics as a way of indicating Spain's modern attitudes (215).[1]

To begin, I ask students to consider how dishes and ingredients acquire national identities. Priscilla Parkhurst Ferguson describes how the culinary discourse found in genres as diverse as literature, philosophical treatises, journalism, and cookbooks "secures the transitory experience of taste" in print. It "reconfigures an individual activity as a collective enterprise" and creates an "archive of culinary attitudes, ideas, techniques, and usages" (17). To tease out these culinary attitudes, I assign Mariano José de Larra's essay "La fonda nueva" (1833) and selections of chapters from *Montes de Oca* (1900) and *O'Donnell* (1904), novels that are part of Benito Pérez Galdós's *Episodios nacionales*.[2] These selections describe foreign innovations in Spanish dining habits and present students with several conversations about national gastronomy. With these texts I encourage students to identify the dominant characteristics of a would-be Spanish "taste community" (Parkhurst Ferguson 17), among them insufficient money, questionable quality, and the overwhelming presence of foreign attitudes and practices, not necessarily particular dishes or ingredients. Additionally, two entries, "Jigote de lengua" ("Chopped Tongue Stew"; 11–19) and "Lengua escarlata ("Scarlet Tongue"; 27–39)," from the epistolary *La mesa moderna: Cartas sobre el comedor y la cocina* (1888; "The Modern Table: Letters on Dining and Cooking"), by Thebussem (Mariano Pardo de Figueroa) and "un cocinero de su majestad" (José de Castro y Serrano), compound this impression (Pardo de Figueroa).[3] These readings take opposing sides in an ongoing debate about Spanish modernization wrought in culinary terms, disputing the proper language of royal menus, the role of the rustic *olla podrida* as Spain's national dish, and complications presented by regional variations in food names. My framing of these authors' perspectives as part of a broader debate—one occurring in the same period in literature, as exemplified by Galdós's prescription for a Spanish national novel in his essay "Observaciones sobre la novela contemporánea en España" ("Observations on the Contemporary Novel in Spain")—primes students to recognize how Pardo Bazán addresses these issues and develops her distinctive position.

Additionally, criticism on the role of cooking in nation building outside Spain—such as in Italy, France, Mexico, and India—offers comparative contexts to prepare students for studying Pardo Bazán's cookbooks.[4] In "How to Make a National Cuisine: Cookbooks and Contemporary India" (1988), Arjun Appadurai studies the explicitly integrationist techniques cookbook writers use to incorporate the varied regional cuisines of the Indian state without diluting the nationalist culinary projects the writers set out to create. Once familiar with techniques from Appadurai's study, students examine Pardo Bazán's recipes for comparable strategies. This exercise can lead to discussions about how certain types of dishes are repeatedly represented throughout Spain, for example, the variations of *caldo* ("brothy soup"), *cocido* ("stew"), and *sopas* ("soups"), which all evolved, according to Pardo Bazán, from the *primitivo* ("rustic") national dish, *la olla castiza* ("Castilian stew"; *Cocina* 19). It can also lead to considerations of how regional variations in recipes for *arroz* ("rice dishes") reflect culinary variations that both compose and coexist with a national cuisine.

In the prologue to *La cocina española antigua*, Pardo Bazán writes that one of her reasons for publishing recipes is her desire to collect and have bound the recipes from her childhood and family traditions (*Cocina* 15). However, in subsequent references to tradition, ethnography, and her comparison of recipes to national relics like medals, arms, and sepulchers, it becomes clear that cooking and recipes are more than merely a personal interest. I ask students to consider what meanings the text creates when it transforms cooking into a national discourse that circulates in print.

Pardo Bazán notes the perseverance required to gather recipes from various regions and acknowledges the incompleteness of her collection. She explains that the difficulty stems from an unwillingness to part with recipes: the methods for preparing dishes "se niegan o se dan adulterados" ("are denied or adulterated"; *Cocina* 16). In a group activity, students discuss the meanings generated by the specific words she uses in the longer version of this passage. First, the knowledge represented by these cooking methods has value both within and outside the community; their value increases when folks are asked to share their recipes. Second, *vejezuelas* ("elderly women") preserve culinary knowledge; their dishes are "'reflejos' del pasado" ("'reflections' of the past") that will disappear when the women die (16). This phrasing indicates that they transmit cooking knowledge orally or by practice, not by written text.[5] Finally, when culinary practices are recorded in writing, Pardo Bazán's *La cocina española antigua* becomes a folklore project.

Pardo Bazán appears to esteem the women whose cooking practices she records in *La cocina española antigua*. However, when students turn their attention to the prologue of *La cocina española moderna*, they encounter a strikingly different focus: the aesthetics of cuisine. The turn from preserving culinary practices of the past to praising elegance and refinement—as a "síntoma" ("symptom") of national progress, regardless of a family's income—sets the stage for our study of Pardo Bazán's treatment of women (*Cocina* 215).

In preparation for students' work on this topic, I assign readings that include Bridget Aldaraca's prologue to *El ángel del hogar: Galdós and the Ideology of Domesticity in Spain* (25–32); selections from chapter 3 of Geraldine Scanlon's *La polémica feminista en la España contemporánea* ("The Feminist Polemic in Contemporary Spain") (122–58), which details the legal status of women; and María de Pilar Sinués de Marco's chapter "Goces y esplendores del hogar" ("The Pleasures and Splendors of the Home") from *La dama elegante* (1880; "The Elegant Lady") (269–303), a contemporary domestic manual. These texts introduce students to women's social role and legal status during the period and provide a framework for understanding the arguments that Pardo Bazán makes in her feminist essays "La mujer española" (1890; "The Women of Spain") and

"La educación del hombre y la de la mujer" (1892; "The Education of Men and Women"). Additionally, Sinués's text exposes students to the genre of practical manuals and provides examples of the behaviors that bourgeois culture deemed appropriate for women. With these historical and cultural contexts in mind, students return to the cookbooks to consider how Pardo Bazán addresses her women readers.

On one level, the materials on the status of women in nineteenth-century Spain prepare students to see the cookbooks' potential for subversion: does Pardo Bazán embed distinctly feminist messages in order to bring thinking women into a national project that includes many of the products of their labor? In a course on women's writing, this is a rich path to explore and takes into account the work of North American feminist scholars on women's culinary writing.[6] Additionally, instructors can encourage students to recognize in Sinués's writing the subversive potential of a text that presents the professional work of a woman writer to a female reading public (Sánchez-Llama 28–29). And the cookbook prologues provide a provocative counterpoint to Pardo Bazán's progressive treatment of women in her novels *Insolación* (1889; "Sunstroke") and *Memorias de un solterón* (1896; "Memoirs of a Confirmed Bachelor"), regular offerings in undergraduate courses.

However, with close reading, students note the pessimism of Pardo Bazán's comments in *La cocina española antigua* that the appeal of feminism to Spanish women is "aislado" ("isolated") and "epidérmico" ("superficial") and that the author's publication of cookbooks represents for women a return to the "senda trillada" ("conventional path") (*Cocina* 15). Students contrast this attitude with her feminist essays, which criticize the structural inequality that keeps women from participating in public life and from access to good education.[7] Most striking are the similarities students identify between Sinués's work, which textualizes middle-class anxieties about maintaining class status (Sánchez-Llama 346), and Pardo Bazán's sustained admonitions in *La cocina española moderna* that readers attend to the aesthetics of the meals they prepare. The vividness of her warnings against the *abuela*'s dirty tablecloth and against olives floating in unappetizing, yellowish cloudy water indicate an obsession with appearances that Noël Valis identifies in *The Culture of* Cursilería (2002) as a defining characteristic of the Spanish middle class. The focus on appearances gives the impression that women are expected to adhere to convention instead of advocating for change within the Spanish modernization process. Students are able to develop their critical thinking by identifying contradictions and ambiguities in Pardo Bazán's treatment of women in these texts.

By comparing and contrasting two distinct types of women that Pardo Bazán represents — *vejezuelas*, the guardians of regional culinary traditions, and the middle-class, reading women who might purchase the books but are anxious about household budgets — students begin to see the clear class differences that she establishes. Defining the middle class was difficult in Pardo Bazán's time and continues to be difficult for students today. The cookbooks represent culinary labor—and in *La cocina española antigua*, the codification of popular prac- tice—in textual form; literacy and language therefore become important win- dows to Pardo Bazán's thinking on social class. The cookbooks are directed to women who read and who have disposable income with which to purchase the books. These would-be buyers are also seeking guidance about organizing their households. Like Sinués's *Dama elegante, La cocina española moderna* serves as a guide to the recipes and attitudes Pardo Bazán deems appropriate for middle- class Spanish households. The women of these households may not do all of the cooking, but even those who can pay skilled cooks must keep tabs on kitchen activity (215). Pardo Bazán plays to her readers' likely class anxiety, highlighting dishes that present a touch of refinement (217) and offering advice to women eager to serve foods that do not look like they were just dumped from the pot (218). I ask students to find in the prologue to *La cocina española moderna* indi- cations of the class status and financial wherewithal of the women Pardo Bazán imagines as her readers. Students also study a selection of recipes to identify the frequency and quantities of more expensive ingredients, like meat; using data from the historian Pedro Carasa and the anthropologist Isabel González Turmo, students consider Pardo Bazán's recipes in the light of the average food expenses for Spanish households of different social classes. The woman who can choose a new recipe from a book and can afford special ingredients does not eat accord- ing to a "taste for necessity" (Bourdieu 372). Indeed, as González Turmo indi- cates, any compilation of recipes into book form, despite their popular origins, already indicates the mediation of the middle class (307). A question to pose to students, then, is why the author would present this style of cooking to women whose finances might not be sufficient to prepare it.

In both volumes Pardo Bazán frequently mentions the importance of the Span- ish words used to discuss food. Resigned to accept imported terms like *bechamela* or *gratín* (216), she asserts, in defense of the national language, that a Spanish cookbook should be written in "castellano castizo" ("pure Castilian"; 18). Her at- tention to culinary vocabulary also appears in her 1911 article for her Cartas de la Condesa column in *El diario de la marina*, "Sobre la huelga, la filología de la cocina, el *Diccionario de la Academia*" ("On the strike, culinary philology, the *Dic- cionario de la Academia*"). Likely inspired by the declaration of a general strike in 1911 and its accompanying violence, this brief article presents a vivid condemna- tion of the worker and peasant uprisings of the period. According to Pardo Bazán, strikes merely parody past legitimate uprisings: the working class uses the lan- guage of revolution to justify material desires rather than to promote legitimate social change (144). She proposes an escape into culinary philology as a way to distance herself and her readers from the violence of contemporary events. Stu- dents can be asked to identify assumptions that her proposal makes about the interests of workers. On the one hand, she indicates that they have no interest in philology, a field she considers a national cultural treasure (149). On the other, she expresses hostility toward the plight of workers and feels no responsibility to respond to their struggles (145).

Finally, I ask students to compare Pardo Bazán's condemnation of worker uprisings and her meditation on culinary philology with two separate mentions she makes of working-class *cocineras* ("cooks"). The first comes from her prologue to Manuel Puga y Parga's *La cocina práctica* (1905; "Practical Cooking"). This *cocinera* cooks from instinct; not suffering the "enfermedad" ("illness") of literacy, she neither weighs the salt nor measures the milk (9). The second *cocinera* is mentioned at the conclusion of *La cocina española antigua*'s prologue: Pardo Bazán advises leaving to the *cocinera* the smelly chores of handling onions and garlic so that the reader does not soil her own hands or clothing in the kitchen (18). Cookbooks like *La cocina española antigua* may archive the essential culinary knowledge of the *pueblo*. But when students attempt to reconcile that the protesting working class Pardo Bazán condemns also constitutes part of the *pueblo*, as do the *cocineras* who do not read cookbooks but labor in middle-class kitchens, they comprehend that middle-class literacy becomes a prerequisite for participation in the nation-building project.

My approach to teaching Pardo Bazán's cookbooks allows students to learn that the political tensions and conflicting ideologies found in conventional literary writing can also enter texts intended for audiences marginal to existing literary debates — in this case, the practical, domestic manuals used by Spanish women. Additionally, studying the cookbooks reveals a more conservative side, particularly on issues of social class, of a writer more often associated with progressive ideas with respect to women's equality; students and instructors can bring this knowledge to bear on Pardo Bazán's fiction and other writings.

NOTES

[1] I cite a 2009 edition that includes both cookbooks in one volume, *Cocina española antigua y moderna*. All translations are my own.

[2] I assign chapter 1 of *Montes de Oca* (5–15) and chapters 17 and 18 of *O'Donnell* (159–77). I am grateful to Mary Kempen for these suggestions.

[3] English translations of these chapter titles only incompletely capture the authors' wordplay. "Un cocinero de su majestad" is the pseudonym of José de Castro y Serrano.

[4] See Helstosky; Parkhurst Ferguson; Pilcher. On Spain in particular, see Ingram; Anderson; Moreno.

[5] For more, see Goody's work on the recipe (78–90); Certeau et al.

[6] For more on women's culinary writing, see Avakian and Haber.

[7] Pardo Bazán's pessimism is evident in other texts about the cookbooks: see Pardo Bazán, "Mi libro"; Bravo-Villasante 279–81 ("Carta a Alejandro Barreiro").

Pardo Bazán's Galicia: Representations of Gender, Nature, and Community

Francisca González Arias

Emilia Pardo Bazán's narrative world is informed and enriched by her native region. Galicia is the setting, or an important backdrop, for some fourteen of the author's novels and over one hundred of her short stories (a sixth of her short story production). Four of her short story collections are set in Galicia: *Cuentos de Marineda* (1892; "Stories of Marineda"), *Historias y cuentos de Galicia* (1900; "Stories and Tales of Galicia"), *Cuentos del terruño* (1907; "Stories of the Native Land"), and *Cuentos de la tierra* (published posthumously in 1922; "Stories of the Land"). This essay shows how several recurring themes in Pardo Bazán's Galician narratives are enhanced by the author's familiarity and identification with her region: her knowledge of the history and culture that shaped its community, her sensitivity to Galicia's natural landscape, and her feminism. The aim of this essay is to help instructors select and study texts that reflect Galicia's role in Pardo Bazán's body of work.

The thematic constellation of the author's Galician narratives — community, nature, and women — enables the exploration of multidisciplinary connections with fields outside Spanish literature, like anthropology, sociology, women's studies, folklore studies, economic and labor history, and ecocriticism. These intersections open up a range of pedagogical possibilities. I offer short analyses of illustrative texts and mention lesser-known, similarly themed stories to help guide text selection and to encourage instructors to draw from a largely untapped corpus that offers many opportunities to enable students' engagement.

Joseba Gabilondo points to the recurrence of Galician words and expressions in Pardo Bazán's texts as a sign of her dual identity as Galician and Spanish. These "traces of the other language and geography (Galicia/n)" ("Towards" 249) emphasize the importance of Galicia in the author's creative trajectory. Pardo Bazán herself alluded to linguistic concerns in her memoir, "Apuntes autobiográficos" (1886; "Autobiographical Notes"), confessing that she had given up on her project to write a novel with peasant characters because capturing authentic speech would result in "a monstrosity" (728).[1] She believed that a novelist should portray dialogue realistically — she faulted Émile Zola for failing to do so (728) — and that the novel must reflect the writer's community in a way that is true to life. In her short stories she succeeded in depicting a largely rural society by devising strategies to effectively reproduce Galician speech patterns in an unobtrusive way. As demonstrated in my article "La poética de Galicia en los cuentos de Emilia Pardo Bazán" ("The Poetics of Galicia in Emilia Pardo Bazán's Stories"), the author incorporated such techniques as sprinkling characters' dialogue with Galician words and expressions (she included a glossary of Galician terms at the end of *Historias y cuentos de Galicia*) and replicating Galician grammar and word order in Spanish. Online Galician-Castilian-English dictionaries, like the one available on the *Xunta de Galicia* Web site, can help teachers and students approach the unfamiliar vocabulary in Pardo Bazán's Galician narratives.

From childhood Pardo Bazán was intimately acquainted with her region's natural landscape and its people. As attested in "Apuntes autobiográficos" and the essays of *De mi tierra* (1888; "Of My Land"), she was exposed to all social classes through the different neighborhoods of her native city, and she was driven to explore every corner of Galicia's coast, mountains, and valleys. She transposed her knowledge into many texts, creating a comprehensive portrait of the Galician people that recalls the anthropologist Renato Rosaldo's proposal for "forms of writing that . . . enable the descriptive to approximate people's lives from a number of angles of vision" (62). Teachers can make rural Galicia more accessible to students by encouraging them to compare it with remote areas of the United States like Appalachia, with its mountain culture and particular dialect, or northern Maine. Instructors could introduce students to work by North American anthropologists: Heidi Kelley and Ken Betsalel's comparative work on Galicia and Appalachia and Sharon Roseman's studies on women and rural communities in contemporary Galicia are particularly helpful in this regard. Teachers could also ask students to share stories passed down in their families about their regions of origin.

Pardo Bazán's observations of Galician popular culture in her essays and narratives ran parallel to the birth of anthropological studies in Spain. Prodded by the folklorist Antonio Machado y Álvarez, father of the poet Antonio Machado, Pardo Bazán founded the Society of Galician Folklore in 1884 and soon after compiled a questionnaire of 445 topics embracing all aspects of Galician life that was intended to guide members in collecting data (Sociedad). Students could undertake a similar compilation of questions addressing culture and customs in their own community. To introduce students to Galicia's cultural richness, instructors can ask them to identify examples of Pardo Bazán's observations of legends, rituals, celebrations, traditional costume, and native architecture in her Galician stories. For example, "Un destripador de antaño" (1890; "The Heart Lover"; *Cuentos completos* 2: 5–21), the chilling tale that introduces *Historias y cuentos de Galicia*, describes in detail rural houses, the clothing of well-to-do peasants, and the rowdy merrymaking that often accompanied millwork.[2] The mourning ritual, the *pranteo*, appears in "Consuelos" (1903; "Comfort"; 2: 320–22) in the description of the wailing women, or *choronas*, that accompany the coffin of a child. In "El molino" (1900; "The Mill"; 2: 187–91) the tradition of the *enchoyada*, the competition between two young men to improvise couplets to impress a young woman, enriches the portrayal of rural courtship customs. Instructors can then help students see how Pardo Bazán not only recorded popular traditions but also highlighted their impact on people's lives. Students can explore stories that illustrate, for example, how ancestral beliefs helped people cope in the face of poverty and wretched conditions. In "Atavismos" (1912; "Atavisms"; 3: 246–49) an old peasant woman clings to her belief in the evil eye in order to make sense of her children's disappearance. In "La 'Compaña'" (1901; "The 'Holy Company'"; 2: 175–77)[3] the only diversion of Caridad, a young boy forced to steal from other people's fields to survive, is to listen to his grandmother's stories of ancient superstitions, like that of the *santa compaña* referred to in the title. Caridad can be paired with Minia of "Un destripador de antaño," whose devotion to her patron saint, widely venerated in the area, helps her endure her aunt and uncle's cruelty.

The *Rexurdimento*, comparable to the Catalan *Renaixença*, was the nineteenth-century movement that sought to recuperate Galician identity, language, and culture after centuries of Castilian domination. Despite her comprehensive portrayal of Galicia in her narratives, Pardo Bazán was shunned by the leaders of the Galician renaissance. Carmen Pereira-Muro shows that the author's gender played a role in this rejection (*Género* 97–106). As Paredes Núñez has observed, Pardo Bazán regularly produced stories of "un feroz verismo, de barbarie bestial" ("a savage, brutal realism"; *La realidad* 229).[4] Because of such stark portrayals, she was perceived by Manuel de Murguía, one of the *Rexurdimento's* leading figures, as having transgressed the feminine code of Galician literature, comprising "sweetness, . . . vagueness, and melancholy" (qtd. in Pereira-Muro, *Género* 98). Studying Pardo Bazán's stories that depict harsh realities and disconcerting juxtapositions can illustrate for students how Pardo Bazán transcended the gender limitations of Galician literary discourse. For example, the idyllic scenes of the grape harvest in "Racimos" (1922; "Clusters"; 3: 297–300) are followed by the observation that Rosiña's aversion to wine stems from the abuse her drunken father inflicted on her mother and her. The pastoral setting of the mill of Tornelos in "Un destripador de antaño" belies the horrific crime that the mill's inhabitants are to commit. The story narrating the gruesome acts of vengeance that two warring peasant families wreak on each other is ironically titled "Geórgicas" (1893; "Georgics"; 1: 216–18). "La ganadera" (1908; "Earnings"; 3: 307–09) depicts a coastal people's custom of slaughtering shipwreck survivors in order to rob them of their valuables.[5]

Pereira-Muro reminds us that while *galleguistas* (Galicianists) believed that language was the link that connected all Galicians, most intellectuals of the Galician renaissance wrote in Castilian and that, lacking a literary tradition, they turned to nature as their principal referent (*Género* 95). Nature—equated with the people and their history and accessible to all social classes (96)—was the agglutinating symbol offered by the theorists of the *Rexurdimento*. The identification between landscape and nation—to use the title of María López Sández's book *Paisaxe e nación*—was compellingly expressed by the poet Rosalía de Castro in her *Cantares gallegos* (1863; "Galician Songs"), the work that initiated Galicia's literary revival. Galician topography, landscape, and climate are essential components of Galicians' social imaginary, and Pardo Bazán famously excelled at describing Galicia's natural world. Yet Murguía accomplished his goal of banishing Pardo Bazán from the Galician canon by portraying her as unnatural (Pereira-Muro, *Género* 97) as well as unfeminine.

In her introduction to the *Cantares*, Rosalía emphatically contrasts the parched, barren flatlands of Castile with the rugged, lush Galician countryside (261–62). The same Castile-Galicia dichotomy expressed by Galicia's foremost poet resonates in Pardo Bazán's short novel *Insolación* (1889; "Sunstroke"). Set among Madrid's aristocratic and popular classes, *Insolación* exemplifies the tension between concrete territory and imagined space that, as Eugenia Romero observes, underlies the identity of Galicians absent from the homeland (105). Several passages from the novel illustrate to what degree the tactile memory of the native landscape resides in a Galician's subconscious. The dream sequence of *Insolación*'s protagonist recreates the voyage that Pardo Bazán herself made in the spring of 1887 from Madrid to A Coruña and during which she conceived the idea for the novel (Pardo Bazán, "*Miquiño mío*" 70 [letter to Benito Pérez Galdós]). In the novel's dream sequence, Asís's train advanced " . . . al través de las eternas estepas amarillas, caldeadas por un sol de trópico. ¡Oh! Castilla la fea, la árida, la polvorosa, la de monótonos aspectos, la de escuetas lontanzas. . . . ¡Oh! calor, calor del infierno. . . . " (". . . through the eternal yellow steppes heated by a tropical sun. Oh! Castile, so ugly, arid, and dusty, of monotonous and spare distances. . . . Oh, hellish heat!"; 276).[6] At last, Asís is revived by the sight and feel of her native land: "Salimos del país llano. . . . ¡Montes queridos! . . . más y más montañas, revistidas de frondosos castañares, y por cuyas laderas . . . se despeñan saltando manantiales, cascaditas, riachuelos, mientras allá bajo caudaloso y profundo, corre el Sil. . . ." ("We leave behind the flatlands. . . . Beloved hills! . . . ever more mountains, covered with lush chestnut trees . . . springs, waterfalls, streams tumble down their slopes while below the Sil flows fast and deep. . . . "; 277). The image of Galicia's rainy skies sparks a fit of weeping during Asís's dreamlike state, unleashing her repressed guilt over her Madrilenian escapades with Pacheco. To help students comprehend the different landscapes from one region of Spain to another and the bond Asís feels with her native landscape, they can be asked to create a *PowerPoint* presentation with images of the novel's locales in Madrid and in Galicia, ranging from coastal Vigo (the protagonist's native city) to the interior's mountains and valleys.

Gender transcends class in Pardo Bazán's approach to women in both her critical and creative writing. As Pereira-Muro observes, Pardo Bazán subverted patriarchal discourse by reincorporating women and Galicia into the national literary discourse (*Género* 112). Galicia must be recognized for its role in awakening the author's feminism and in her ongoing portrayal of the plight of both urban and rural women. Her knowledge of Galicians' socioeconomic conditions and the impact of emigration on women were crucial in her creative process. Her daily visits over two months to A Coruña's cigar factory yielded *La Tribuna* (1882; "The Tribune"), her third novel. Her observation of four thousand women at work aroused her sympathy and educated her about factory work ("Apuntes" 725). Teachers could engage students with research assignments intended to draw parallels between the novel and American labor history—for example, between A Coruña's *cigarreras* and Lowell's nineteenth-century female textile workers (who formed the first union of women workers in the United States) or between Amparo as the *lector* ("reader") in *La Tribuna* and the role of the *lector* in the cigar factories of turn-of-the-century Tampa.

Instructors could also ask students to compare how government and community groups address domestic and sexual violence against women in Spain or in the United States today with how violence against women was treated in Pardo Bazán's time. "El indulto" (1883; "The Pardon"; 1: 122–27), set in a working-class community of Marineda (the fictionalized version of A Coruña), introduces the recurring subject of domestic violence.[7] It highlights women's solidarity in response to the failure of the patriarchal justice system to protect the washerwoman Antonia from a violent husband. In "Rabeno" (1912; 4: 151–54), an unknown man who harrasses young women is thought to be a reapparition of the satyr-like figure of Galician lore named in the story's title. Patricia Carballal Miñán argues that the story's conclusion, in which a girl's accusation leads villagers to administer their own justice against the man, reflects Pardo Bazán's despair at the authorities' inefficacy in protecting women. "Las medias rojas" (1914; "The Red Stockings"; 3: 195–97) depicts the parental abuse of a peasant girl, Ildara, which dashes her dream of a better life in America, while the red stockings of the title hint at the vulnerability of Galician women emigrants to sexual exploitation. Ildara can be paired with Maripepa of "La advertencia" (1922; "The Warning"; 3: 207–09): summoned from her Galician hamlet to Madrid to be a wet nurse, Maripepa is equally vulnerable.

Pardo Bazán published "La gallega" ("The Women of Galicia"), an essay on the women of rural Galicia, in Machado y Álvarez's series on the popular traditions of Spain (1884). The essay begins with the invocation of an imaginary ethnologist: the author assures the scientist that the same types of women described in the essay will indeed be found in Galicia (164–65), thus demonstrating the article's intention as a serious document that transcends a costumbrista aesthetic. Pardo Bazán paints the wretched living conditions of rural women and the unrelenting manual labor they perform in the fields and in the home. Here, as in her short stories, she describes how Galician women found sporadic relief from grim realities in popular customs, dressing in traditional garb and dancing the *muiñeira*, the ancient miller women's dance. Tellingly, in her overview of anthropological studies on Galician women, Mar Llinares García traces the first mention of ethnographic topics related to Galician women back to Pardo Bazán's folklore studies.

Pardo Bazán offers numerous examples of resolute women who are physically stronger than their male companions, like Mariniña of "El molino," the protagonist of "La Mayorazga de Bouzas" (1886; "The Mayorazga of Bouzas"; 2: 21–27), and Camila de Berte of "El aire cativo" (1922; "The Evil Air"; 3: 301–04). The roots of these strong Galician women are pre-Roman: Galicia was portrayed as a matriarchy by the Greek historian Strabo, who, in his *Geography*, called ancient Galicia's customs "uncivilized" and described how Galician men, not women, gave dowries (qtd. in Llinares García 11). Lourdes Méndez notes the historical parallels between Galician law and Celtic society, both of which gave women the right to own and inherit property (25).

Massive waves of male emigration from Galicia in the nineteenth century reinforced the autonomy of women. Rosalía de Castro addressed the impact of emigration when she described the wives left behind as "viudas d'os vivos" ("widows of the living"; 520). In the last half of the nineteenth century seventy percent of emigrants did not return (Cagiao Vila 41), a situation that resulted in a kind of "forced matriarchy" (49) as Galician society recognized the self-sufficiency of women who alone worked the fields and managed the family finances. Gender roles in family life were reconfigured as women became both mothers and fathers to their children. To address the topic of Galician emigration in Pardo Bazán, instructors could assign the short story "El tetrarca en la aldea" (1892; "The Master in the Village"; 2: 62–65), in which Marcos de Loureiro, who had emigrated to Uruguay after being unable to provide for his wife and children, is confronted upon his return with six children instead of the three he had left behind. Apprised by his neighbor that the landlord's administrator was responsible, Loureiro nonetheless shows himself capable of reasoning that befits "el hombre verdadero" ("the true man"; 63) by acknowledging the marked improvement in his family's living standards compared with when he left. Finally, the memory of his own infidelities "allende los mares" ("beyond the seas"; 65) determines Marcos's immediate reinstatement in his marriage.

Using Susan Walter's study of narrative frames in Pardo Bazán's short stories, teachers can show how the frames of some Galician stories forcefully represent Pardo Bazán's engagement with the community she portrayed. An example is "Viernes santo" (1891; "Good Friday"; 2: 55–62), which also introduces students to the world of Los pazos de Ulloa (1886; "The House of Ulloa") and La madre naturaleza (1887; "Mother Nature"). Here the narrator's interlocutor, Father Eugenio, intersperses his narration with observations that reveal the narrator's gender—"Ya verá usted, señora" ("You shall see, madam"; 61)—as well as the narrator's knowledge of the French and Russian novel (a trait shared with the author). The priest relates how the local cacique (political boss), Lobeiro, ordered the murder of the gentleman farmer nicknamed Cristo on Good Friday, driving the townspeople to engineer his death in a way that recalls the peasants' collective action against the tyrant in Lope de Vega's Fuenteovejuna (1619).

With the portrayal of the villagers' evolution from long-suffering, terrified victims of the cacique's cruelty to determined plotters of his death, Pardo Bazán corrected in fiction her earlier observation, in her review of the Cancionero popular gallego, that Galicians' traditional fear of authority had allowed rule by local caciques to flourish in Galicia as nowhere else in Spain ("El Cancionero" 909). The priest's identification of Lobeiro with the "Sacretario" in Lamas Carvajal's O Catecismo d'o labrego (1888; "The Peasant's Catechism"), the wildly popular satire against Galician officialdom, lends verisimilitude to Pardo Bazán's fiction. By situating a character resembling herself in the same environment, and among the same characters that inhabit *Los pazos de Ulloa* and its sequel, the author embraced the struggles of both her real and her fictional worlds. I suggest initiating a discussion in which students address the issues that spur protest in their communities and the forms that collective action take.

The story "Planta montés" (1890; "Native Plant"; 2: 38–41) is ideal for conveying to students Pardo Bazán's engagement with Galicia because it represents how the author shared in her Galician heritage and reflects her awareness that culture defines and binds together a community. The story's narrator relates the events that unfold after her decision to pluck a peasant boy from her ancestral village to serve in her home in the city. Pardo Bazán's own communications with rural Galicians are mirrored in the narrator's adoption of the boy's native language when addressing him. Instructors could ask students to translate the dialogue between Cibrao and his mistress and encourage them to role-play versions of these interactions. Another opportunity for role-play is to have students identify and re-create the comparisons that Cibrao's father makes between farm animals and his son to market him to his future employer.

Contrary to the narrator's expectations, Cibrao proves immune to the distractions of city life and unsuited for work away from his natural world. Like the native plant of the title that cannot thrive in unfamiliar soil, he gradually withers away. When his father refuses to take him back, Cibrao takes to his bed, and, convinced that a dog's howling one stormy night augurs his end, he dies soon after. Having herself heard the dog howl on the night of Cibrao's death, the narrator acknowledges the shared Celtic legacy that links them: "los que nacimos en la brumosa tierra de los celtas agoreros" ("we who were born in the misty land of Celtic seers"; 41). Rattling windowpanes and the sounds of echoing footsteps on narrow streets accompany the narrator's recording of this epiphany. The description recalls the account in *De mi tierra* (327–29) of similar sights and sounds around the author's home in A Coruña's old quarter, the model for the fictional neighborhood in which the story is set. The story's conclusion suggests the image of Pardo Bazán herself in the act of writing, intensifying the identification between the author and her Galician universe and highlighting Galicia's enduring presence in her narrative world.

NOTES

[1] I cite "Apuntes autobiográficos" in *Obras completas* 3: 698–732.
[2] I cite Pardo Bazán's stories in Paredes Núñez's four-volume edition, *Cuentos completos*.
[3] The *santa compaña* of Galician lore is a procession of ghosts that appears on roads or in cemeteries, usually at night, foretelling the death that year of any person encountering it.
[4] All translations are my own.

[5] Paredes Núñez shows that these stories were often inspired by actual crimes that Pardo Bazán commented on in her column La vida contemporánea in *La ilustración artística* (*La realidad* 235).

[6] I quote from the 2001 Cátedra edition of *Insolación*.

[7] The *La Tribuna* research group's recent discovery that Pardo Bazán's paternal grandmother died at the hands of her second husband sheds new light on the author's compelling and ongoing portrayal of violence against women (Grupo).

Pardo Bazán and the Pedagogy of Realism

Hazel Gold

The writings of Emilia Pardo Bazán have earned a prominent place in a wide range of undergraduate and graduate courses in Spanish literature and culture, ranging from first-year seminars (commonly taught in English) and introductory classes in literary analysis to historical surveys of Peninsular literature and advanced topics-based seminars organized around critical issues in Hispanism: for example, the emergence of a contested modernity in Spain; the configuration of gender; the historical development of specific literary and discursive genres (the novel, short story, and critical essay); and the position of Spanish letters vis-à-vis European culture. These courses inevitably intersect with Pardo Bazán's engagement, as an author and literary critic, with realism, the dominant mode of expression characterizing narrative prose from the 1860s through the early decades of the twentieth century.

Including readings by Pardo Bazán in discussions of the consolidation of the realist aesthetic in Spanish fiction is not without its challenges. For one, unfamiliarity with the historical and cultural circumstances in which she wrote and to which her texts refer presents a potential stumbling block to comprehension. Her concern with social themes is difficult for students to analyze in the absence of at least a rudimentary understanding of key events (the 1868 revolution, the Bourbon Restoration of 1874, and the collapse of the Spanish empire in 1898) and prevailing historical currents (Spain's immersion in free-market capitalism, the creation of a working-class proletariat, urban expansion, industrialization, women's increasing participation in the public sphere). Adequate background knowledge of these developments enables students to recognize and appreciate the tensions that repeatedly arise in her narratives with respect to individual rights versus duties to family or nation, metropolitan rhythms versus long-established modes of rural life, scientific empiricism and philosophical positivism versus religious belief systems, and tradition versus progress. Assigning relevant selections from political, economic, and cultural historians can provide contextualization on key issues students will encounter as they read.[1]

Familiarizing students with Pardo Bazán's historical moment and positioning her production within the landscape of nineteenth-century culture open the door to an understanding of why realism triumphed at this juncture. Gradual improvement in literacy rates and the introduction of new commercial printing technologies led to an increase in the number of readers and to the ever more rapid circulation of texts. The majority of these readers hailed from Spain's rising middle class, whose power was confirmed by the Glorious September Revolution. These middle-class readers had leisure time and income to spare; they read for recreation as well as for instruction. However, they were no longer stirred by the faraway, long-ago exoticism of Romantic tales. Instead, they wished to read closely observed portrayals of the contemporary moment in which they themselves were like the protagonists — either as actors in scenes of bourgeois life or as voyeuristic spectators of alien milieus, social classes, and psychological states. The dramatic changes that transformed Spanish middle-class society destabilized personal identity, social relations, and literary models. Philosophically and formally, realism reflects this upheaval: "realism is what it is because it is in crisis" (Valis, " 'Tell' " 198). Alongside a conviction in the validity of representation, realism abounds in paradox, irony, and contradiction, recurring conditions of Pardo Bazán's texts to which students should be attuned when they encounter the unreliable narrators, equivocal titles, and unresolved endings that characterize many of her texts, as exemplified in *La Tribuna* (1882; "The Tribune") and the short stories "En Babilonia" (1902; "In Babylon"; *Cuentos completos* 3: 8–10), "En tranvía" (1890; "On the Streetcar"; 2: 97–101),[2] and "Restorán" (1901; "Restaurant").

Another challenge for literature instructors is that students inevitably approach nineteenth-century realism through their twenty-first-century experience as cultural consumers. Although the middlebrow best sellers they read and most of the films and television programs they view conform to classical realist models, this repeated exposure often blunts their perception of how realism operates qua representational system. Contemporary forms of reality-based art — unscripted television programming, memoirs, autobiographical confessions — lay claim to a putative authenticity that belies the degree of self-conscious contrivance or mediation that intervenes between life in the raw and "life as art" (Shields 166).[3] Owing to this process of naturalization, students may have only a fuzzy understanding of the premises that foreground realist texts or how writers work to conceal those very devices that create the illusion of verisimilitude. Asking students to explain the meaning of "The Realness" in hip-hop titles by Cormega, Beezie, Mitch G, and J-Wanz or to examine the presuppositions of shows like *The Real World* or *The Real Housewives* franchise can serve as a first step toward exposing realism's binary nature as a social document and a manufactured web of discourse. Students often confuse the concept of literary realism with the commonsensical use of *realistic*; supposing that realism only encompasses *dispositio*, with no room for *inventio* or imagination, they may incorrectly surmise that realism precludes formal experimentation. Consequently, teaching examples of Pardo Bazán's fiction can be enriched by first exploring with students the dynamics of realism as a historically and culturally bound system of writing that exploits a set of representational conventions emphasizing linear plots, meticulous psychological characterization, manipulation of point of view and narrative voice, exhaustive description, framing strategies, and geographic and temporal specificity, all in the service of the creation of a "reality effect."[4] In Robert Scholes's salutary reminder regarding realism, "[a]ll writing, all composition, is construction. We do not imitate the world, we construct versions of it" (7).

Mapping a realist poetics becomes a pressing task precisely because realism, defined as a form of artifice or "intrinsic masquerade" (Furst, *All* viii, 25), has acquired in one strand of critical thought a negatively charged valence. Realism is always positioned in opposition to the classical or Romantic paradigms that preceded it or to the modernist (and later, avant-garde) art that dethroned it. Modernism repudiated realism as aesthetically inadmissible, viewing it as ideologically reactionary because of its association with a dominant bourgeoisie whose transcendent view of the real was no longer considered viable (Jameson, "Beyond" 7, 9);[5] the truth claims of realist writing were deemed "philosophically naïve" or a deliberate act of bad faith (Furst, *All* 12, 25). By the mid-twentieth century realism had come to be judged disreputable at worst and "banal, programmatic and even cheap" at best (Kazin). Such denigrations of realism as anachronistic or contaminated by humanist ideology do a disservice to the formal complexity and historical insight of Pardo Bazán's narrative production, especially her understanding of character as a location of social forces at play. Relying on unexpected plot turns (the surprise endings of "En tranvía" and "En Babilonia"), painstaking depictions of place (*La Tribuna*'s domestic and industrial interiors; the workaday Madrid in "En Babilonia" that disappoints Luis when it fails to conform to his sexualized, orientalist fantasies), and a deliberate focus on linguistic forms (the transcription of regional and lower-class dialects in *La Tribuna*; the Italianized Spanish spoken by foreign street performers in "Restorán"), Pardo Bazán presents to her readers a known world and confirms their faith in its objective materiality. Yet these same techniques unsettle readers' perceptions and expectations. *La Tribuna* exemplifies this double movement: its political message is conservative (Amparo and her fellow workers in Marineda's tobacco factory are mistaken in placing their hopes for the future in a republican government about which they know little), while its social implications are progressive (there is value to women's work and joy in their shared solidarity; gender inequality, especially across class lines, creates disastrous consequences for women like Amparo, who is seduced by an effete military officer). The dual meaning of the title of the novel's final chapter, "¡Por fin llegó!" ("It/He finally arrived")[6]—a reference to the birth of Amparo's illegitimate child and the proclamation of the First Spanish Republic—summarizes the contradictory logic that governs the story, the double bind of the social structures that delimit class and gender roles, and the mixture of melodramatic and realist narrative modes that Pardo Bazán exploits to invest readers in the novel's outcome.

In guiding students toward a working definition of realism, one productive strategy is to ask them during the first week to compose the title and first page(s) of an original realist novel; then, in peer review, to compile a taxonomy of the plots, character types, and narrative conventions they have used to structure their compositions. Later in the course, students can be asked to reflect critically on what they wrote: What did they initially think realism is and how has their understanding of it changed after reading Pardo Bazán's fiction? Instructors will of course want to underscore that realism is literary writing characterized by cognitive and aesthetic dimensions; it privileges secular and rational forms of knowledge originating in the Enlightenment and is predicated on the conceptual triumvirate of empiricism (factuality, materialism, particularity), mimesis (verisimilitude, verifiability), and communicability (language used to represent an exterior world and subjective responses to it) (Morris 9–12).

Supplementary readings may be assigned to amplify this definition. For instance, Erich Auerbach, in *Mimesis*, emphasizes the democratizing impulse of realist fiction: the expansion of the repertoire of characters to include socially and psychologically marginal subjects and a broadening of novelistic content to include hitherto proscribed topics, such as prostitution, incest and other forms of sexuality, and alcoholism. (*La Tribuna* offers several such instances, including a graphic childbirth scene [261–66] and the scene in which the army violently breaks up the strike by the *cigarreras* in the tobacco factory [237–47].) In *Problems of Dostoevsky's Poetics* and *The Dialogic Imagination*, Bakhtin assesses the roles of polyphony and heteroglossia in realist fiction, which contribute to the creation of texts that signify multiple, often mutually contradictory truths, and he elaborates on the concept of the chronotope (the interconnectedness of time-space relations); these elements, signaling authors' engagement with social reality, subvert the notion of language and ideology as monologic, that is, characterized by single-voiced, cohesive discursivity. Nancy Armstrong, in *Fiction in the Age of Photography*, and Peter Brooks, in *Realist Vision*, link realism to the emergence of new technologies for seeing everyday life.[7]

While more advanced students will profit from reading selections by these contemporary theorists, the logical place to start is Pardo Bazán's writings, which in themselves constitute a pedagogy of realism. In her critical essays the author displays a vested interest in explaining and defending the philosophical and literary underpinnings of realism; her fiction exemplifies how these foundational principles inform her narrative practice. Teachers may choose to introduce her views on realism by assigning short texts such as the preface to *Un viaje de novios* (1881; "A Wedding Trip") and the prologues to the first editions of *La Tribuna*

(1882) and *El cisne de Vilamorta* (1884; "The Swan of Vilamorta") or by using passages drawn from her lengthy study of the genealogy of realism and naturalism in the contemporary novel, *La cuestión palpitante* (1882; "The Burning Question").[8] Distinguished by clarity of exposition and logical argumentation, opinionated yet not doctrinaire, they are ideal texts with which to inform students of the Galician author's position in the critical debates surrounding realism's instatement as the dominant literary paradigm.

In the preface to *Un viaje de novios* Pardo Bazán stakes out her overarching claims: realist texts and the polemics surrounding them are signs of the novel's vitality, an indication that this genre has entered a new phase; no longer simply entertainment, the novel is "ascendiendo a estudio" ("rising to the level of a study"; 52) that demands of the novelist powers of observation and analysis. This contemporary novel, which is a "traslado de la vida" ("copy of life"; 52) shaped by the author's distinctive way of viewing the real, participates in a national Spanish tradition that rejects the extremes of French naturalist impassivity before the laws of nature on the one hand and, on the other, the sermons of novelists who preach a particular moral or political credo. While realist fiction may—indeed, should—teach the reader, it should only do so indirectly and without excluding idealism, given that the human condition conjoins matter and spirit. These ideas are revisited in the prologue to *La Tribuna*, described as a "study of local customs" (57) interwoven with recent political events whose setting, the fictional Marineda, is a microcosm of the author's native A Coruña. In her pursuit of artistic verisimilitude Pardo Bazán relies on "[e]l método de análisis implacable que nos impone el arte moderno" ("the method of unsparing analysis that modern art imposes on us"; 58), combining close examination of the subjectivity of her female working-class protagonist, prolific descriptions of the ills of factory life (which she had documented personally), and distinctive regional speech patterns. That there is a "propósito docente" ("educational intention"; 58) is undeniable, but, she avers, she did not impose it a priori on the text; rather, it was revealed in the course of her contemplation of the social class she set out to portray. The prologue to *El cisne de Vilamorta* makes a similar point, although in this instance she is defending her novel not from accusations of crude naturalism, as in *La Tribuna*, but its opposite, a tendency toward Romantic idealism. Denouncing critics who mistakenly divide reality into mutually exclusive spheres (the intellect versus the senses), she maintains that the same objectives inform both novels: to examine and artistically depict people and places she knows well, thereby creating fully developed novels rather than simplistic costumbrista sketches.

La cuestión palpitante elaborates at greatest length Pardo Bazán's objections to naturalism as embodied in the works of Émile Zola: when, in the experimental novel, a human being is deterministically reduced to a machine or a beast of nature and human passions and intellect are similarly reduced to physiochemical reactions, they are banished from the domain of poetry and literature, transforming the novelist into a sociologist, a criminologist, or a politician. For Pardo Bazán, realism offers a broader and more complete canvas than naturalism: "Comprende y abarca lo natural y lo espiritual, el cuerpo y el alma, y concilia y reduce a unidad la oposición del naturalismo y del idealismo racional" ("Realism comprises and contains the natural and the spiritual, body and soul, and reconciles and reduces to unity the opposition between naturalism and rational idealism"; 46). In wording and concept, her statement is markedly similar to Benito Pérez Galdós's search in realist art for a "perfecto fiel de balanza entre la exactitud y la belleza de la reproducción" ("perfectly faithful balance between the exactitude and the beauty of reproduction"; "La sociedad" 159). Spanish literary realism is scientific, based on the observation of the individual and society, but it also professes the cult of artistic form, which it practices with richness and analytic perspicacity. Here Pardo Bazán is especially insistent that the spread of Spanish realism is less a new movement than a continuing evolution of a perennial tendency epitomized by Miguel de Cervantes, Diego Hurtado de Mendoza, Saint Teresa of Ávila, Diego Velázquez, and Francisco de Goya and whose current exemplars are Galdós, José María de Pereda, Juan Valera, and Pedro Antonio de Alarcón (63–64): hers is a pedagogy of realism that is historicized and nationalized.

Of the many qualities Pardo Bazán ascribes to realist writing, three aspects seem most germane to her own narrative practice: visuality, mobility, and the *Bildung* narrative pattern, which traces the process of apprenticeship and self-cultivation that culminates in a character's acculturation and acquisition of wisdom, typically through disillusionment but also through rebellion. Visuality evokes the recording of the "thing-ism" (Brooks, *Realist Vision* 16) of the world through sight, underscoring the role of outward appearances in a society of and as spectacle. Extreme contrasts between poverty and wealth (in "En tranvía"; *La Tribuna*) are communicated in dense descriptions of pure physicality, generating catalogs of faces and bodies, inventories of clothing and household goods. The placement of characters in the spotlight of public scrutiny (the transfigured Amparo, reading aloud to her coworkers or addressing a political delegation; the destitute mother in "En tranvía" who becomes an object of public charity during a streetcar ride; Jacobo, alias Restorán, on display in a lurid carny show) likewise reminds readers of Pardo Bazán's foregrounding of visual regimes. Thus, an effective classroom approach is to contrast textual passages with visual analogs in nineteenth- and early-twentieth-century painting and photography. What sort of dialogue emerges from the juxtaposition of *La Tribuna*'s factory scenes with Vicente Cutanda's *Una huelga de obreros en Vizcaya* (1892; "Workers' Strike in Vizcaya") or Gonzalo Bilbao's *Interior de fábrica de tabacos de Sevilla* (1915; "Interior of Tobacco Factory in Seville")? Or looking at middle-class family portraits by Joaquín Sorolla—such as *Mis hijos* (1904; "My Children) and *Clotilde sentada en un sofá* (1910; "Clothilde Seated on a Sofa") or by Marcelina Poncela de Jardiel—such as *Mis muñecas* (1904; "My Dolls")—paired with descriptions of the Sobrado family in *La Tribuna* or the well-attired, self-satisfied passengers of the streetcar in "En tranvía"? Or photos and paintings exalting the mother-child bond (by Antonia de Bañuelos, in *El despertar de un niño* [1890;

"A Child's Awakening"]; by Mary Cassatt, in *Breakfast in Bed* [1897] and *Mother Feeding Child* [1898]; and by Berthe Morisot, in *The Cradle* [1873]) compared with the verbal images of maternity that conclude "En tranvía" (a blind baby in the arms of his beggar mother), *La Tribuna* (Amparo and her newborn illegitimate child), and "En Babilonia" (the unidentified mother whose child is dying in the hotel room adjoining Luis's)? Students can draw equally productive comparisons between Mariano Fortuny's staged, orientalizing paintings of female sensuality (*La odalisca* [1861; "The Odalisque"]; *Sueño de la odalisca* [1860; "Dream of the Odalisque") and "En Babilonia." If students today are visually oriented learners, then "visual and spatial ways of knowing" (Jones 270) become important tools for teaching realism.

Mobility, too, is a distinguishing element of Pardo Bazán's realist fiction. Travel is a constant theme in her works. Streetcars and trains crisscross the Spanish landscape and the European continent, bringing young men from the provinces to the city (Chinto in *La Tribuna*, Luis in "En Babilonia"), transporting marginal subjects beyond the city limits ("En tranvía"), and bringing foreign entrepreneurs to Spain ("Restorán"). Mobility refers as well to notions of circulation and exchange—of money, certainly, but also of blood ("Restorán") and even language itself, as we find in the slippage from metonymy to metaphor (Furst, *All* 160–73) that characterizes the account of the infernal circles of Marineda's factory in *La Tribuna*. Mobility is likewise associated with the shifts in point of view and narrative voice—from first to third person, from dialogue to interior monologue—essential to facilitating readers' entry into the varied topographies of consciousness these texts encompass.

Finally, the *Bildung* pattern, a form of mobility across time, is a device especially favored by Pardo Bazán. In *La cuestión palpitante* she asserts that psychological analysis, which is linked instrumentally to the developmental model of self-formation in narrative, is the most rewarding territory the realist writer can explore (182). At the conclusion of *La Tribuna*, misled by a faithless lover and betrayed by her utopian belief in the ameliorative power of federal republicanism, Amparo is left to fend for herself in an uncertain future, enduring the deception that Pardo Bazán's women protagonists so often experience in love or marriage. Jacobo, the orphaned *golfo* ("delinquent") in "Restorán" who was employed to let a flea circus suck the blood from his arm, ends up a pickpocket; having learned his lesson well, the previously victimized host now becomes a parasite on society. The disenchantment of the protagonist of "En Babilonia" is equally definitive: expecting to encounter in Madrid the debauchery of nocturnal orgies attended by voluptuous concubines, Luis instead discovers something radically different—not the "supreme mysteries" (10) of sexual initiation but the shadow of mortality hanging over an incurably ill child. Luis's is not a sentimental education; rather, he receives a crash course in the destruction of illusions and the loss of youthful innocence.

Visuality, mobility, and *Bildung*—how to see, how to move, how to live—lie at the heart of Pardo Bazán's realist enterprise-cum-lesson in history and literary art. The author uses these strategies and conventions creatively rather than slavishly to create fictional worlds that, in their orientation toward social reality, encourage readers to compare her reports of human experience with their own, to assess where change is needed—in essence, to stimulate critical thinking. In her essays and narratives this critical faculty of realism is never far from her mind, hardly surprising given her well-documented interest in pedagogical reform efforts. No doubt she would have read with approval Rafael Altamira's commentary (1886) on the doctrine of literary realism:

> La tendencia realista, proclamando el principio de la experimentación, como fundamento de la creación literaria, aspira á educar las funciones de la juventud estudiosa, á *educir* sus facultades latentes, para (dándoles base) ponerlas en ocasión de ejercer *realmente*, de que tengan un verdadero concepto del mundo en que han que actuar.
> Así viene á ser el Realismo la pedagogía de la literatura.   (515)

> The realist tendency, in proclaiming the experimental principle as the foundation of literary creation, aspires to train the capabilities of studious youth, *to draw out* their latent faculties, so that, giving them a base, they will have the opportunity to *really* develop them, so that they will have a true concept of the world in which they will have to act.
> Thus Realism becomes the pedagogy of literature.

For Pardo Bazán, realism is no mere theory of reflection, nor is its actualization in her writing simply a matter of resorting mechanically to some master code of narrative conventions. However, to construct fictional worlds that closely resemble her own she makes ample use of the instruments in her literary tool kit. The value of realism for her is that it does not simply show the reader something recognizable but also moves the reader to thought and potentially to action—a point well worth remembering when teaching her texts to our students.

NOTES

[1] Suggestions include Carr, *Modern Spain* 1–15, 31–46; Fontana 351–84; Tortella Casares 1–21; Shubert 31–41, 51–55, 104–18, 133–43; Scanlon, *La polémica* 58–121, 122–58; Nash, *Mujer* 7–60. See also Gómez-Ferrer Morant, *Vida*, especially 59–82 and 279–98, dedicated to Pardo Bazán's positioning in fin de siècle intellectual culture and women's education.

[2] I cite "En Babilonia" and "En tranvía" in Paredes Núñez's four-volume edition, *Cuentos completos*.

[3] Shields contends that contemporary culture is obsessed with a "reality hunger" precisely because reality is so rarely experienced in our scripted and artificial world, which is based on the simulacra of postmodern hyperreality (81).

[4] For the concept of the reality effect, which Barthes coined, see his "L'Effet de reél," which is still required reading for scholars of literary realism. See Barthes, "Reality Effect" for an English translation.

[5] Jameson explores the opposition created between the "ideology of the text" and the "ideology of realism"; the former, based on the positive valuation of self-conscious, open-ended textuality advanced by structuralism and poststructuralism, condemns the latter for trafficking in a deceptive vocabulary of transparency and naturality ("Ideology" 239–46). Such attacks, Jameson says, can be traced to "the idea that the literature of realism has the ideological function of adapting its readers to bourgeois society as it currently exists, with its premium on comfort and inwardness, on individualism, on the acceptance of money as an ultimate reality. . . . [T]he realistic novelist has a vested interest, an ontological stake, in the solidity of social reality, on the resistance of bourgeois society to history and to change" (*Antinomies* 5). Moreover, the supplanting of bourgeois class culture by the global consumerism of late capitalism renders obsolete the "privileged content" of nineteenth-century realism (6).

[6] All translations are my own.

[7] Recommended theoretical readings include Auerbach 454–92, 493–524; Brooks, *Realist Vision* 1–20; Armstrong 1–31; Bakhtin, either *Problems* 5–46 or *Dialogic Imagination* 259–422 ("Discourse in the Novel").

[8] The prologue to *La Tribuna* is contained in the 2006 Cátedra edition (57–59). The prologue to *El cisne de Vilamorta* appears online at the *Biblioteca Virtual Miguel de Cervantes* (*El cisne* [Alicante]). *La cuestión palpitante* appeared as a series of articles in *La época* in 1882 and was published in book form the following year. This essay cites the 1970 edition by Carmen Bravo-Villasante. I cite the preface to *Un viaje de novios* in Marisa Sotelo Vázquez's edition (51–56); it is also anthologized in English translation in Becker (261–65; "On Spanish Realism"), which also includes the translation of Leopoldo Alas's prologue to *La cuestión palpitante*, here titled "What Naturalism Is Not" (266–73). For a more recent compilation of realist manifestos and theoretical interventions, see Furst's *Realism*.

Explaining Nineteenth-Century Spanish Literature: Pardo Bazán's Literature Lessons

Íñigo Sánchez-Llama

In *Retratos y apuntes literarios* (1908; "Literary Portraits and Notes"), Emilia Pardo Bazán included a series of critical studies that incorporate texts that originally appeared in the prestigious journals *Nuevo teatro crítico* (1891–93) and *La lectura* (1901–20), along with lectures delivered in distinguished cultural institutions such as Madrid's Ateneo Científico, Literario y Artístico (Scientific, Literary, and Artistic Atheneum). Because *Retratos y apuntes literarios* constitutes an impressive summary of her critical texts, it is an effective centerpiece of a graduate seminar that examines the text's assessment of the primary aesthetic trends of the nineteenth century. Its references to classicism, Romanticism, and realism provide engaging references to familiarize graduate students with these literary movements. Students in this seminar read Pardo Bazán's works along with the evaluation of literary texts that belong to the artistic movements analyzed. The seminar gives students the opportunity to understand Pardo Bazán's critical perspective, a perspective that is both timely and relevant to understanding the way nineteenth-century Spanish literature articulated a discourse of modernity.

Useful complementary material for the introduction of the seminar includes nineteenth-century texts that define the role of criticism. Manuel de la Revilla's essay "Principios a que debe obedecer la crítica literaria" (1883; "Foundations of Literary Criticism"; *Obras* 535–65); reflections by Leopoldo Alas developed in "El libre examen y nuestra literatura presente" (1881; "Impact of Free Thinking in Contemporary Spanish Literature"; *Solos* 62–76); or the academic lecture of Juan Valera, "La poesía popular como ejemplo del punto en que deberían coincidir la idea vulgar y la idea académica sobre la lengua castellana" (1862; "Popular Poetry as an Example of How Popular and Academic Interpretation of Castilian Language Should Interact"; *Discursos* 1: 5–53) are valuable references for understanding the modern critical perspective that emerged in Spain in the last third of the nineteenth century.

The seminar can introduce the importance of classicism, Romanticism, and realism in nineteenth-century Hispanic literature. These literary movements generated intense debate in Spanish criticism around the concepts of artificiality, authenticity, originality, and artistic beauty. Pardo Bazán participated in this debate with a favorable view of the artistic merit of the works she analyzed. Romanticism questioned classicism during the first third of the nineteenth century by drawing on a universal reference point—the classicist perspective—that was considered incompatible with the creation of an authentic Spanish literature. After the Glorious Revolution of 1868, however, the proponents of realism questioned Romanticism's representation of artistic sensitivity, which likewise failed to achieve full literary authenticity. Debates in Spain about classicism and Romanticism harkened back to the lack of artistic vigor of both literary movements. Pardo Bazán, addressing these criticisms, promoted a perspective that integrates cosmopolitanism, an attempt to renovate Spanish cultural habits, a modern aesthetic awareness, and a modernized approach to the vindication of local traditions. These values define how the concept of modernity was articulated in Spain beginning in the 1870s.

In *Retratos y apuntes literarios* Pardo Bazán assesses the classicist author José María Gabriel y Galán and the Romantic authors Miguel de los Santos Álvarez, Ramón de Campoamor, and Gaspar Núñez de Arce, who were not included in the canon of modern Spanish literature at the time. Her analysis is important not so much because it highlights prestigious figures of her time as because it allows students to understand in accurate terms the critical readings of classicism and Romanticism by those who promoted Spanish literary modernity. Her discussions of the poetry of Gabriel y Galán offer a detailed appraisal of classicism and criticize the lack of originality in eighteenth-century lyricism (*Retratos* 83–116). She celebrates Gabriel y Galán's classicism for embodying "no el clasicismo atildado de un académico que se viste a la antepenúltima moda . . . sino el fuerte y sano clasicismo tradicional, que procede de haberse enjuagado frecuentemente la boca con vino añejo, con Fray Luis, con los bucólicos de la Arcadia" ("not the stylish classicism of an academic who wears last year's fashion . . . but a strong and healthy traditional classicism, which comes from having been rinsed with old wine, with Fray Luis, with the bucolic academics of Arcadia"; 103). Gabriel y Galán's classicism is considered acceptable not only for its reference to the Renaissance tradition but also for its expression of textual indebtedness to the popular literature of Spain. Pardo Bazán also highlights the prestige of Gabriel y Galán's work within the Castilian agricultural community (86). The writer believes that "el poeta más grande será el que más enteramente se comunique" ("the greatest poet is the one who most fully communicates"; 116). The poetic canon grants aesthetic merit to works that fuse artistic originality with local literary tradition while at the same time communicating effectively with their audience. This critical perspective accords a favorable evaluation to Gabriel y Galán's regionalist, classicist poetry.

Pardo Bazán's inclusion of Spanish classicizing literary texts provides a critical reference point for measuring the significance of her assessments. José de Espronceda's article "El pastor clasiquino" (1835; "The Little Classicist Shepherd"), Carolina Coronado's poem "A un poeta clásico" (1845; "For a Classicist Poet"; *Poesías* 375–76), and Juan Valera's essay "De lo castizo en nuestra cultura en el siglo XVIII" (1871; On the National and Aesthetic Purity of Spanish Culture in the Eighteenth Century"; *Crítica* 239–58) are representative of how eighteenth-century Spanish classicism was interpreted during the nineteenth century. Such texts are important to aid students' understanding of Pardo Bazán's distinctive critical reading of classicist literature.

Retratos y apuntes literarios also reflects on Romanticism by including detailed critical analyses of the lyrical works of Campoamor, Núñez de Arce, and Santos Álvarez (5–82, 357–71). As she does for Gabriel y Galán, Pardo Bazán highlights the importance of Campoamor based on the enduring success of his work "que atraviesa medio siglo sin producir indiferencia ni cansancio" ("that spans half a century without showing signs of indifference or fatigue"; 46); she notes that a literary work that aspires to long-lasting significance must display a certain artistic value. Romanticism also conveys an appreciation of creative genius: "la exaltación del yo, el lirismo ha venido, con el romanticismo y la disociación de los ideales colectivos, a predominar en nuestra mejor poesía moderna" ("the exaltation of the self, lyricism, with Romanticism and the dissociation of collective ideals, has begun to dominate our best modern poetry"; 69–70). Pardo Bazán vindicates the epic poetry of José Zorrilla for reaching "la rara excelencia de la integridad poética" ("a rare level of excellence in poetic integrity"; 70). The Galician writer offers a thought-provoking discussion of the poetry of Espronceda and reflects on his poem "A Jarifa en una orgía" ("For Jarifa in an Orgy"). She asserts that in this work the poet develops "una abstracción filosófica, símbolo de la inania de las cosas y pretexto para desahogar su desesperación" ("a philosophical abstraction, symbol of the innateness of things and a pretext to express his despair"; 363). She celebrates Romantic poetry for its individualistic lyricism, popular success, and intuitive ability to reflect the philosophical crisis of the nineteenth century. These judgments link her perspective to similar interpretations of the complexities of nineteenth-century Western culture formulated between the 1830s and the 1850s by Jules Michelet in his *Introduction á l'historie universelle* (1830; "Introduction to Universal History") and Auguste Comte in his *Catéchisme positiviste* (1852; "Positivist Catechism").

Romantic poems or observations on Romanticism are productive supplements for analyzing Pardo Bazán's interpretation of Romanticism in the classroom. Espronceda's poem "A Jarifa en una orgía" (1840; *Poesías* 259–63); the well-known essay by Juan Valera, "Del romanticismo en España y de Espronceda" (1864; "Romanticism in Spain and Espronceda"; *Estudios* 1: 161–201); and *Discurso sobre la poesía* (1887; "Lecture on Poetry"), delivered as a lecture by Núñez de Arce at the Ateneo, help contextualize Pardo Bazán's enthusiastic regard for Romanticism.

In *Retratos y apuntes literarios* Pardo Bazán also develops her theories on the art of the nineteenth-century novel, focusing on three authors: Pedro Antonio de Alarcón, Juan Valera, and Luis Coloma (117–355). The writer argues that Alarcón is one of the Spanish novelists whose work "sirvió de puente entre el romanticismo más descabellado y huero y el realismo más castizo y donoso" ("served as a bridge between the most absurd and vacuous Romanticism and the most authentic and witty realism"; 118). She describes the development of the nineteenth-century Spanish novel as a well-paved path to modern realism, which was fully developed by the last third of the century; other contributions to modern realism are Golden Age narratives and the "realismo popular" ("popular realism") of the costumbrista prose of Fernán Caballero (167). The best works of Alarcón and

Valera, in the author's opinion, are those that respond to this aesthetic expectation. Among Valera's novels, in which an "evolución al realismo" ("evolution to realism"; 274) can be discerned, Pardo Bazán considers *Pepita Jiménez* (1874) the ideal example of the "momento áureo y culminante de [su] vida literaria" ("golden moment and highlight of [his] literary life"; 266). Among Alarcón's works, she considers *El sombrero de tres picos* (1874; "The Three-Cornered Hat") as "el punto culminante de la inspiración alarconiana" ("the highlight of Alarconian inspiration"; 144). She asserts that the realism in this novel is particularly interesting for its fusing of local tradition and originality: "todo es de la misma castiza y jugosa cepa; todo es añejo y fresco a la vez, como vino embotellado junto con dorada uva" ("Everything together is pure and delightful; everything is mature and fresh at the same time, as bottled wine with golden grapes"; 188). She also celebrates the "poder plasmante" ("expressive power") of Benito Perez Galdós's narrative for its "facultad inventiva que, aun partiendo como no puede menos, de los datos reales, obra a su manera de crisol con el metal, derritiendo e imprimiendo nueva forma al tesoro de datos que suministra la experiencia propia y ajena" ("inventive quality, even when based on no less than real facts, he models his craft as if working with metal in a crucible, melting and imprinting a new form on the trove of information gleaned from his own personal experience and that of others"; 164). Pardo Bazán, using a discursive strategy similar to the one she used in assessing classicism, stresses the importance of dignifying the techniques of the realist literary movement through its association not so much with French narratives but with fictional works of the Spanish Golden Age (303). In short, she articulates a realist discourse defined by modernity, cosmopolitanism, and identification with local literary heritage.

Retratos y apuntes literarios contains critical opinions that validate the talent of nineteenth-century women writers of narrative. Pardo Bazán's perspective is original because of its explicit distance from the most influential critical evaluations of the Bourbon Restoration period. Revilla censures the Valerian character Pepita Jiménez for being "más voluptuosa que una odalisca, más filósofa que Hipatia, y más salada que las salinas de Cardona, que tenía por costumbre entregarse a Cupido después de disertar sobre metafísica mística" ("more voluptuous than an odalisque, more philosophical than Hypatia, and saltier than the salt mines of Cardona, [and] who often surrendered to Cupid after lecturing on mystical metaphysics"; *Críticas* 2: 293). The renowned critic perceives the "figura marmórea" ("marble figure") Doña Luz from *Pepita Jiménez* as "más que criada en las regiones andaluzas, parece doña Luz matrona romana o nacida a las orillas del Rhin" ("rather than raised in the Andalusian region, Doña Luz appears to be a Roman matron or someone born on the banks of the Rhine"; 2: 294). Pardo Bazán, however, defines Pepita Jiménez as "la figura juvenil de una mujer honesta, apacible, algo teóloga también a ratos, lo cual no es inverosímil en los pueblos. . . . He conocido tipos muy análogos al de Pepita en la vieja ciudad universitaria de Santiago de Compostela" ("the youthful figure of an honest, gentle woman, also somewhat of a theologian at times, which is not implausible in the villages. . . . I have met people very similar to Pepita types in the old university city of Santiago de Compostela"; *Retratos* 270–71). Likewise, her opinion on *Pequeñeces* (1890) by Luis Coloma departs from other criticism on the novel. Juan Valera minimalized its importance because of its satirical didacticism, "la novela hubiera sido mejor sin ser sátira; y la sátira, mejor sin ser novela; y el sermón, retemejor si no hubiera sido ni novela ni sátira" ("the novel would have been better without satire; and the satire would have been better had it not been a novel; and the sermonizing would have been even better had it not been a novel or satire"; *El arte* 308). Pardo Bazán, however, highlights the aesthetic merits of "tan hermosa novela" ("such a beautiful novel"; *Retratos* 295). According to her, Coloma transcends the format of satire, and even transcends sermonizing, through his skillful execution of the novel's plot. The Galician author indicates that she only reproaches satire and sermonizing when they "echa a perder la obra de arte" ("spoil the work of art"; 301). In her view the formal features of the text rather than its author's worldview determine the artistic value of *Pequeñeces*. Her defense of the novel is important because, as she states, society exhibits "una prevención sorda y tenaz" ("a silent and tenacious mistrust"; 299) of literature written by women and of authors such as Coloma who were linked to religious orders.

Discussing the novels that Pardo Bazán analyzes helps students understand the aesthetic foundations of their critical evaluation. Reading *Pepita Jiménez* or *Pequeñeces* allows students to consider whether or not these works dialogue with the artistic expectations developed by Pardo Bazán. Incorporating the criticism of the novels by, respectively, Revilla (*Críticas* 2: 263–97) and Valera (*El arte* 302–31) also helps students understand Pardo Bazán's feminist perspective vis-à-vis the masculine bias of the prevailing criteria used to define aesthetic value.

Retratos y apuntes literarios reflects on the challenges faced by nineteenth-century Spanish women writers. A certain irony about gender stereotypes may be noted when Pardo Bazán anticipates her female readership's disappointment over her refusal to comment on the love life of the authors she analyzes (25–26). She praises women who wrote during the reign of Queen Isabel II (1833–68) for works that aligned with prevailing artistic values. She describes Caballero as an "eminente mujer" ("outstanding woman") and an "ilustre novelista y costumbrista" ("illustrious novelist and costumbrista writer"; 282). Gertrudis Gómez de Avellaneda is considered a "poeta de estro ardiente y clásica dicción, alma de fuego, impetuosa y varonil" ("poet of profound inspiration and classical diction, an impetuous, virile, impassioned soul"; 283). Pardo Bazán also connects the height of Romanticism with a sensitivity linked to the female gender: "los poetas líricos son mayores cuanto más impregnan a sus versos el aroma femenino, comunicándole sabor de tristeza infinita" ("lyric poets are even better when they fill their verses with a female fragrance conveying an infinite sadness"; 51). She recognizes that sexism causes Spanish women writers to become "*escritores maniatados*. Rompen sus ligaduras, claro está, pero la gente recoge los pedazos y les azota con ellos el rostro" ("*handcuffed writers*. They break the ties that bind them, of course, but people pick up these ties and lash them across the face with them"; 299). With these observations she poses the complex articulation of artistic creativity developed by female writers in a sexist society. The association of literary Romanticism with so-called feminine traits does not legitimize literature written by women so much as it magnifies the expressive possibilities available to male writers.[1] Pardo Bazán perceives that nineteenth-century Spanish women writers, even if they gained the respect of cultural institutions by working in dominant aesthetic modes, continued to suffer gender bias by entering a domain — the literary arena — associated almost exclusively with men. Describing Spanish women writers as "handcuffed" is a powerful way to explain the difficulties they faced. Likewise, stressing the feminine traits associated with Romantic lyricism elucidates the contradictions inherent in patriarchal prejudices against nineteenth-century Spanish women writers of literature.

Various supplementary materials effectively illustrate for students the connection between Pardo Bazán's feminist perspective in *Retratos y apuntes literarios* and the gradual evolution of a feminist consciousness in modern Spanish literature. Newspaper articles by Gómez de Avellaneda, published in 1860 as "La mujer"; Concepción Arenal's essay *La mujer del porvenir* (1869; "Women of the Future"); and Margarita Nelken's watershed analysis from 1930 on the importance of Romanticism in the development of Hispanic literature written by women in *Las escritoras españolas* ("Spanish Women Writers";187–88, 221–23) offer a theoretical foundation for understanding Pardo Bazán's vital contribution to modern Spanish feminism. Celia Amorós's cogent analysis on the importance of modernity in the genesis of contemporary feminism (292–308) also constitutes a recent critical appraisal that may be useful in interpreting the feminism inscribed in Pardo Bazán's critical works.

NOTES

This essay was translated by Lisa Nalbone, who also provided the translations of the Spanish quotations.

[1] For an analysis of the difficulties faced by modern European and American women writers in this regard, see Boyd 26–27; Korsmeyer 29–31; and Moi 3–120.

Pardo Bazán as a European Intellectual: Naturalism, Spiritualism, and Idealism

Denise DuPont

Emilia Pardo Bazán, arguably the most important Spanish woman writer of the nineteenth century and a leading light of Spain's first-wave feminism, will be of particular interest to those interested in pedagogy, since she was a teacher in many senses and at a time when women were not expected to perform a didactic role in society in the high-profile way that she did. As she explains in her short autobiography, "Apuntes autobiográficos" ("Autobiographical Notes"), she saw Spanish literature as special and distinctive and yet also part of the ongoing project of European letters (719).[1] For this reason, she felt called to inform her reading public and those who attended her lectures about literature from other countries, particularly France and Russia, and to promote mutual awareness in the international community of readers. She spent her early years at a French school, and she traveled several times to the neighboring country, where she met French literary luminaries and Russians who introduced her to their national literature and culture (Faus Sevilla 1: 79–80, 347, 352, 359–64). She enlightened foreign contemporaries, including Spanish Americans, with respect to Spanish letters past and present and addressed the same topic to her compatriots, many of whom she saw as lacking a healthy pride in their national literature.

Pardo Bazán's transnational literary interests make the author an ideal subject for study in a comparative literature or world literature classroom. Students in a comparative literature course could be asked to explore their non-Spanish nineteenth-century interests, particularly French or Russian topics. Students familiar with George Eliot or Madame de Staël could be encouraged to research the connections and differences between those authors and Pardo Bazán, who is often seen as the Spanish counterpart to those writers. Visual culture can engage students and ground their literary studies in images from the author's time; almost any museum with collections of European art of the second half of the nineteenth century or the beginning of the twentieth would be relevant to aspects of her work.

Pardo Bazán's desire to situate Spanish literature in the larger European context irked some of her contemporaries. The author recognized that she was labeled unpatriotic because of her attention to literature outside Spain; in response, she recalled the example of Peter the Great, who wished to provide his country with a window to the West. Spain needed a similar window, she argued in *La revolución y la novela en Rusia* ("The Revolution and the Novel in Russia"), in order to keep an eye on developments in European thought (*Obras completas* 3: 761). She saw her nation as afflicted with a misguided instinct for independence, which led Spaniards to confuse influence with domination and to fear looking past the country's borders. Some intellectuals deemed curiosity about foreign literatures a threat to Spanish originality, but she argued against this view of her country's culture as fragile and susceptible to absorption or eclipse by other nations.[2] She saw herself as one of few Spaniards equipped to evaluate cultural developments in the rest of Europe, since most of her compatriots denied the existence of any thought or aesthetic life beyond the Pyrenees, an error she believed was quickly corrected when the mountain range was crossed (Faus Sevilla 1: 353 [letter to Narcis Oller of 12 Oct. 1866]). In her campaign against xenophobia, closed-mindedness, intolerance, insecurity, and fear, she enthusiastically promoted international travel and engagement with other cultures.

The author was well aware that many of her contemporaries, in addition to accusing her of an excessive preoccupation with literature from outside Spain, found fault with her shifting attention from one country to another, which they described as superficial and connected to her gender. The literary historian Marcelino Menéndez Pelayo, a good friend of Pardo Bazán's, argued in his prologue to one of her books that her eminently feminine character predisposed her to follow external influences with docility, in contrast to men, who were equipped for creativity (xi). The novelist and critic Juan Valera commented that since it was natural for women to wish to dress fashionably he was not surprised that "Doña Emilia" was styling herself a naturalist (qtd. in Pereira-Muro, *Género* 61).[3] Pardo Bazán's association with Émile Zola's naturalist movement, of which the author's collection of essays titled *La cuestión palpitante* (1882; "The Burning Question") is the best example, drew much attention from her contemporaries and continues to shape her critical reception today. Her critical study was the first in Spain to deal systematically with the questions raised by Zola, even though, as she herself points out in *La cuestión palpitante*, she had been excluded from relevant discussions in Madrid's Ateneo Científico, Literario y Artístico (Scientific, Literary, and Artistic Atheneum) the previous year on the basis of her gender (Faus Sevilla 1: 196–202). Her interest in Zola's movement was particularly jarring for Spanish men of letters, some of whom glossed over her disagreements with Zola in order to paint her as his devoted follower. However, she did not accept the determinism that formed the basis of French naturalism, cautioned against other extremes of the movement, avoided scabrous detail and licentiousness in her own fiction, and lamented the pessimism of the French school. She promoted naturalism only insofar as she believed that a realist approach to fiction offered an alternative to escapism and had the potential to remedy poverty, social inequality, and limited opportunities for women. Her short story "Un destripador de antaño" (1890; "The Heart Lover"; Pardo Bazán, *Cuentos completos* 2: 5–21) is a good example of stark realism in the service of this social agenda, as is the popular "Las medias rojas" (1914; "The Red Stockings"; 3: 195–97). Both these short pieces leave an impression on students, who are shocked by the desperation produced by poverty and ignorance and the violence experienced by the young female characters.

The judgment by Pardo Bazán's compatriots that the author's attention to the French literary school was improper appears attributable to gender bias. Although she was one of the most important authors of the Spanish realist novel, her male contemporaries tended to characterize the genre in masculinizing terms (Jagoe, "Disinheriting"), leaving Pardo Bazán in the remarkable position of leading a literary movement that attempted to exclude her (Pereira-Muro, "Maravillosas supercherías"). Despite sexist dismissals of her work, she continued to lead efforts to break through the Spanish prejudices that identified anti-intellectualism and a lack of curiosity with patriotism. Spanish realism, she argued in the preface of her novel *Un viaje de novios*, was an eminently patriotic literary style, given its roots in the work of Miguel de Cervantes, Tirso de Molina, Diego Velázquez, and Francisco de Goya (*Obras completas* 3: 571–73). Pardo Bazán, as well as other Spanish authors such as Benito Pérez Galdós, believed that when the ugly excesses of French naturalism were eliminated, the playful, satirical, and even bawdy realism at its core was a homegrown literary and artistic genre of which Spanish painters and writers were the unquestioned originators and masters. In the preface to *Un viaje de novios*, a good short reading on the author's views on naturalism, Pardo Bazán called for a return to a native Spanish realism that laughs and cries—a realism that is comic, dramatic, indirect, unconscious, detailed, and full of inspiration. The Spanish realist tradition, which she encourages contemporary Spanish authors to cultivate, combines spirit and matter, heaven and earth, and does not disdain idealism.

Accused of too closely imitating French naturalism and of lacking originality, Pardo Bazán was also criticized for relying on too few sources and for drawing heavily from them without giving credit. The author responded to such charges by arguing that her task was to teach her nation about the world of letters beyond the Pyrenees by presenting the international literary panorama in an engaging way, liberated from sources and documentation. Working from this idea, a discussion of teaching methods and goals can be initiated with students with the following prompts: When teaching about developments in any field, should the professor synthesize and generalize or prioritize specificity and specialization? Can these approaches be harmonized, and if so, how? Pardo Bazán often denied being scholarly and acknowledged that she lacked mastery of the topics she discussed. Erudition and authoritativeness were not her goals, nor did she aspire to possess an exhaustive, encyclopedic knowledge of literature and its history. She was an expert on no topic, yet she knew how to play to her strengths as a brilliant writer with a quick grasp of complex literary and social issues. The later decades of her career were increasingly devoted to chronicling culture in modern life, such as in her columns La vida contemporánea and Un poco de todo and in the short pieces she wrote for *La nación*, the Buenos Aires newspaper. Committed to literary experimentation, she remained receptive to artistic trends throughout her career. In 1916 she received the honor of being named professor of contemporary Romance literature at the Central University in Madrid. She described this appointment to her friend Miguel de Unamuno as a miracle, "dadas las varas de tela que penden de mi cintura" ("because of the many measures of cloth that hang from my waist" [that is to say, because she was a woman]; qtd. in Faus Sevilla 2: 247 [letter of 20 Mar. 1916]). She may not have participated in or recognized every new development—she claimed there was no new novel in Spain in the generation after hers, dismissing the novelistic boom of 1902 despite being acquainted with some of its authors—but she did recognize the value of innovation, as shown by her support for the Catalan modernists in Cau Ferrat (Faus Sevilla 2: 87–97).

For Pardo Bazán, another important quality of great literature was its connection to the spiritual, a lesson she wished to impart to her readers on the occasions in which she adopted a quasi-ministerial role in her writings. The belief that literature might offer spiritual sustenance led her away from French and toward Russian naturalism, which she saw as embodying ideals and nourishing the soul. Mad reformers and quixotic dreamers like Saint Francis of Assisi appealed to her because she was herself a spiritualist; in *La revolución y la novela en Rusia*, she wrote, "así creemos los espiritualistas" ("as we spiritualists believe"; *Obras completas* 3: 805).[4] She saw such eccentric figures as representing humanity's desire for something more than material well-being: spiritual visionaries embodied the painful aspiration to attain something beyond worldly experiences. In 1890 she argued in "Últimas modas literarias" ("Latest Literary Fashions") and in "Edmundo Goncourt y su hermano" ("Edmond de Goncourt and His Brother") that readers had been exhausted by the exaggerations of naturalism and declared that its gloomy French school had run its course (*Obras completas* 3: 932–39; 951–64). Though she had previously taken an interest in French naturalism, in the final decade of the nineteenth century she became convinced that modern French writers struggled to follow Russian models of spiritual literature and argued in "Edmundo Goncourt" that writers such as Leo Tolstoy and Fyodor Dostoyevsky set standards for the turn-of-the-century European novel. The idealism of the Russian novel, she explained in "Últimas modas literarias," coincided with humanity's turn-of-the-century spiritual disposition, which she saw developing in Spain as well as in France.

Pardo Bazán's insistence on the connection between the novel and Europe's spiritual development correlated with her belief in literature's commitment to the social. For her, literature had a distinct role to play in the restoration of charity in society. Yet, at the same time, she wrote frequently about artistic freedom, arguing for art for art's sake in the face of religious intolerance and a censuring mentality she identified especially among politically intransigent neo-Catholics in Spain. She supported the Catholic Church as an institution and Catholicism as an abstract ideal, more so than many of her male contemporaries. She parted ways, however, with right-wing political applications of Christianity, particularly when they hindered literary expression. She rejected fiction composed in the service of a political agenda, while she accepted texts that were true works of art but happened to carry a spiritual message. She increasingly emphasized fiction's capacity to communicate spiritual and moral values and thus to stimulate cultural regeneration in Spain and in Europe, which she saw as spiritually adrift. Her conception of literature as a remedy for national ills can be tied to the Spanish crisis of 1898, when the country's intellectuals confronted the loss of their nation's traditional, imperial identity in the wake of the Spanish-American War. Facing her country's cultural depression and apathy, Pardo Bazán renounced her detachment from sociopolitical questions and noted the weakening of her faith in disinterested aesthetics. Committing her pen to national salvation, she called for "una literatura de acción, estimulante y tónica despertadora de energías y fuerzas" ("a stimulating literature of action, a tonic to awaken energy and strength"; "Asfixia").

As a logical extension of these ideas, around the turn of the twentieth century Pardo Bazán began to model her approach to fiction after Tolstoy's, which, she believed, reconciled true art with the teachings of Christ. She shifted from an approach based on literary aesthetics to thesis novels devoted to feminism, criminology, and the decadence of contemporary Spain, among other topics (Faus Sevilla 2: 25). Her admiration for Tolstoy's talent for propagating ideas and worldviews through artistic literature is evident in the Christian novels she wrote in the last part of her career. In the prologue to *Doña Milagros* (1894) she presents herself as a storyteller chosen by God; the notion of a divinely elected author sets the tone as well for *La quimera* (1905; "The Chimera"), *La sirena negra* (1908; "The Black Siren"), and *Dulce dueño* (1911; "Sweet Master").[5] Her spirituality is apparent in these last three novels—the last she wrote—in which her personal beliefs harmonize with international literary trends (Faus Sevilla 2: 261).

Pardo Bazán's belief in the redemptive function of literature drew her attention back to France during the devastation of World War I. As a university professor and cultural commentator, in the final years of her life Pardo Bazán returned to the allegiances of the earliest years of her intellectual formation. Two important texts to consult in this regard, both from 1916, are "El lirismo en la poesía francesa" ("The Lyricism in French Poetry"), the second course Pardo Bazán taught at the Central University of Madrid (published posthumously as a book in 1923), and the short piece "El porvenir de la literatura" ("The Future of Literature"), a lecture she delivered at Madrid's Residencia de Estudiantes (*Obras completas* 3: 1543–51). In these pieces she argues that unbridled "lyricism," originated by Jean-Jacques Rousseau and cultivated in the Romantic period and beyond, led to the anarchic, antisocial individualism of many talented writers. Culminating with Nietzsche, she explains in "El porvenir," the idea of the free man, the total individualist, has caused the dissolution of the institutions that humanity laboriously created over time: these valuable institutions and customs have now been summarily dismissed as conventions of a slave morality (1549). The selfish individuality of the intellectual artist then produced a backlash that correlates with the dehumanization caused by the World War I and the loss of the individual to mass movements. With hopes that the war is drawing to an end, Pardo Bazán envisions a redeemed France, purged of the antisocial tendencies of Rousseau and his literary descendants, which could awaken in Europe a concern for community, hospitality, charity, generosity, and social integration without sacrificing the healthy expression of individuality. Prewar nationalist ideals will be replaced by the union of peoples and races and by moral, social, religious, and human ideals embodied in mercy and philanthropy (1548–49). The author sees this trend toward spiritual renewal in Spain as well, as is evident in her sensitive treatment of the cathedrals of León and Santiago de Compostela in articles from June of 1915, both of which would be interesting pieces for a course focusing on the international impact of World War I and the resulting return to idealism.[6]

At the end of her life, while Pardo Bazán insisted on literature's role in healing society, she also defended art from the pressure to be utilitarian, a defense she made throughout her career. She had suffered the traumas of the early twentieth century, and her contradictory reactions in "El porvenir" will shock students when they realize to what extent the war's destruction of life and dehumanization of society led the author to question human progress. Taking an apocalyptic stance, she states that she gives her confession as did the first Christians, understanding that all human existence will soon end and that rushing toward extermination is nothing but the fulfillment of an unavoidable law (*Obras completas* 3: 1543). She mentions approvingly Ernest Renan's doubts as to whether (degraded) modern lives are equal in value to those of the medieval serfs who created the great Gothic monuments (1543). And yet, as the war demonstrated, even those monuments can be destroyed—the artistic form most likely to survive the apocalypse to testify to the human condition is literature, she argues, with its infinite number of copies. Her predictions for the development of postwar European culture thus point in two directions. On the one hand, if humanity survives, a new literature grounded in international religious awakening will guide European society in the reconciliation of individual spiritual genius and humanitarian concerns. On the other, if human beings hasten their divinely ordained end, literature will remain as the monument to their lost culture. With this essay Pardo Bazán, a dedicated teacher, gives today's students a testament of Europe in crisis and a vision of hope for its future that are sure to spark debate and discussion in the classroom.

NOTES

[1] I cite "Apuntes autobiográficos" in *Obras completas* 3: 698–732.

[2] The question of whether Spanish culture and literature relied too heavily on French models had been debated since the establishment of the Bourbon dynasty on the Spanish throne in the early eighteenth century, and some degree of resistance to France continued into Pardo Bazán's day, having been exacerbated by the imperialism and anticlericalism of the Napoleonic occupation (1808–14). To teach this topic, I use a *PowerPoint* with anti-French prints from the Spanish War of Independence, in which Napoleon appears

to be counseled by the devil and defiant Spaniards defecate on the constitution he attempts to write for Spain. A good source for these prints is *Estampas*.

[3] For a thorough discussion of the idea of Pardo Bazán as a woman at the mercy of fashions, see Pereira-Muro, *Género* 61–62. See Faus Sevilla (1: 471) for an analysis of the antipathy generated by Pardo Bazán, whose career was met with hostility to which her male contemporaries were generally immune.

[4] Translations are my own. Here Pardo Bazán uses the term *spiritualist* to mean someone interested in spiritual matters rather than the more common meaning of someone who attempts contact with the spirits of the dead.

[5] The character Minia Dumbría in *La quimera* is perhaps Pardo Bazán's best-known author surrogate. Minia facilitates the conversion of her dying protégé, the artist Silvio Lago, a figure based on the Galician painter Joaquín Vaamonde. See Faus Sevilla 2: 255–60.

[6] *La ilustración artística*, no. 1746, 14 June 1915, p. 398; *La ilustración artística*, no. 1747, 21 June 1915, p. 414.

A Fruitful Dialogue:
Pardo Bazán, Poe, Maupassant, and Chekhov

Susan M. McKenna

Masterful storyteller and influential critic, Pardo Bazán played a pivotal role in redefining the Spanish short story. Emboldened by superb linguistic skills and irrepressible curiosity, she corresponded with both the leading Spanish intellectuals of the day and their European counterparts.[1] She transcended national boundaries and embraced modern tenets of Continental philosophy and culture, interweaving these advances into the fabric of her craft. "En prosa como en poesía todo el mundo, quiera que no quiera tiene antecesores y maestros" ("In prose as in poetry, like it or not, everyone has ancestors and teachers"; 719), she affirms in "Apuntes autobiográficos" ("Autobiographical Notes"), the prologue to the first edition of *Los pazos de Ulloa* ("The House of Ulloa").[2] Accordingly, this essay foregrounds the fruitful outcome of intertextual exchange by examining Pardo Bazán in conjunction with three recognized masters of the short story: Edgar Allan Poe (1809–49), Guy de Maupassant (1850–93), and Anton Chekhov (1860–1904). Comparative close readings of their representative works will serve as a model for instructors of world literature courses.

No discussion of the short story is complete without recognizing Poe's role in defining the genre. He was the first to praise the story as a superb literary art form and, more important, to formulate a set of artistic principles specific to it. The term *art* here is not incidental: in an essay written in 1842 for *Graham's Magazine* in which he reviews Hawthorne's *Twice Told Tales*, Poe sought to legitimate the story as a literary genre (Poe, "Review"). Poe does not merely validate the genre, however, but extols the story as a unique literary medium that provides "the finest field for the exercise of the loftiest talent" (115). The story, he continues, has a "point of superiority" even over the poem because "the story allows for the expression of truth" (117). Essential to Poe's definition of the short story are brevity and the "unity of effect or impression" (117). Because brevity and unity are interdependent, unity, Poe maintains, can be preserved only in those "products" whose reading can be completed in one sitting: those that require "from a half-hour to one or two hours" (116; McKenna 14–15).

In Spain, Poe's stories first circulated in Baudelaire's French translations published in 1856. The first Spanish version of Poe's *Extraordinary Tales* appeared two years later. In the following decades, Poe's stories were published in Spanish individually in journals and later collected into volumes. These tales influenced the works of Pardo Bazán and those of her contemporaries, including Pedro Antonio de Alarcón, Fernán Caballero, Benito Pérez Galdós, Leopoldo Alas (Clarín), and Pío Baroja.[3] Reading Poe's "The Black Cat" (1843) in tandem with Pardo Bazán's "El espectro" (1909; "The Specter"; *Cuentos completos* 3: 73–76) underscores the general effect the fantastic mode had on Spanish literature as well as the depths of Pardo Bazán's intercultural knowledge and exchange.[4]

The fantastic mode, as defined by Tzvetan Todorov, requires the fulfillment of three conditions. First, the text must oblige the reader to consider fictional characters as a world of living persons and to hesitate between a natural and supernatural explanation of the events described. Second, because this hesitation is often experienced by a character, the reader's role is entrusted to that character. Both reader and character seek a rational explanation for the events; in a naive reading, the reader is identified with the character. Third, the reader must adopt a certain attitude with regard to the text, rejecting allegorical as well as "poetic" interpretations (33). Hesitation, or the vacillation between a rational or supernatural account, thus becomes one of the themes of the work. Following this designation of the fantastic, the response of the reader to both "The Black Cat" and "El espectro" is tantamount to making meaning, what literary critics call signification. Comprehension demands the reader's engagement in the storytelling process itself.

In addition to brevity, intensity, tension, tone, unity of form, and unity of effect or impression, the short story's formal conventions of narrative endings and beginnings are also noteworthy. The short story theorist Peter Rabinowitz maintains that beginnings and endings hold "privileged positions" within a literary text, for they are places of special emphasis for both authors and readers. These advantaged positions provide a "core around which to organize interpretation" by informing the reader how best to focus attention (300–02). Hence the reader assumes an integral role in textual production by actively participating in the construction of meaning.

"The Black Cat" presents an unreliable, first-person narrator: a man who is condemned to death for the murder of his wife and who outlines for the reader the series of household events that led to his downfall. Many standard conventions of Poe's tales manifest themselves in the story's opening lines: sanity, madness, fear, dread, horror, awe, disbelief, and the phantasm. The artifice of the narrative design and the importance of the reader's dynamic contribution to the storytelling process are also evident. Speaking directly to the reader, the nameless narrator explains, expounds, and qualifies his version of the events. Instead of telling his story plainly, as promised, he endeavors to manipulate the reader's response. He trusts that an intellect calmer, more logical, and far less excitable than his own will perceive in his story an ordinary succession of natural causes and effects. The horror of Poe's story, then, lies not in its murderous impulses, mutilated corpses, and frightening felines. Instead, true horror, as Richard Badenhausen maintains, originates in the reader's realization that the narrator, preoccupied with arguing the case, rejects his one last opportunity "to humanize the self through a confrontation with death" (490). Expressing neither remorse nor shame, he entrusts the final judgment of both his sanity and his tale to the reader.

Similarly, the narrator of Pardo Bazán's "El espectro" opens with an ambiguous statement concerning the sanity of his friend Lucio Trelles, which nonetheless emphasizes Lucio's seemingly normal and well-balanced qualities. Next, the narrator compares the importance of one's psychological well-being in contemporary society with the importance of possessing pure Christian blood in an earlier era. The narrator ends this section refuting Lucio's hypothesis that everyone is a little unbalanced, whether they show it or not. As in "The Black Cat," madness, superstition, fear, and mental illness are introduced in the text's opening paragraphs, but in this story Lucio's sanity, not the narrator's, is in question. Lucio is haunted by his killing of his mother, which he blames on the actions of a white cat. Lucio's guilt stems from the allegedly accidental shooting and from his mother's deathbed reproach—the burden of her eternal suspicion. In the text's final paragraphs, the careful reader discerns Lucio's hesitation to respond to the narrator's query: Did the mother indeed have cause to fear her son? Lucio refuses to answer the question and never again discusses the case. The story concludes with Lucio's unnerving equation of the white cat to a ghost (*espectro*). For him the two are psychically linked.

The textual circularity of "El espectro" informs the reader that Pardo Bazán's narrative could alternatively be called "The White Cat," which makes the reference to Poe clear: a murderer is haunted by a cat, but is it a vengeful ghost or just a cat? Cats (white and black), ghosts (real and imagined), houses (inhabited and uninhabited), characters plagued by guilt, diseases of the mind and the body, violence, passion, murder, and hubris occupy these two dark landscapes. Despite the sixty-year gap between their compositions, their critiques of modern society, explorations of the human psyche, and playful dialogues with the narrative process make for a perfect exercise in comparative analysis. After studying "The Black Cat" and "El espectro," students may develop their own intertextual readings of Poe and Pardo Bazán.[5] Pardo Bazán's stories "Presentido" ("The Premonition"; *Cuentos completos* 4: 104–06) and "Confidencia" ("The Secret"; 1: 166–69) work well in this respect for studying thematic aspects, narrative techniques, and the use of language.

Pardo Bazán's short stories aim to engage the reader quickly: in the first paragraph, the first few sentences, even in the title itself. Likewise, the intensity of the narrative, the gradual diffusion of psychological terror, and the unexpected ending or twist are all effective devices. Reading Pardo Bazán's stories alongside those of Guy de Maupassant also increases our understanding of the Spanish author's approach to the genre. In 1880, under the tutelage of Gustave Flaubert, Maupassant published his first great short story, "Boule de Suif" ("Butterball"), which was instantly and tremendously successful in both France and Spain. Like Pardo Bazán, Maupassant produced dozens of stories annually; the period from 1880 to 1891 was the most fertile of his career. Maupassant's influence on Pardo Bazán can be observed in her careful attention to detail and concentrated interest in psychological inquiry. Nonetheless, her distinctive style becomes evident in two pairings of her stories with stories by Maupassant: "Eximente" (1905; "The Defense"; *Cuentos completos* 2: 379–82) with "Le Horla" (1889; "The Horla") and "La calavera" (1893; "The Skull"; *Cuentos completos* 1: 173–77) with "Lui?" (1884;

"The Terror" ["Him?"]). Juan Paredes Núñez argues that there are many thematic similarities between "Le Horla" and "Eximente" (*Los cuentos* 113–19). In both stories a suicidal narrator uses the confessional form to justify the motives for his conduct. Both narrators suffer from an inexplicable terror that leads to hallucination, insomnia, and the fear that they are not alone. They attempt to flee, successfully at first, from the torment but finally realize the impossibility of escape and resort to suicide. Nevertheless, the differences between the stories are great. Maupassant's is much longer and therefore better developed; it includes accounts of the haunted Brazilian ship and the fire that destroys the narrator's home. While Maupassant allows his unnamed narrator to relate his tale directly through a series of journal entries, Pardo Bazán employs an artificial frame and then makes use of a "found" diary. Finally, the reader learns of Monsieur's suicide only in the last line of "Le Horla" but knows of Federico Molina's from the first word of "Eximente." Beginnings and endings once more prove paramount. A comparative reading of these two stories enriches students' comprehension of the sophistication, inventiveness, and modernity of Pardo Bazán. Ever at the forefront of European literary innovation, she continued to cultivate the psychological narrative throughout her career.

Reading Maupassant's "Lui?" (1884) together with Pardo Bazán's "La calavera" (1893) reveals similar parallels (Feeny). Both stories explore the deterioration of the psyche into madness. Male narrators, who live alone, relate their own versions of the events that precipitate their downward spiral into insanity. Each unsuccessfully seeks refuge in his bed at night and traces the onset of his illness to his first encounter with the title characters: in Maupassant, the terror (apparition) and in Pardo Bazán, the skull. Madness, fear, and an emphasis on the telling of the tale present themselves in both texts' opening and concluding paragraphs. Maupassant's first-person narrator starts by asking if his listener thinks the narrator is losing his mind, and Pardo Bazán's story begins and ends by underscoring the word "el chiflado" ("the crazy one"; *Cuentos completos* 1: 173). In "Lui?" the protagonist admits that the apparition exists only inside his mind and that he must marry to avoid being alone with his thoughts, doubts, and hallucinations. The protagonist of "La calavera" succeeds in throwing away the skull at the end of his story but confesses that the fear now resides within him. In "Lui?" the fear of going mad torments the narrator; in "La calavera," the fear of death. For both Maupassant and Pardo Bazán, the supernatural is a symptom of the protagonist's troubled mind.

In addition to penning more than five hundred short stories, Pardo Bazán devoted hundreds of pages of literary criticism to the short stories of her contemporaries, both Spanish and foreign. Her analysis of Maupassant describes the melancholy thoughts, vague terrors, and the fears of characters suffering from nervous psyches that permeated his fantastic stories (*La literatura* 3: 149–70).[6] Affected by his own descent into illness and madness, the French author, she argues, artistically rendered in his stories his negative conception of life, characterized by pessimism, sensuality, and cruelty. The stories that immortalized him, she continues, are dramatic, tender, sorrowful, or ironic, not merely entertaining. In conclusion she praises the quintessentially French character of his stories and the naturalness of their form. She extols their impeccable execution, clean prose, unaffected vocabulary, clever composition, and sober style. The possibilities for textual exploration are countless when we read her own writings through the artistic and critical lenses with which she examined her contemporaries. Incorporating her critical writings further enhances the classroom experience.

The fictional self-consciousness of the short story lends itself to a variety of imaginative and theoretical methods. Any discussion of the modern short story in a world literature class is bereft without Chekhov, for many the most significant practitioner of the genre in the twentieth century. His elusive style, wherein what is left unsaid is often more important than what is said, rejects traditional emplotment and the conventional transformation of the protagonist. Because they read more like impressionistic sketches, Chekhov's narratives do not so much impose moral judgments as they elicit the reader's subjective response. The most important element of any Chekhov story is the internal drama experienced by a given character and the reader's response to it. Suggestion is everything.

The influence of Chekhov on the short story was immense. He combined a keen use of brevity with poetic and symbolic sensibility. His best stories reflect a deep sense of psychological realism and reveal the desolate undercurrents that inform commonplace situations. In his stories life is often defined by cruelty, want, boredom, and misunderstanding, with only occasional intervals of happiness or serenity. His language is free from the emphatic, the florid, and the rhetorical. Like Chekhov, Pardo Bazán exploited the inherently concise structure of the story format to convey the tragedy, banality, and sometimes the humor in the everyday lives of her protagonists. One subject ripe for exploration in the classroom is the representation of marriage in stories by Chekhov and by Pardo Bazán.[7] Chekhov's "Before the Wedding" (1880) and "Wedding American Style" (1880), for example, examine the challenges encountered before couples exchange their vows and portray marriage as a bleak, contractual exchange reduced to a loveless, monetary transaction. "The Chemist's Wife" (1886), "The Husband" (1886), and "The Wife" (1891) further develop the alienation, isolation, and the absence of intimacy in Chekhov's renderings of marriage. Pardo Bazán, too, confronts the complexity and fragility of marriage in stories such as "La culpable" (1893; "The Guilty Woman"; *Cuentos completos* 1: 303–04), "La novia fiel" (1894; "The Faithful Fiancée"; 304–07), and "El encaje roto" (1897; "Torn Lace"; 331–33). While these stories explore the restrictive social mores, hardships, and conditions endured by women during the engagement period, "El indulto" (1883; "The Pardon"; 122–27) and "Casi artista" (1908; "Almost an Artist"; 3: 101–04) examine the mistreatment, exploitation, and abuse women suffered once married. The potential for thematic, structural, and narratological comparisons centered on these ten stories by Chekhov and Pardo Bazán multiplies when the dynamic element of the reader's response is considered.

By reading Pardo Bazán in fruitful dialogue with her literary ancestors and contemporaries and by comparing her absences—that which is left unsaid—with those of Chekhov, students will comprehend her wide-ranging erudition and her bold modernity.

The great number and variety of short stories Pardo Bazán wrote throughout her career suggests that she used the form as a vehicle for experimentation, entangling her craft with other masters of the genre. Accordingly, their vast array of themes and literary techniques provides instructors with a wealth of textual material and the perfect foundation for cross-cultural literary exploration. Transcending national borders, the subjects, structures, approaches, and theories that Pardo Bazán's stories share with those of Poe, Maupassant, Chekhov, and others remind us what makes these texts so compelling and why we continue to read them.

NOTES

[1] On Pardo Bazán and her contemporaries, useful essays include DeCoster; Feeny; and Paredes Núñez, "Paralelos."

[2] I cite "Apuntes autobiográficos" in *Obras completas* 3: 698–732. All translations are my own.

[3] See Cantalupo; Llácer Llorca et al.; May.

[4] I cite Pardo Bazán's stories in Paredes Núñez's four-volume edition, *Cuentos completos*.

[5] If time allows, reading Poe's "The Fall of the House of Usher" in conjunction with Pardo Bazán's *Los pazos de Ulloa* may deepen the analysis.

[6] Pardo Bazán devotes an entire chapter of her study *La literatura francesa moderna* (3: 149–170) to the French realists and naturalists, including Maupassant.

[7] Purves's exemplary and detailed analysis read in conjunction with that of Quesada Novás (*El amor* 187–207) may serve as the springboard for this discussion.

Short Stories and Journalism:
Writing the Mind

Harriet Turner

Approaching midlife in 1895, "counting"—perhaps even "dissembling"—the ineluctable fact of her forty-four years,[1] Emilia Pardo Bazán found herself at a turning point in her controversial career as a woman writer in late-nineteenth-century Spain. Already she had published eleven major novels, more than a hundred short stories, innumerable articles in newspapers and journals, and, as kind of a capstone, she had completed her monthly periodical *Nuevo teatro crítico* (1891–93; "New Critical Theater"), a "liberating forum" for new ideas and storytelling (McKenna 34).[2] Yet by September of 1895, she felt a palpable unease about the public reception of her literary endeavors. Two years earlier she had complained that "la novela no se lee ni se hace el drama, y la literatura, en definitiva, tiene poca prosperidad y poco influjo" ("people are not much interested in novels or plays, and literature, in general, hardly prospers and actually has little influence").[3] She began to wonder what other venues for writing and publication she might pursue and how she might negotiate the interconnection between reporting facts and opinions and storytelling.

The periodical press with which Pardo Bazán was already familiar presented an enticing opportunity. Since mid-century, the growth of the periodical press in Spain had fostered the formation of an intellectual middle class and, as a result, had increased national literacy.[4] By 1895 she had already published short stories in Spain and abroad as well as costumbrista sketches of local manners and mores in regional and national newspapers and journals.[5] As the century drew to a close, she also had begun to participate in the foremost crisis of the times, defined broadly as the "incompatibility between an unmodern past and the present need for modernization" (Krauel 26). She felt this pervasive cultural divide keenly: while loyal to the traditional region of Galicia where she resided half the year, she had nonetheless developed a cosmopolitan sensibility, spending the other part of the year in Madrid, where she attended lectures, concerts, and expositions, and traveling abroad to Paris and other European capitals.

The tensions between tradition and modernity strongly color the comparative writing style of her journalism and her fiction. In an essay subtitled "De París y de aquí" (1899; "About Paris and about Here") she writes: "Mis observaciones acerca de París tienen por fuerza que referirse a otras análogas observaciones acerca de Madrid, pues observar es comparar" ("My observations about Paris necessarily refer to observations about Madrid, for to observe is to compare"). Parisan dresses, for example, are so low-cut as to leave a woman practically naked—"la manga ha desaparecido, el busto surge entero del corpiño" ("sleeves have disappeared, bosoms pop out of corsets"), whereas in Madrid, "todavía se lleva ropa interior, enaguas y mangas en los cuerpos" ("dresses remain flounced with undergarments, crinolines, and the modesty of sleeves"; *La vida* 131). Her habit of moving regularly between Paris and Madrid seems to have encouraged her innate analogical way of thinking—simile and metaphor enliven her pungent, digressive style of reporting: "Aunque no suelo hablar aquí de mis viajes, por hacerlo en otra parte," she notes in another essay subtitled "París vs. Madrid" (1901), "la influencia de los lugares que visito no puede menos de sugerirme reflexiones que involuntariamente acuden a la pluma, y suelen presentarse en forma de comparación" ("Usually I don't talk about my travels, having written about them in other venues, but the influence of the places I've visited keep prompting reflections that come unbidden to my pen, often as comparisons"; 192).

"To observe is to compare," she declares in "De París y de aquí," offering a perspective we may take in teaching her journalistic writing style. In Paris, for example, a newspaper account of thievery is so brief that it fits rolled into "un papel de fumar" ("a cigarette paper"); people alert one another to inadvertent losses in the street, which her own experience verifies: "En París se me cayó ayer, desabrochándose de la cintura, una bolsa de seda donde llevaba el portamonedas, el pañuelo, los gemelos, el lápiz, mil menudencias necesarias. Ocho o diez gritos me advirtieron" ("Yesterday in Paris, my silk purse with wallet, handkerchief, eye glasses, and a pencil, along with a thousand indispensable little things, slipped unbuckled from my waist. Several passersby cried out to let me know"; 192).

This example of *honradez* ("honorable conduct") and *servicialidad* ("social courtesies") in Parisian street life is contrasted with Madrid, where petty theft happens everywhere: "no es posible distraerse un minuto en parte alguna" ("one has to be always on the lookout"). If, in Madrid, an object gets snagged amid "el remolino de la bajada" ("the rustle of skirts as ladies alight [from a coach]"), "[d]os segundos después, el objeto ha desaparecido para siempre" ("two seconds later it's gone forever"; 192). This observation gives rise to another quick sketch of her own experience of being robbed on the street of the jeweled frame of her eyeglasses. In the telling, ingenuity—her own as well as the thief's—is worthy of a picaresque novel. Her journalistic style, as evinced in "De París y de aquí" and "París vs. Madrid," highlights how her analogical imagination seeks to capture the flux of old and new that marked the practice of journalism at the turn of the century in Spain.

In the years leading to 1895 a flourishing periodical press promoted the essay, a genre that had emerged as the literary preference of the intellectual movement known as *Regenerationalismo*; debates about empire, literary movements, and Spanish cultural identity had begun vigorously to claim public attention. As Javier Krauel has observed, the essay's many forms, especially in the aftermath of the 1898 crisis, display three principal features:

> [A]ll are highly personal pieces of writing that foreground the lived individual experience of the author above and beyond any concern for systematic or theoretical elaboration; . . . all discuss subject matter critical to the general, educated readers of the late nineteenth and early twentieth

centuries; and . . . all presuppose and appeal to the reader's sympathy and invite her collaboration in the production of meaning precisely because the essay is an open, fragmentary literary form that can only offer a limited, provisional truth. . . . [A]ll can be described as hybrids of art and science. (28)

These features were aligned closely to Pardo Bazán's own way of thinking and writing, particularly as the notion of hybridity applies to her blended style of journalism and fiction.

In such circumstances, in 1895, restless and somewhat discouraged about the public reception of her novels and stories—particularly those that had caused public discomfort and even outrage—Pardo Bazán decided to renew her attention to journalism. Even as she considered herself first and foremost a novelist (*La vida* 7), it is easy to imagine how the author would have picked up her skirts (clothing and fashion are ubiquitous topics) to look to her future. With her dynamic and practical personality, she knew it was time to change course, take a different stance, and consider fresh options (8). She embarked upon an innovative journalistic project: writing opinion and social commentary essays on a fortnightly basis from 1895 to 1916 in a column called La vida contemporánea for *La ilustración artística*.[6]

Pardo Bazán's journalism displays an inconsistent appreciation for the tastes and opinions of the common reader. On occasion she would rebuff the public for its predilection for spectacle: "El lector pide extensas revistas taurinas, del género inaguantable, con los ceceíllos patosos y barbarismos achulados tan en moda . . . [o] el drama conyugal o el crimen de pasión" ("Readers clamor for magazines about bullfights, a despicable genre with its slipshod, slurred ways of speaking now in fashion, dandified posturing, and barbarous gestures . . . [or] about a marital drama or crime of passion"; *La vida* 129). Significantly, however, her respect for the social responsibility of the popular press was to remain undiminished throughout her journalistic career. When, in the commemoration of the centenary of the Spanish War of Independence (1808), she notes the "frialdad del espíritu público" ("cold-hearted public spirit"; 363), she also affirms the positive role played by the periodical press in broadening the perspectives of *la grey*, her term for the reading public at large. On that celebrative occasion in 1908, no matter the jumble of expectations of *la grey*—"sus prevenciones, sus sentimentalidades, sus desorientaciones y sus antipatías" ("their misgivings, sentimentalities, waywardnesses, and dislikes")—such a vital flux of preferences drives journalism and in turn shapes public opinion. While some think that *la grey* holds sway over "la oligarquía gráfica e intelectual" ("the intellectual oligarchic elites of the printing industry"), Pardo Bazán acknowledges the reciprocity between elites and public opinion (363).

Such shifts of perspective recur in Pardo Bazán's journalism—Spain, she avers, has been called the country of reversals ("el de los viceversas"; 81). She recognizes that the popular press exerts a kind of pressure that keeps the public open to new ideas and thus "en un estado de equilibrio inestable" ("a state of unstable equilibrium"; 363). Studying her journalistic writing must take into account her appreciation for the various components that make up the public, for in her view the designation of the "public spirit" is suitably "vague" ("el espíritu público es una palabra muy vaga"; 363). Her appreciation for the public is balanced by her insistence that the periodical press deserves respect. At the same time, she retains a strong sense of herself as la condesa de Pardo Bazán (the Countess of Pardo Bazán) and takes pleasure in exclusive social settings.

On occasion Pardo Bazán describes her journalistic prose pieces as *crónicas* — timely reports of civic, social, political, and historical events that function as op-eds and offer privileged access to her writing mind. Initially they carried the signature "Emilia Pardo Bazán"; however, in 1908, as she explains in a confidential aside to her readers — "Mis lectores encontrarán al pie de esta crónica alguna variación en mi firma" ("My readers will find at the close of this column a change in my signature"; 366) — a recent social distinction called for writing as "la Condesa de Pardo Bazán," a signature now owed to the Spanish king's formal recognition of her family's nobility. Like Pardo Bazán's short fiction, the *crónicas* are hybrids, defined by Susan M. McKenna as "a story form that combined the journalistic article with literary fiction" (24). The notion of hybridity suggests how readers must tease out the ways that Pardo Bazán, by combining reporting and storytelling, pictures the news: the initial act of reporting gives rise to stylistic features that approach novelistic experiments in realism — the compelling sight and sound of that tumultuous "rustle of skirts" or, in Paris, of the secreted, bulging roundness of her silk purse.

She describes walking about "ese ombligo" ("that navel") of Madrid and entering a carpentry shop, now suitably pictured as "el teatro de la escena" ("a stage with props") — the metaphor built on the business of carpentry and crafted by a skilled storyteller, for "a stage with props" is also a social critique of Madrid. In the shop, she comes upon the "espectáculo triste" ("sad spectacle") of a man crumpled against a wall. In conversation with the owner of the shop, she learns that the man is an alcoholic — jobless, homeless, forsaken. A story ensues, based on her eyewitness account, of heavy manual labor ("Yo les he visto mover, entre risas y chanzas, el enorme sillar o viga desmesurada" ["I've seen them move, laughing and joking, a huge stone block or outsized beam"]); she understands that in this kind of work there's no place for a debilitated alcoholic. Who or what is to blame for the man's predicament? In this piece Pardo Bazán proposes to give utterance to "todas las voces" ("all voices"); thus, the episode ends not with her words but with the complaint of the distraught man: "Yo no puedo andar esa distancia" ("I can't walk that far"), he protests, lacking the strength to make it even to the free housing the shop owner provides. Such are the consequences of the lack of social "props" on the "stage" that defines the center ("navel") of Madrid (546).

In another untitled *crónica*, Pardo Bazán investigates the public outcry about mice extermination. Politicians propose poison; Pardo Bazán argues that cats "enroscado[s] sobre un almohadón y ronroneando" ("curled up on a cushion, purring") could solve the problem and thus avoid exposure to poison. She notes, with regret, that the politicians' masculine, supposedly more scientific approach (poison) outweighs the common sense of housewives (cats). She also reports a conversation with the British consul, giving the flavor of his "jerga pintoresca" ("picturesquely garbled speech"): "Con mí no poder ratonsito. El abrir bujero y yo tapar bujero. El volver abrir, yo volver tapar. El abrir aún, yo volver tapar. El abrir aún, yo tapar aún. Cansarse ratonsito y largarse" ("No mouse get the better of me. He open hole, I close hole; he open hole, again I close. He still open, again I close. Mouse get tired, go away"; 361).

The lively charm of the episode about mice expresses the writer's great sense of humor, displayed again in her enthusiasm for cooking: "No sé por qué se me viene a la pluma hablar de cocina" ("I can't explain how it happens that my pen keeps going on about cooking"). Just as she sees how male politicians have bungled the case for the extermination of mice, she also notes how gender-inflected changes in culinary art have taken place over the centuries.[7] In the past, she writes, "Yantares eran aquellos muy de varones, de arrieros y trajinantes, de buscadores de vida, de bravos soldados y atezados labriegos. . . . El trago sigue al bocado, al bocado al trago, y creemos asistir a una escena de novela pintoresca" ("Olden-type meals were set out for men, mule drivers and itinerant workers, men on the make, fierce soldiers, and sunburned peasants. . . . A gulp here, a mouthful there, and we saw ourselves facing a scene from a picaresque novel"). But tastes change along with the pervasive influence of France: "Privan ahora los sutiles *purés*, los vaporosos *mousses* o espumas, las gelatinas . . . todo lo que disfraza la glotonería y la rebosa en golosina, en algo de arte, de gentileza, y cortesía, no ya con los invitados sino consigo mismo" ("Now delicate *purées*, whipped *mousses*, frothy sponges, gelatin custards take pride of place . . . everything that masks gluttony, topped off with something sweet, artistic, and refined, in sum, a courtesy, not just for guests but for oneself "; 360). The author's references to practices in cooking, eating, and manners show the conflation of private and public experiences—a conflation that opens narrative spaces, similar to those of her short fiction, inviting the reader to interact with the text, to reinterpret experiences, and to develop new ideas.

In Pardo Bazán's prose journalism, central to the notion of hybridity is point of view, a narrative device essential to the author's storytelling.[8] Once she styles herself as a storyteller, her reporting voice begins to live inside the essay, engaging in reminiscences and self-reflections as she sees herself looking, reacting, and talking as much to herself as to her interlocutors and readers. Her newspaper articles are both autobiographical—for example, she offers that as a child she didn't like to play with dolls (304)—and biographical—in an essay subtitled "Embajadas. Un libro argentino. Nuñez de Arce" ("Embassies. An Argentine Book. Nuñez de Arce"), Pardo Bazán draws the reader so close to celebrated writers like Rubén Darío that the reader can imagine Darío is in the room with her.[9] Darío's *España contemporánea*, a compilation of essays he wrote for the Buenos Aires newspaper *La nación*, is the "Argentine book" that becomes a "mirror" for

Pardo Bazán: "Así es que el libro de Rubén Darío . . . es un espejo donde nos contemplamos para interpretar nuestra fisonomía moralista, nuestra *facies* poco tranquilizadora para el pronóstico de nuestro porvenir" ("Rubén Darío's book is a mirror in which we see ourselves and so may understand our moral being, our own disquieting *actions* that foretell the future"; 181).

Using the editorial *we*, Pardo Bazán describes her journalistic writing style as spontaneous and open: "Escribimos sin cautela, con espontaneidad, dejando siempre abierta una ventana del espíritu, por la cual (como suponen algunos astrónomos que sucede a las famosas manchas) se ve el fondo de nuestro ser" ("We write without any reservations at all, always spontaneously, leaving a window open to the spirit through which [as astronomers claim we can do with those famous sun spots] to glimpse the depths of our being"; 295). She confesses to lapses and distractions: "¿Por qué iba yo diciendo todo esto? ¡Ah! Ya recuerdo. . . . " ("Why was I saying all this? Ah, now I remember. . . . "; 279).

In a piece dated 1905, for example, she shifts from thoughts about "sentimientos fundamentales" ("basic feelings") to conjure before us, in a storytelling manner, one of her readers: "Se me ocurre todo esto que voy *ensartando a cuento* de haber recibido dos o tres cartas de letra de mujer, fina y menuda" ("It's just occurred to me that—having received two or three letters written in a refined, delicate feminine style—I'm already *weaving a story*"; my emphasis); further, she knows this writer is a woman because there aren't many "señoritas que gastan una caligrafía completamente masculina, grande y alta" ("young ladies who shape letters as large and as tall as men do"). The unknown, female letter writer, full of questions about Silvio Lago, the dreaming artist in Pardo Bazán's novel *La quimera* (1905; "The Chimera"), thus begins to take shape not only as a reader but as a fictional figure. This transformation occurs in the moment that Pardo Bazán herself approaches Silvio—a fictional character—as if he were a real person: she begins questioning Silvio's motives, desires, and artistic possibilities while referring to the way that Silvio questions his own motives and desires. Further, as her own best critic, Pardo Bazán spiritedly contests how her friend, a certain "señor Villegas," "me puso a Silvio de hoja de perejil" ("gave her a hair-curling critique of Silvio"; *La vida* 298). In effect, an alleged conversation about *La quimera* cuts four ways—through a letter, a novel, a critique, and a newspaper essay—and in four voices that converge in the essay: Pardo Bazán's, the female reader's, Silvio Lago's, and the critic Villegas's. These voices arise in various spaces, times, and texts, endowing this particular journalistic entry with the roundedness of character and plot.

Conversation provides a captivating frame for the opinion pieces and sketches of Pardo Bazán's column. In an essay titled "Románticos," the author listens to a friend recount the suicide of Mariano José de Larra in 1837. Horrified, yet curious and compassionate, she feels compelled to recreate "la tremenda escena" ("the tremendous scene"), styling the episode as a twice-told story. In the end, however, the truth of that tragic event proves elusive, and, since Pardo Bazán cannot locate a portrait of Dolores, the fateful married woman to whom she refers as "la señora de C . . . ," she re-creates an alluring portrait of Dolores, describing her hair piled high, curls framing her face, and a dress so provocatively cut in the French manner as to shape an "escote insolente" ("brazen neckline"). But, Pardo Bazán reasons, in the end it's really better not to know what Dolores actually looked like, because " . . . ¿y si era fea, bigotuda, amarillenta, chata? No nos acerquemos demasiado a la realidad" (" . . . what if she were ugly and squat, with a hairy lip and yellowed skin? Let's not get too close to what's real"; 179).

Once again, Pardo Bazán's notion of an "unstable equilibrium" defines her narrative persona as it evolves through the hybridity of her journalistic writing. Her predilection for figurative language allows her to refer to one thing under the guise of another in order to capture the deepest registers of thought and feeling. Yet as she moves in and out in her blended roles as author, narrator, character, and reader, her writing mind always remains in balance, consistently true to herself as a journalist and writer of stories.

NOTES

[1] This sly, benevolent aside about Doña Emilia comes from Carlos Dorado, in the introduction to his edition of *La vida contemporánea* (2005), a collection of Pardo Bazán's journalistic essays named after the title of her long-running column in *La ilustración artística* (8). Some essays in the volume carry subtitles, while others only use the general heading La vida contemporánea. All translations are my own.

[2] The eclectic *Nuevo teatro crítico* was "suitably named to honor Benito Jerónimo Feijoo and his grand Enlightenment encyclopedia *El Teatro universal o discursos varios en todo género de materias para desengaño de errores omunes* (1726–39)" (McKenna 33). Feijoo, a mentor to Pardo Bazán and a fellow Galician, was the subject of a biographical study by Pardo Bazán; her good friend and colleague, Benito Pérez Galdós, also appropriated the name and persona, adapting it to don Evaristo Feijoo, the elderly retired military officer who offers humane, enlightened counsel in *Fortunata y Jacinta* (1886–87).

[3] Quoted by Dorado in the introduction of Pardo Bazán, *La vida contemporánea* (8). Originally published in the *Heraldo de Madrid*, 8 June 1893, p. 1.

[4] See Botrel, "Contribution" and "Narrativa." McKenna also gives pertinent statistics about literacy in late-nineteenth-century Spain: "According to the census data of 1877, 15 percent of women were literate; almost 19 percent in 1887; and in 1900, the number had grown to more than 25 percent" (27).

[5] Dorado points to some examples of Pardo Bazán's occasional pieces called "Instantáneas," which profiled local types, behaviors, and styles of living, each sketched with a quick hand and subsequently published in 1883 in *Las provincias*, a regional daily paper: see Dorado's introduction in Pardo Bazán, *La vida contemporánea* (9).

[6] *La ilustración artística* covered science, history, art, politics, and literature. Issued weekly and lavishly illustrated, it was founded in 1882 in Barcelona by the publisher Montaner y Simon, which also published a similar journal, *La ilustración americana*. These journals are available in Madrid at the Hemeroteca Municipal and at the Biblioteca Nacional.

[7] Pardo Bazán's first cookbook, *La cocina española antigua* ("Traditional Spanish Cuisine"), came out in 1913. A few years later she published *La cocina española moderna* ("Modern Spanish Cuisine").

[8] For insightful discussions of Pardo Bazán's innovative narrative techniques, see Tolliver, *Cigar Smoke*; Tolliver's introduction and commentary to Pardo Bazán, *"El encaje roto"*; McKenna; and Walter.

[9] The prose and verse of the Nicaraguan writer Rubén Darío (1867–1916) sparked the *modernismo* revolution in letters across Latin America and Spain. *Azul* (1890), *Prosas profanas* (1896), and *Cantos de vida y esperanza* (1905), as well as his short stories, are major works in Hispanic literary modernity.

Verdad versus Realidad:
Teaching Pardo Bazán's Theater in the Context of National Regeneration

Margot Versteeg

Few people know that Emilia Pardo Bazán, famous for her novels and short stories, also wrote for the theater. In fact, she produced a number of plays that, although unsuccessful in her time, are of great interest to readers today. In this essay I argue that her play *Verdad* (1906; "Truth"), because of both its subject matter and its dramatic construction, is exceptionally suited to introduce graduate and upper-division undergraduate students to Pardo Bazán's drama, especially when read in dialogue with Benito Pérez Galdós's well-known play *Realidad* (1892; "Reality"). Keenly aware of the limitations of the contemporary Spanish stage, both Galdós and Pardo Bazán moved away from the melodramatic paradigm instituted by José Echegaray (1832–1916), a now almost forgotten engineer-turned-dramatist whose prolific output and notorious stagecraft made him the undisputed master of the Spanish stage during the final decades of the nineteenth century. Echegaray's hegemony—he produced sixty-seven plays—reduced Spanish drama to a set of conventions that allowed artistic expression only when cloaked in morality and conformism. As an alternative to the Echegarayan model, Galdós strived to create "a more natural theater, based on the development of character and on the realist representation of the problems of contemporary society" (Ríos-Font 138). While Pardo Bazán lauded Galdós's intentions, her plays, written from a female point of view, imagine the nation in very different ways.

Melodrama was the dominant dramatic genre in Spain from the late eighteenth century through the middle of the nineteenth. The melodramatic was also a moral and aesthetic mode that pervaded almost all theatrical production of the second half of the nineteenth century. Students can familiarize themselves with the general characteristics of melodrama by reading the first chapters of Peter Brooks's *The Melodramatic Imagination* (1–23) and Wadda Ríos-Font's *Rewriting Melodrama* (9–49). They could also read and discuss Echegaray's most popular melodrama, *El gran galeoto* (1881; "The Great Galeoto"), in which a man's platonic love for a married woman is intentionally misunderstood. *El gran galeoto* makes clear the point to which the Calderonian honor code still permeated nineteenth-century society and obsessed the Spanish playwright.

Galdós's *Realidad*, staged in Madrid's Teatro de la Comedia in 1892, is often hailed as a critical turning point in Spanish theatrical production and the first successful foray into realist drama. *Realidad*, which was based on a homonymous dialogue novel by the same author (1890), aroused ample public debate. While some critics praised the ingenuity of *Realidad*, others resented the author's break with the tradition of honor plays (Ríos-Font 138). After reading the play with students, instructors could ask them to imagine why critics were divided when it came to appreciating Galdós's style. Pardo Bazán, who had assisted Galdós throughout the rehearsal process, wrote one of the most in-depth reviews of the play in her cultural magazine *Nuevo teatro crítico* ("New Critical Theater"), which students could be assigned to read (Pardo Bazán, "Realidad").

In *Realidad* Galdós stages a traditionally melodramatic conflict based on adultery and gives it a treatment that is contrary to melodrama's spirit. The cuckolded husband, Orozco, pardons his adulterous wife, Augusta, instead of murdering her. By dismantling melodrama's Manichaean worldview and portraying both wife and husband as neither entirely innocent nor entirely guilty, Galdós depicts the traditional Spanish honor code as irrelevant at the turn of the twentieth century. At the end of the play, the main female character (played by a very young María Guerrero) is not killed for her transgression of social norms. The review by Pardo Bazán of *Realidad* expressed appreciation for Galdós's theatrical innovation. In her opinion, Galdós had tried to invigorate the weak Spanish dramaturgy by imposing on the stage the analytical and human content of the modern novel ("Realidad" 52). While she agreed with Galdós that the Spanish stage should focus on issues relevant to contemporary society, she did not agree with his assessment of that same society. However, it would take her more than ten years to conceive a theatrical answer to Galdós.

In 1906 Pardo Bazán produced her play *Verdad*, which ferociously criticized her male colleague for what she considered a complete misrepresentation of reality (Pardo Bazán, *Teatro* 103–67). In *Verdad*, written a decade after *Realidad* and after the disastrous events of 1898, Pardo Bazán's feminine perspective is quite different from Galdos's point of view: *Verdad* effectively relegates Galdós's rational rejection of wife murder to the domain of mere wishful thinking. If Galdós, in *Realidad*, is keen to avoid a final act of wife murder, Pardo Bazán opens *Verdad* with a monstrous crime. Contrary to the benevolent and generous Orozco, Pardo Bazán's Martín is a misogynist psychopath who, after a presumed attack on his honor, does not hesitate to strangle his female companion. In her journalistic prose, Pardo Bazán often highlighted wife murder as a leading cause of death for women. In *Verdad*, she recycles the outdated melodramatic conventions with new elements from gothic literature, crime fiction, and Henrik Ibsen's theater to convey a highly critical message about the vulnerable situation of Spanish women.

Verdad, Pardo Bazán's first full-length play, premiered in Madrid's Teatro Español on 9 January 1906, with actress María Guerrero playing both Irene, the main female character, and Irene's sister, Anita, and Guerrero's husband Fernando Díaz de Mendoza as Martín. The actress's earlier performances in many Echegarayan melodramas and in *Realidad* make *Verdad* what Marvin Carlson has called a "haunted production" (96); the memories associated with the actress's previous roles must have steered the audience's reception of the play. Despite the famous actors, the premiere of this prose drama in four acts met with the explicit reprobation of numerous critics. After assigning reviews of the play by Pardo Bazán's contemporaries (see Nunemaker; García Castañeda; Schiavo and Mañueco Ruiz), instructors could ask students to reflect on why the reviewers disliked the play. With a few exceptions, the critics disapproved of the "revolting" plot for which the audience, in the critics' opinions, was not prepared. One of them even recommended "¡Que se vaya a hacer calceta!" ("Let her start knitting!"; qtd. in García Castañeda 121).[1] And indeed *Verdad*, with its violent and fantastic story, is anything but the kind of play that the middle-class audience of the recently remodeled Teatro Español expected.

If Galdós was unable to escape the conventions of melodrama, Pardo Bazán consciously recycled these same conventions. In the first act of *Verdad*, she starts off with a miniature melodrama that revolves around a shocking assassination that takes place right in front of the spectators. At his country estate, Martín de Trava has a secret rendezvous with Irene de Ourente, a socialite he hopes to make his mistress. After prevailing upon her to confess past love affairs, in a fit of jealousy Martín strangles her to death. His servant, Santiago, covers up all evidence of the crime. Successive acts of the play each end with horrifying dramatic effects. In the second act, Martín returns to his estate after six years of absence. He is now married to Irene's sister, Anita, who is determined to discover the source of her husband's unhappiness. The act ends with the appearance of Anita, whose sinister resemblance to her sister provokes several observations from Santiago regarding the "return of the death," which force Martín to confront his past. The spectators, from the outset well aware of the truth, start to worry that the truth will be revealed. That is indeed what happens at the end of the third act, and in the fourth act Martín is killed.

Instructors can discuss with students how and why Pardo Bazán uses melodramatic devices to provoke a strong emotional reaction in the audience. The melodramatic formula, writes Ríos-Font, is defined by a struggle between good and evil in which clearly defined antithetical characters (heroes and villains) are opposed. Melodrama is a hyperbolic formula, characterized by an excess of sentimentalism, an exaggerated acting style, and the use of all sorts of far-fetched devices. It supports a conservative ideology: at the end the villains will be punished and order restored (9–49). Pardo Bazán does not use the melodramatic mode just to play with the audience's emotions. She has a different purpose. Spanish theater audiences were used to plays that let them feel and not think, but when Jacinto Octavio Picón wrote that Galdós's *Realidad* made the audience think, Pardo Bazán did not consider this a complete achievement (Picón). She wanted to create plays that made her audience not only think but also feel, and by stirring up the audience's emotions she intended to provoke disgust for a social reality that she believed the audience should disapprove of both emotionally and rationally. In this way she hoped to mobilize spectators against the false morality, especially regarding women, in which Spanish society was anchored. She discusses her ideas in more detail in the article "Más clínica" ("More Clinical Notes;" *De siglo* 232–43), which instructors could recommend students read alongside *Verdad*.[2]

After shaking up the complacent theatergoers, Pardo Bazán uses the excess of melodrama to foreground the wickedness of Martín and the implications of his crime. The melodramatic conventions ensure that the villain is punished. The assassin and his accomplices are responsible for no less than three violent murders: those of Irene, Martín himself, and Santiago's mother. Although Martín feels remorse—remorse that Pardo Bazán elaborates on stage, as we shall see, with techniques borrowed from Poe and Ibsen—melodrama has no tolerance for characters that have crossed certain lines. Pardo Bazán, who explicitly approved of the end of Galdós's *Realidad* ("Realidad" 60), believed that while some transgressions, such as marital infidelity, could be pardoned (62), others, such as wife murder, could never be (*De siglo* 241). In melodrama the revelation of truth implies the triumph of virtue, but in *Verdad* the truth only causes destruction. Pardo Bazán obviously judged this destruction necessary to create a more just society. Using melodrama's structure to polarize good and evil, Pardo Bazán assigns all the male characters in *Verdad* to the category of villains. These invariably sexist and often aggressive and violent male characters are connected by strong homosocial bonds, offering one another mutual protection and covering up one another's crimes. Their alliances cut across social classes, illustrated by the sympathy that the strangler Martín feels for the throat-cutter Sangre Negra, whom Martín meaningfully calls "brother" (154). These bonds even transgress death: Santiago, the excessively servile butler and *hermano de leche* (108; "milk brothers" are children breastfed by the same woman) sacrifices his own mother to protect his master. Martín underscores the extremity of this male solidarity—his victim is not his own wife but the adulterous spouse of another man. Pardo Bazán gives the archetypical melodramatic conflict between feelings and duty an interesting twist—as if all the men in the play are frantically trying to protect themselves from an elusive and menacing femininity.

While *Verdad* seems at first to present a melodramatic conflict between good and evil, Pardo Bazán problematizes this conflict by injecting other conceptually contradictory genres and forms into the paradigmatic conflict. She thus distances her spectators from melodrama's false reassurance that the world, despite its villainy, is fundamentally good. One of these other genres is the gothic. To introduce this idea to the classroom, students could be asked to investigate the characteristics of gothic literature and then to look for gothic elements in *Verdad*. As in melodrama, in gothic literature the world's forces are divided in binaries: light and darkness, natural and supernatural, good and evil. But if melodrama supposes the confrontation of clearly defined antagonists and the expulsion of villains, in gothic literature the villains cannot be expulsed and evil cannot be controlled. The methods of gothic literature, denying melodrama's effort to order reality in reassuring moral categories (Ríos-Font 192), allow Pardo Bazán to undermine a worldview that she considers too simple.

Martín's death at the end of the play shows how Pardo Bazán combines gothic and melodramatic elements. The villain is being punished, but the punishment is instigated by the villain's wife, Anita, who incites Santiago to kill her husband.

The servant must live with the same remorse that had tormented his master. Anita's conflict is identical. While she had begged Santiago to prevent Martín from turning himself in, she understands too late that her motivation sprang from the desire to know what had caused him to murder Irene. The murder of Martín is in this sense a reenactment of Martín's murder of his first wife (Bretz, "Theater" 44); Anita's confession, in the final lines of the play, of complicity in her husband's death reveals that the melodramatic paradigm will not be maintained.

The gothic, with its mixture of fantasy, cruelty, and horror, allows Pardo Bazán to take a feminist approach to a set of problems — machismo, abuse of patriarchal power, the double standard between men and women, female disempowerment, spousal abuse (Pérez, "Naturalism" 155) — that threaten the well-being of the family and, by extension, the nation. She purposefully situates the play not in Madrid, which theatergoers were accustomed to, but in a liminal space, Galicia, and gives it a mysterious and uncanny gothic setting in a ruinous castle on the shores of the Miño, the river that delineates the Spanish-Portuguese border. Montserrat Ribao Pereira has identified a series of mythological symbols that establish a comparison between the Miño and the Styx, the river that in Greek mythology formed the boundary between the earth and the underworld ("Estudio preliminar" 27–29). Across the Styx, the souls of the newly dead were transported into the underworld, which can be understood analogously to Spanish colonial losses and the repatriation of the remains of thousands of soldiers killed in the Spanish-American War. The Miño separates Spain from Portugal, where Irene used to live a cosmopolitan life. Elizabeth Ordóñez points out that Pardo Bazán identified the Portuguese national project of modern renewal with the freedom enjoyed by women in the Portuguese capital; in this sense Portuguese women had achieved social progress in ways that Spanish women had not yet (21).

Pardo Bazán uses the gothic convention of the double to underscore on stage the dual nature of her characters and to show that appearances sometimes hide secrets. The uncanniness that Freud assigns to doubles (*Uncanny* 142) appears in the macabre sympathy that Martín feels for Sangre Negra and in the resemblance between Irene and Anita. While on a surface level Irene seems a transgressive femme fatale and Anita a virtuous woman, Pardo Bazán's female characters eschew this reductionism. Played by the same actress, Irene and Anita both represent complex identities and gender roles in flux. Moreover, Irene's reincarnation in Anita suggests a lack of male control over the female body. Pardo Bazán's use of gothic conventions approximate the play to 1940s Hollywood film noir. These film narratives, writes Helen Hanson, pass through several stages: romance, suspicion, investigation or discovery, confrontation or confession, and resolution (56). As an in-class activity, students could work in small groups to identify these stages in *Verdad*. Anita, whose suspicions may be a reason for her attraction to her husband, tries to uncover the repressed secret of her sister's disappearance, but when Martín confesses to Irene's murder, Anita refuses to accept the truth — "[e]sa verdad, no" ("[n]ot this truth";

156)—and distorts any reasonable argument: "La prueba de que no me quieres es que a mí . . . no me matarías" ("The proof that you don't love me is that you would never kill me"; 158). By instigating Martín's murder, Anita proves a sisterly solidarity. The specter of the dead woman has seemingly risen from the grave to take vengeance.

As usual in melodrama, the villain is condemned at the end, but Pardo Bazán also punishes Martín in another way when she has him gradually lose his mental faculties. In gothic literature it tends to be the heroine who loses her mind, becoming incarcerated in a house against her control. Pardo Bazán subverts this convention and has Martín wander aimlessly on the stage to underscore the fragility of traditional masculinity.

Alienation, not social pressure, gives Martín the urge to confess. Here *Verdad* suggests a connection to a short story by Edgar Allan Poe, "The Imp of the Perverse" (1850), in which a murderer whose crime has gone undetected suddenly feels compelled to confess, an urge that can be attributed only to the spirit of the "perverse." Like Poe's story, *Verdad* is an account of what cannot or should not be told: wife murders and Irene's "disgracia" ("disgrace"), "aquella cosa . . . que no tiene nombre" ("that . . . which does not have a name"; 155). Students can be encouraged to read Poe's story alongside *Verdad* and to explore these similarities more fully in a short paper.

In *La nueva cuestión palpitante* (1892; "The New Burning Question") Pardo Bazán rejects the notion of the "born criminal" as proposed by Cesare Lombroso in 1876 and by Max Nordau in 1892 (402).[3] In *La revolución y la novela en Rusia* (1887; "The Revolution and the Novel in Russia"), she claims that Dostoyevsky's *Crime and Punishment* makes a case that no one is innocent, and especially not men (374–80). In *Verdad* she has Martín say, "Somos malos todos los hombres" ("All men are bad"; 134). The actions of the greatest criminals, she writes, are often not so different from those of normal men (*De siglo* 238; Cate-Arries 207), implying that apparently normal men could commit unimaginably cruel wife murders.

Pardo Bazán gives Martín a human touch; he seems to be a normal man distraught by a mental conflict. He lives in the past and can't see the future. Martín's retrospection and introspection connect *Verdad* with the theater of Ibsen. The Norwegian playwright, who was well known in Spain, introduced the technique of autoanalysis and the notion that the past forms part of the present (Gregerson 13, 69). His plays do not present an intricate accumulation of events but focus on an individual's inner struggles. Ibsen analyzes personal relationships and tries to reveal the lies between members of society, presenting a series of unpleasant truths intended to make the audience think. Like Ibsen's heroes, Martín is tormented by the ghosts of the past. Gradually, his struggle with these dark forces begins to suffocate him, and he wants to take responsibility for his actions and face the bitter reality: "Es tarde. Se ha despertado mi conciencia. . . . Yo quiero acusarme de mi crimen" ("It is late. My conscience has awakened. . . . I want to admit to my crime"; 162).

Martín's awakened conscience is clearly a metaphor for the Spanish nation after 1898. The play makes it evident that Pardo Bazán blamed Spanish men for the pitiful reality that Spaniards, and above all Spanish women, had to face after 1898. Titling her play *Verdad*, she especially wants her spectators to see the bitter truth and to distance themselves emotionally and rationally from a society governed by a caste of dysfunctional males who are focused on the past and who destroy the integrity of the family while promoting a false morality, especially regarding women. She aims to convince the audience that this brotherhood must come to an end—homosocial alliances that cut across social classes and even transgress death will never contribute to the regeneration of the Spanish nation. She suggests that, on the contrary, regeneration will have to come from Spanish women. If Spanish women accept a new role as acting and thinking subjects Spain may become a modern and industrious nation, not one burdened with hypocrisy and drained by military expenditures—in short, a safe place for both men and women. Only in this way will Spain evolve from a brotherhood of men into a community in which both genders make important contributions to the impending regeneration of the nation.

NOTES

[1] Translations are my own.
[2] This essay cites the Administración edition of *De siglo a siglo*.
[3] This essay cites the Bercimuel edition of *La nueva cuestión palpitante*.

From Page to Screen:
Teaching *Los pazos de Ulloa* and
La madre naturaleza through Adaptation

Linda M. Willem

On 2 August 1979 Spain's minister of culture, Manuel Clavero Arévalo, signed an order calling for proposals from Spanish film companies for miniseries projects, preferably based on "grandes obras literarias españolas" ("great Spanish literary works"), to be broadcast on Televisión Española (TVE), Spanish public television ("1.300 millones"). This alliance between cinema and TVE would establish serial adaptation of classical novels as the hallmark of quality Spanish television and initiate a decade-long flourishing of the genre. Among the adaptations of this period is Gonzalo Suárez's *Los pazos de Ulloa* ("The House of Ulloa"), which adapted Emilia Pardo Bazán's novel of the same name along with its sequel *La madre naturaleza* ("Mother Nature") into a four-part miniseries that was televised in Spain in December of 1985. In this essay I will discuss how this adaptation can be used in an advanced undergraduate Spanish classroom to supplement and extend discussions of the novel *Los pazos de Ulloa*.[1]

TVE has a long history of adapting classics of Spanish literature, but in the 1970s there was a sea change in its approach, primarily due to the phenomenal success of the new formula for literary adaptations that the British Broadcasting Corporation (BBC) initiated in the mid-1960s, which coupled a more serious and sophisticated treatment of style and content with a highly effective miniseries format (Giddings and Selby 26). The BBC's commitment to high production values quickly set the international standard for classic novel adaptations from the 1970s onward. In Spain, TVE began to imitate the BBC model, moving from low-budget, predominantly in-studio productions to well-financed, on-location miniseries such as *Cañas y barro* (1978; "Reeds and Mud") and *La barraca* (1979; "The Cabin"). In the 1980s cinema-quality miniseries adaptations were brought to the small screen through the collaboration of the television and film industries, with additional coproduction financing from other European countries (Diego 26–31). These works further emulated the BBC formula by employing well-known actors, using elaborate costumes and props, alternating intricate sets with on-location shooting, and coordinating music with the visual narrative.

The BBC serial adaptations of classic novels in this period adhere to its long-standing tradition both to entertain and to educate the public in the canonical masterpieces of national and world literature. As a result, these adaptations attempted to accurately represent the novels upon which they were based. In addition to *Los Pazos de Ulloa* (1985), other Spanish miniseries adaptations of the 1980s and 1990s—such as *Fortunata y Jacinta* (1980; "Fortunata and Jacinta") and *La Regenta* (1995; "The Regent's Wife")—followed the BBC's lead in paying careful attention to the nineteenth-century classic novels that constituted the source material.

The field of adaptation studies has been bedeviled by the issue of fidelity since its origins in the 1950s. Because adaptations are based on source texts, comparative studies traditionally look to identify similarities and differences and conclude that the source is superior to the adaptation. Since basing assessment on fidelity privileges the literary source while positioning the adaptation as a derivative text, new ways of conceptualizing fidelity were needed to validate the adaptation as an artistic work in its own right. Consequently, three categories have emerged for speaking about the intertextual connection between source material and screen adaptation. In the first, literal adaptations, the literary elements of the source text are followed as closely as possible. Few elements are dropped, and little is added. This type of adaptation stresses literary conventions over those developed for the screen. The second category includes adaptations that attempt to capture the spirit of the literary work through the conventions of the nonliterary medium of film. Most of the literary elements of the source text are retained but are dealt with in cinematic terms—that is, visual and auditory techniques are used to convey the written text. Similarities are expected, but additions and changes are present as well. This approach is typical of the vast majority of televised serial adaptations of classic novels from the 1980s and 1990s. Finally, in the third category, transformational adaptations, the source text serves as raw material that the adaptation alters freely and considerably. The literary elements are treated as a point of departure for creative reworking. This type of adaptation reconfigures the novel into something new and different while retaining traces of the original. The field of film studies has succeeded in establishing the status of adaptations as autonomous creations, but hierarchical thinking persists, specifically in the growing preference for the transformational mode.

Recently, however, some scholars have sought to critically redefine the relation between novels and adaptations with approaches that neither privilege the source material over its adaptation nor place one type of adaptation over another. For example, Linda Hutcheon, in *A Theory of Adaptation* (2006), writes of adaptation as a process of interpretation, creation, and reception: each adaptation is the product of where, when, how, why, by and for whom it was made, and of what form it takes. This is a particularly fruitful approach for classroom teaching because an adaptation can be examined within its own context. Thus, TVE's *Los pazos de Ulloa* can be discussed both as Gonzalo Suárez's creative interpretation of Pardo Bazán's novels and as the result of the circumstances of its production.

Below I suggest a plan for incorporating Suárez's television adaptation into advanced undergraduate Spanish literature and culture courses. It presupposes that students already have read and discussed Pardo Bazán's *Los pazos de Ulloa* but are not familiar with its sequel, *La madre naturaleza*. This will allow students to have two entirely different viewing experiences. For the first three episodes of the miniseries students will be what Hutcheon calls "knowing" viewers, who "oscillate" between their memories of the literary text and their experience of watching the adaptation; for the fourth episode students become "unknowing" viewers, watching "without the palimpsestic doubleness that comes with knowing" (120–27). "Knowing audiences have expectations," writes Hutcheon (122), and the pleasure they derive from watching a program *"as an adaptation"* comes from its "repetition with variation," wherein their remembrance of the novel combines with their surprise in seeing how it is interpreted on the screen (4–6). "Unknowing" audiences have no such expectations and do not view the program *"as an adaptation"* (120). Knowing viewers engage in comparative acts while unknowing viewers do not, and this difference in audience reception will affect class discussions of the miniseries as a whole. The following five-step sequence is designed to guide students' intertextual involvement with the written and visual texts.

First, just as novels are analyzed by making reference to literary conventions, so too should screen adaptations be analyzed based on cinematic elements. Instructors can prepare students for the task of viewing and discussing the *Los pazos de Ulloa* miniseries on its own terms by assigning readings on mise-en-scène (including setting, lighting, costume, and actors), camera work, editing, and sound and music from David Bordwell, Kristin Thompson, and Jeff Smith's excellent textbook *Film Art: An Introduction* (113–302). These readings will give students a clear understanding of the concepts, after which they can learn the corresponding Spanish terminology listed in the appendix of cinema vocabulary of John Underwood's *Hablando del cine* ("Speaking of Cinema") (A1–A3).[2]

Second, students should view the first three episodes of the miniseries. Applying what they've read about film style, they should choose one or two scenes per episode that they find cinematically interesting, noting their location (in minutes and seconds) and using Spanish terminology to jot down specific film elements that contributed to the impact of the scenes. These written observations can help instructors prepare for classroom discussion in the next step.

The third step begins with students viewing two supplemental video clips, "*Los pazos de Ulloa*: Presentación oficial en A Coruña" ("*Los pazos de Ulloa*: Official Presentation in A Coruña") and "Entrevista a Gonzalo Suárez" ("Interview with Gonzalo Suárez"), available on the *Los pazos de Ulloa* page of the *RTVE* Web site, as an introduction to the adaptation and to Suárez as both an adapter and as a writer and director of experimental and imaginative art films ("*Los pazos de Ulloa*: Presentación"; "*Los pazos de Ulloa*: Entrevista"). Instructors then should contextualize the adaptation by giving the students background information about its production (Hutcheon's when, where, how, what, why, and by and for whom).

A classroom discussion of how Suárez uses the media-specific techniques of cinema to convey his interpretation of the spirit of Pardo Bazán's literary works can follow from discussion of the film's production. Since Suárez is known for his innovative methods of presenting character perspective, instructors can begin by examining how the character Julián's subjective mental states are conveyed through a combination of mise-en-scène, camera work, and sound. For example, instructors can play a clip from the first episode (13:40–16:50) to show how the demonic associations that the priest attributes to the women in Sabel's nightly gatherings of friends in her kitchen are communicated through their fire-lit faces that are shot in close-ups to give them the appearance of ugly witches with hairy moles and goat hooves for hands. The soundtrack also has an infernal, other-worldly quality that combines their cackling laughter with jarring music and unidentifiable noises. Furthermore, the shot-reverse-shot editing (moving back and forth between the group of women and Julián's face) makes it clear that we are experiencing this scene from his point of view, both physically and emotionally. Julián's eyes become the subjective lens through which we experience how his feelings influence what he sees.

Instructors can then draw on the students' written comments to facilitate class discussion of additional instances of character subjectivity (such as Nucha's dream states) before moving on to other cinematic aspects. Instructors can show clips of student-selected scenes, and the class can reread corresponding portions from the novel. This exercise compares the written and visual texts, so instructors should encourage students to use descriptive rather than evaluative terms to avoid privileging one medium over another. After specific scenes have been discussed, instructors can initiate discussion of stylistic and cinematic elements that are sustained across the episodes to create an overall tone, such as the visual-sonic leitmotif of brief close-ups on water oozing though earth, leaves, stones, and grass.

Turning next to characterization, students can examine how Pardo Bazán's descriptions of the major characters differ radically from the physical appearance of the actors chosen to portray those roles. Fifty years old at the time, the actor Omero Antonutti was much older than the roughly thirty-year old marqués he played, and Victoria Abril's beauty did not correspond to the novel's reference to Nucha's "pocos encantos físicos" ("few physical charms"; 187). Such comparisons can lead to discussions of how extratextual production concerns can influence casting decisions. The Italian Antonutti was given a leading role in part because the miniseries was a coproduction of TVE and RAI (Italian public television), and Abril's celebrity explains why she was chosen as the female lead. Furthermore, Antonutti and Abril lent prestige to the television series through their association with Spanish art-house cinema; Antonutti had recently played the lead in Víctor Erice's *El sur* (1983; "The South"), and Abril was fresh from her performances in Mario Camus's *La colmena* (1982; "The Beehive") and Jaime Chávarri's *Las bicicletas son para el verano* (1984; "Bicycles Are for the Summer").

The class can also discuss how the miniseries intensifies aspects of Pardo Bazán's characterizations, for example, the way the marqués and his coterie devour their food emphasizes their animal-like qualities. Added scenes can also develop aspects of characterization that are suggested but not depicted in the novel, such as the way Rita's facial expression and bodily movements while riding the rocking horse reveal her sexuality. This discussion can lead to examining how Pardo Bazán's descriptions of setting are visualized on the screen. For example, Suárez blurs the line between the interior and exterior of the Ulloa manor house by having dry leaves blowing within the house, evoking both natural and social decay. The contrast between city (as civilization) and country (as nature) is visualized through the mise-en-scène of both locations as well as through the camera work used to focus attention on specific aspects of each.

Finally, students can discuss how sound effects and music can create mood, reflect emotion, raise audience expectations, and influence the viewer's affective response. For example, the foreboding music that accompanies el Tuerto's various appearances builds suspense, and the clashing sound of percussion instruments communicates Perucho's fear after he witnesses the shooting of his grandfather. The use of bagpipe music suggests the regionalism of the Galician setting, while the jarring effect of the main musical theme sets an uneasy tone for the entire series.

The fourth step is watching the final episode of the miniseries, preferably in class so that all students experience it together as "unknowing" viewers. Students approach this final episode as a sequel—but not as a literary sequel. Since they have not read *La madre naturaleza*, they experience the fourth miniseries episode as a filmic sequel to the first three episodes rather than as an adaptation of a literary work. Students can examine how the fourth episode of the miniseries continues the lives of characters or the outcomes of events, building on and expanding elements of the original story. For example, the incest theme can be linked to Pardo Bazán's naturalism, and the casting of Abril in the dual role of Nucha and Nucha's daughter can be discussed in terms of Abril's extratextual star status. Students can also explore how issues of gender, religion, and politics are further developed in the sequel. Finally, students can identify examples of how the fourth episode renders nature in visual and auditory terms.

In the fifth step, students, working in groups, design a remake of the miniseries in the transformational mode of adaptation. The act of rewriting against the grain of fidelity allows students to creatively develop the latent potentialities of the plot and characterizations in both the literary and televised versions. Each group of students should choose one of the following strategies for turning the source material of Pardo Bazán's novel and Suárez's miniseries into raw material to be reworked into a new adaptation:

Elevate a secondary character to the status of protagonist. For example, by centering the story on Sabel or on Rita, students could examine anew the gender and class dynamics of the story. Alternatively, by focusing in the fourth episode on Perucho instead of on Gabriel, students could reframe the ethical dilemmas presented in the sequel.

Identify a possible course of action that was raised but not realized in the story and then imagine it being realized. There are many such possibilities to choose from. What would have happened if the marqués had married Rita instead of Nucha? What if Nucha had given birth to a boy instead of a girl? What if the marqués had won the election? What if Nucha had succeeded in escaping to Santiago with her baby daughter, Manuela? What if Nucha's father had taken Manuela to be raised in Santiago after his daughter's death? What if Manuela had married Gabriel? By creatively engaging with these unrealized potentialities, students will see how individual plot elements evolve and have consequences that resonate throughout the narrative.

Update the setting to the present time. For example, students could explore any of the following aspects of the novel and miniseries from a present-day perspective: domestic violence and spousal abuse, religious or political corruption, evolving class and gender norms, expanded educational and career opportunities, and new transportation and communication technologies.

Introduce a character from another nineteenth-century novel into the story. Students could choose characters from other Spanish works studied in class or from well-known English-language novels to imagine how social, political, religious, or ethical issues raised by Pardo Bazán play out in interactions between her characters and a character from a different novelistic world.

Write an alternative ending. Students could carry forward the concluding events of Pardo Bazán's *Los pazos de Ulloa* and write a sequel that differs from the events in *La madre naturaleza* and the fourth episode of the miniseries, or they could extend the narrative beyond the end of Suárez's fourth episode by continuing the stories of Perucho or Gabriel or Nucha.

The adaptation projects should address both what has been changed and how the changes would be cinematically rendered. As a group, students can present details of the new plot line they conceived together. Then, each student can present one scene that he or she designed in terms of mise-en-scène, camera work, editing, sound and music, and dialogue.

Hutcheon has commented that "we often come to see the prior adapted work very differently as we compare it to the result of the adapter's creative and interpretive acts" (121). The five-step sequence this essay describes will help students reexamine Pardo Bazán's novel not only in the light of Suárez's miniseries version but also through their own creative and interpretive acts.

NOTES

[1] The miniseries can be streamed online on the *RTVE* Web site at no charge and without restrictions. It also is available with English subtitles on DVD from Divisa Home Video.

[2] Instructors can create an affordable custom textbook with material from *Film Art: An Introduction* and *Hablando del cine* using the Web site *McGraw-Hill Create*.

A Dialogue with the Arts
in Pardo Bazán's *Dulce dueño*

Carmen Pereira-Muro

Dulce dueño (1911; "Sweet Master"), the last novel published by Emilia Pardo Bazán, is not frequently taught in the Spanish curriculum. The Galician author's classic, realist novels (the Ulloa series) are typically included in courses on nineteenth-century Peninsular literature because they fit a canonical view of Spanish literary history. *Dulce dueño* is written in the *modernista*, fin de siècle style[1] and takes up an uneasy gender agenda. Lina, its protagonist and narrator (and, in the fiction, the author of the text), is a female dandy in pursuit of supreme beauty. Lina resists the idea of marriage and eventually finds her "dulce dueño" ("sweet master") in God, giving up her riches and freedom to be locked up in an asylum (what some critics have deemed the modern version of the convent ending[2]). This essay argues that *Dulce dueño* has valuable pedagogical benefits precisely because of its unusual characteristics. In addition to problematizing traditional linear and geographical approaches to literature, this novel can promote a lively discussion on gender politics: Is Lina a saint or a mad woman? Is the end of the novel feminist or antifeminist? Is the female mystic's surrender of her soul to God a freeing act or a perpetuation of her submissiveness?

In my experience, a successful teaching approach situates these questions in the cultural milieu of the international fin de siècle. Exploring in the classroom the dialogue between this text and various other artistic manifestations of the period (painting, opera, architecture and interior design, fashion, jewelry) fosters class participation and provides a deeper understanding of the cultural transformations that allowed Pardo Bazán to reroute her literary and feminist agendas. In *modernismo*, symbolism, decadentism, art nouveau, and other incarnations of fin de siècle culture there is a blurring of genders along with a struggle to redefine them, an internationalization of culture together with a search for national identity, and a quest for the total work of art (that is, art that seeks to appeal to all the senses, like Richard Wagner's operas) that can supply the jaded modern subject the spirituality that religion has ceased to offer. Analyzing these aspects in the novel vis-à-vis the arts of the time helps elucidate what *modernismo* offered a feminist like Pardo Bazán, who had a lifelong interest in creating a place for women in high culture and in reconciling cosmopolitanism and national culture.

I teach *Dulce dueño* in a seminar on transatlantic *modernismo* in which I pair Pardo Bazán's novel with José Asunción Silva's *De sobremesa* ("After-Dinner Conversation"; published in 1925, but composed between 1887 and 1896, the year Silva died). The contextualization proposed here works for both novels and provides a background against which students can discuss the texts' similar aesthetic principles and different gender dynamics. I organize the discussion as a module taught in five class sessions:

1. Introduction to the novel, emphasizing aspects that will be important in future class sessions
2. Visions of transcendence; painterly references in the text
3. Modernity and inner spaces; architecture and interior design
4. The body sublime; fashion, jewelry, and the construction of femininity
5. Opera as a total work of art; *Dulce dueño* as a synesthetic opera

In this essay I will focus exclusively on Pardo Bazán's novel and, for reasons of space, I will offer expansive remarks only on the introduction and on the dialogue between text and painting (sessions 1 and 2). I will give a brief summary of sessions 3–5. This proposal is designed for a graduate seminar, but it could also work for advanced undergraduate students.

Graduate students should read the entire novel before the first day of discussion.[3] Students are asked to prepare the following before class:

Locate some of the national and international texts that are directly or indirectly presented in the novel.
List the different arts with which this novel establishes a dialogue, indicating the page numbers where they appear.
How do the content, temporal structure, and stylistic changes in this novel reflect both Spain's modernization and its inadequacy for modernity?

This first class session is organized around these questions and a review of *modernista* aesthetics, illustrated with a preview of the artistic examples that the module will feature.

To start, instructors could discuss the crisis of the bourgeois subject, symbolism, synesthesia, and the aim of the total work of art to find completeness in a fragmented universe. They could show a short video clip of Wagner's opera *Lohengrin*, where the music, singing, acting, spectacular staging, and mystic content create a transcendent, unifying viewing experience.

A second point of discussion could be transcendence through the immanent, (con)fusion of interior and exterior, nature and culture, detail and essence.[4] Here instructors could show an image of a *modernista* interior—from Antoni Gaudí's *El Capricho*, for example—pointing out how outside and nature are brought inside by the use of natural light and by the elaborate decoration based on stylized natural motifs.

A third discussion point concerns male anxiety in the face of the alleged feminization of culture at the turn of the century.[5] Visual examples include Aubrey Beardsley's illustrations for Oscar Wilde's *Salome* and art nouveau jewelry with snake motifs that evoke femme fatale figures like Eve and Cleopatra. Instructors should highlight the novel's singular status in Pardo Bazán's production: it is the only one in which the protagonist is a woman writer. Unique among her contemporaries, Pardo Bazán's critical views on symbolism, decadentism, and other fin de siècle movements as positive and renewing forms of spirituality should also be addressed.[6]

The second class session is dedicated to painting. First, as a general introduction to the aesthetics in the novel, students in groups give five-minute presentations about the artistic styles that will be discussed in class—impressionism, Pre-Raphaelism, symbolism, expressionism, art nouveau—and to connect specific passages in the novel to the various styles. The presentations are followed by a reflection on the fact that although Pardo Bazán always has a penchant for evoking artistic compositions, in *Dulce dueño* the pictorial references are paradoxical as well as pervasive because the narrator-protagonist is a hyperaesthetic and well-educated woman. Women became the main object of representation in fin de siècle culture because "modernism had at its base a masculinity that posited the artist as man and possessor and the woman as both 'sexual prey and artistic cipher'" (Hirsh 171). Lina disrupts this masculine attempt to reestablish gender binaries by becoming both artist and work of art,[7] thus fusing subject and object in her text. *Dulce dueño* aims to be an artist's novel, even more so than *La quimera* ("The Chimera"), Pardo Bazán's 1905 novel whose protagonist is a male painter. The text is the product of a *modernista* sensibility that processes Lina's experiences through preexisting artistic models. Many of these models are international, but the novel aims to nationalize them in order to secure a place for Spain (and for women artists) in the international modern community.

Analysis of specific passages in the novel can follow this introduction. A key passage is the story of Saint Catherine of Alexandria. The "author" of this hagiography, the priest Carranza, is said to be "antirromántico" and a man of a national, classical formation, but the story is transcribed for us by Lina with "arrequives de sentimiento o de estética que el autor reprobaría" ("adornments of feeling and aesthetics of which the author may disapprove"; 48).[8] This rewriting corresponds to Lina's more modern and international tastes; after inheriting her fortune, she will similarly modernize her aunt's preferences in furnishings and jewelry. Instructors should call attention to the descriptions of Catherine's sumptuous vestments, jewels, and surroundings; to the strange tension between eroticism and mysticism; to the Byzantine (mixture of Hellenic and oriental) atmosphere; to the ideal of female beauty (honey-colored tresses, fair skin and eyes, body like a classical sculpture of a goddess); and to Catherine's proximity to the femme fatale type—akin to Cleopatra, whose jewels she has inherited—and to Lucrezia Borgia, who was painted as Catherine by the Renaissance painter Pinturicchio. There are echoes here of Pre-Raphaelite art and the aestheticist symbolism of the painters Gustave Moreau[9] and Gustav Klimt; the story also prefigures Lina's later self-fashioning.

A range of imagery is available to help illustrate the aesthetics suggested by the text. For example, Dante Gabriel Rossetti's paintings *Beata Beatrix*, *Venus*

Venetta, and *Lady Lilith* show chromatic and textural richness, Venetian and Byzantine luxury, a mixture of mysticism and eroticism, and the particular ideal of female beauty that this part of the novel expresses: Hellenic facial features, white skin, green eyes, and luxurious, light-colored hair. In Moreau's *Dance of Salome*, Salome's skin is covered with arabesques, making her an *objet d'art* with bejeweled surfaces; the arabesques are reminiscent of liquid and snakes, both associated with women. The Moreau painting can be usefully presented together with the final scene of this section of the novel, where Saint Catherine's hair spreads like Medusa's snakes over the lake of milk that emanates from her severed head (103). Like Moreau (and also reminiscent of Byzantine icons), Klimt, in works such as *Judith II (Salome)* and *Salome*, favors flat, gold, ornate backgrounds in place of naturalistic, perspectival backgrounds, creating a transcendent, mysterious atmosphere; eroticism is accentuated through the contrast between the naturalist treatment of the female figures' flesh and the surrounding abstract, gold, and jewel-like designs. Here the popular fin de siècle motif of the severed male head connected to femme fatales such as Salome and Judith can be contrasted with its opposite in the novel, the severed female head of Saint Catherine.

A passage from the second part of the novel that echoes, with a modern twist, the aesthetics of the first part describes Lina's solitary "fiesta[s] a mí misma" ("parties to herself"; 127), her nights spent in her rooms trying on cosmetics, jewels, and luxurious clothes. The description of her outfits — "vestes," "bordados bizantinos," "línea de mosaico de Rávena o miniatura de misal" ("tunics," "byzantine embroideries," "line of a Ravenna mosaic or a missal miniature"; 129) — matches those of Catherine's and the precious aesthetics of the art described here. However, Lina recognizes that her Spanish looks — she is petite with dark hair — don't fit the aesthetic. Studying herself in the mirror, she concludes that "[h]elénicamente no valgo gran cosa" ("from a Hellenic point of view, I am not worth much"; 128). An average woman, she wishes to re-create herself following "la moda actual, artísticamente pérfida y reveladora" ("today's fashion, artistically perfidious and revealing"; 129) and believes that "el misterio de mi alma se entrevé en mi adorno y atavío" ("my adornment and my clothes give glimpses of the mystery of my soul"; 130). Lina will try to become "divine" (131) by sublimating herself in the modern aesthetics that evoke the spiritual through the material; she piles precious objects on and around herself in an attempt to become an art object — as in Klimt's images of women covered with gold leaf or Moreau's Salome covered in calligraphic body art. The result is an image that mixes genders, transforming her bust into a menacing phallic image: "mi busto brotando del escote como un blanco puñal de su vaina de oro cincelado" ("my bust sprouting from my neck line like a white dagger from its chiseled golden sheath"; 131). To achieve agency as an artist — an agency normally reserved for men — Lina submits herself, paradoxically, to the cultural mandate that women become art objects. Does she achieve this agency? The absence of a clear answer in the text creates a great opportunity for debate in the classroom.

Lina's descriptions of landscapes also reflect her *modernista* artistic sensibility: fall and spring views of the shores of the Jarama as a plein air aquarelle; the Alhambra, Loja, and its sierra as exotic and sensual sceneries; the Swiss Alps as a sublime landscape; the hidden valley where Lina goes to live at the end of the novel as an impressionist depiction imbued with symbolist meaning. Lina's acute sensibility toward the beauty of (solitary) landscapes relates to nineteenth-century plein air painting and impressionistic techniques for capturing effects of color and light as well as to the Romantic painting of the sublime, exemplified in the works of Caspar David Friedrich and Joseph Mallord William Turner, and the symbolist abhorrence of the modern city as a soulless, dehumanizing place, such as in the works of expressionists like James Ensor and Edvard Munch. Lina is repulsed by the crowd of workers, by the philistine operagoers that ruin her sublime Wagnerian experience, by prostitutes who lurk in dark alleys, and by lowly people with whom she must share trains.[10]

Examples from the art of Mariano Fortuny y Marsals and Munch help contextualize Lina's sensibility within the artistic currents of the period—the taste for the primitive and oriental in Fortuny, repulsion of modernity in Munch—strategically placing "oriental" Spain at the center of European modern art. Fortuny's paintings of Granada's Islamic buildings, such as *Patio en la Alhambra* ("Patio in the Alhambra"), *Los Abencerrajes*, and *Odalisca* ("Odalisque") anticipate the Spanish fashion first for French Romantic orientalism, such as Delacroix's *Women of Algiers*, and then for fin de siècle Parisian art. As DuPont has noticed, Pardo Bazán sees Spanish oriental and primitive culture as catering to the antimodernist taste of international modernism and as a means to resituate Spain at the forefront of European culture—hence the ecstasy in Granada of Henri Regnault, who followed Fortuny there and stayed two years ("Cabezas"). Munch's *Anxiety*, an expressionist painting of a lone woman followed by a menacing, faceless male crowd, can be related to Lina's disgust with crowds and their connection with greed and venal eroticism (the ever-present pornography in Paris). Modernism's fear of prostitution is reversed in this painting, as in *Dulce dueño*, where men are the menace and the prostitute will become an "amiga" ("friend"; 269).

In the third class session, devoted to architecture and interior design, I show images of *modernista* buildings and interiors, mostly those by Gaudí, and highlight their roles as inner sanctuaries and extensions of the self as well as their function as signs of social and economic status. *Modernista* design can be related to Lina's refurbishing of her aunt's old-fashioned, bourgeois house and furniture as an exquisite modern dwelling that shields her from the ugliness of the world. In the fourth class session Lina's passion for the new style of jewels and fashion again shows rejection of the old aesthetics and illustrates her paradoxical search for an inner, perfect beauty expressed by costly, precious crafts. Instructors should point out the centrality of the female figure, stylized nature, and oriental and Byzantine motifs in art nouveau jewelry and clothing: the fantastic Venetian designs of Fortuny (the son of the painter) can be introduced as illustrations here.

In the final class session we watch the parts of Wagner's *Lohengrin* that are described in the novel as well as Salome's dance from Richard Strauss's homonymous opera. I suggest that the novel follows the musical structure of having a prelude with motifs that are repeated with variations. We compare how synesthesia in the service of spirituality is present in the operas and in the novel and discuss how *Dulce dueño* both embraces and rejects the gender constructions reflected in the operas.

Lina's trajectory, as illuminated by the novel's dialogue with art, responds to a specific nationalist agenda that not only connects Spanish culture to international modernism but assigns Spanish culture a privileged place as a spiritual repository. Lina goes from Alcalá de Henares, the birthplace of Miguel de Cervantes, where she is exposed to classical aesthetics with Carranza; to the semimodern city of Madrid, where she has her first contacts with the modern aesthetic pleasures of fashion, interior design, and opera; to Granada (oriental, sensual aestheticism); to Biarritz (international aristocratism); to Paris (Baudelarian disgust for the sexual venality of the city); to Switzerland (international crossroads and a search for the sublime); and finally back to Spain, where she is purified of her degenerate modernism by the feared icon of modernity, the urban prostitute. Lina then travels to a remote, hidden Castilian valley; her experience of its landscape is akin to the mystic and symbolic landscapes of the Spanish writer Santa Teresa of Ávila. Finally, in an ironic extreme of dematerialization—as in Miguel de Unamuno's plea to go "adentro" ("inside"; 22)—Lina, locked inside the white, empty walls of an asylum, finally finds inner peace. The suppression of the self propitiates the mystic weddings with the *dulce dueño* intuited in her first encounter with Wagner's *Lohengrin* at the beginning of the modernist odyssey, astutely feminizing and nationalizing them.

NOTES

[1] *Modernismo* is one form of an international aesthetic reaction against prosaism, materialism, and industrialization; it prevailed from the last quarter of the nineteenth century (in the Spanish tradition its beginning is traditionally marked by Rubén Darío's *Azul* in 1888) until World War I. It was called *modern style* in England and the United States, *art nouveau* in France, *Jugendstil* in Germany, *Sezession* in Austria, *liberty* in Italy, and *modernisme* in Catalonia.

[2] For criticism that expresses disappointment with the novel's ending, see Mayoral 32–41; Charnon-Deutsch, "Tenía"; Medina; and Kirkpatrick, "Gender."

[3] Recommended critical readings for the first or second class session are Bieder, "Divina"; Charnon-Deutsch, "Tenía"; Ezama Gil; Kirkpatrick, *Mujer*; Smith, "Women"; Pereira-Muro, *Género* 145–76.

[4] See Olivio Jiménez 19–33; Kirkpatrick, *Mujer*.

[5] For this phenomenon in Western culture generally, see Showalter; Huyssen; Felski. For Spain, see Valis, "Female Figure." For *Dulce dueño*, see Kirkpatrick, "Gender."

[6] See Kronik; DuPont, "Cabezas."

[7] See Kirkpatrick, "Gender" and *Mujer* 108–28. Kirkpatrick compares Lina to the impossible union of artist and work of art (*Mujer* 115), a fusion like that of Pygmalion and Galatea.

[8] All translations are my own.

[9] Moreau's works, and specifically his *Salome*, along with the works of the symbolist painter Odilon Redon, were favorites of Jean des Esseintes, the protagonist of Joris-Karl Huysman's novel *À Rebours*, after whom Lina's reclusive dandyism is modeled (Kirkpatrick, *Mujer* 111–12).

[10] As a contraposition to the solitary Alhambra paintings by Mariano Fortuny and the dead cities (like Bruges) dear to symbolists like Fernand Khnopff, impressionism was fascinated with urbanity and modernity. See, for example, Camille Pissarro's *Boulevard Montmartre*, Auguste Renoir's *Ball at the Moulin de la Galette*, and Claude Monet's *Gare Saint-Lazare*. Lina resorts to impressionistic techniques but does not share the realist taste for the prose of the world.

Mapping the City in *La Tribuna*

María Luisa Guardiola and Susan Walter

[L]a sociabilidad del hombre es la causa del desarrollo de
la urbanización. (Man's socialization is the reason for the
development of urbanization.)
— Ildefons Cerdá, Spanish urban planner (1867)

In this chapter we propose reading Emilia Pardo Bazán's novel *La Tribuna*
(1882; "The Tribune") through the analysis of urban spaces represented in the
text. *La Tribuna* focuses on female solidarity among working-class women and
explores characters' interactions with the spaces of Marineda, a fictional version
of A Coruña, Galicia, against the backdrop of Spain's industrialization and the
political liberalization promoted by the Glorious Revolution (1868). Amparo,
the novel's protagonist, finds work and later develops her career in Marineda's
tobacco factory. She also loves to stroll through the city and is therefore an excellent guide for students to map out the various spaces of Marineda and the
social classes that populated them.

La Tribuna, the third novel written by Pardo Bazán, was one of the first Spanish naturalist works. The novel is set against the historical and social background
of the Sexenio Democrático (1868–74), the six revolutionary years that followed
the 1868 revolution. Amparo's career in the tobacco factory, where she first
reads newspapers aloud to her fellow workers and later becomes the workers'
spokeswoman, takes place during this tumultuous period. *La Tribuna* ends with
the proclamation of Spain's First Republic (1873–74), a counterpart of the main
character, Amparo, whose life experiences narrated in the novel match the de-
mise of the First Republic. Amparo is nicknamed "la Tribuna" because of her
public reading and union activities.

Incorporating *La Tribuna* into a course on urban cartographies allows students
to develop a theoretical understanding of literary approaches to urban studies
and then hone their skills with spatial readings of *La Tribuna* and other texts.
Jorge Carrión's anthology *Madrid/Barcelona: Literatura y ciudad, 1995–2010*
is a useful companion text for this type of course, providing a diversity of short
stories as well as insightful theoretical pieces by Carrión and other important
twenty-first-century Spanish thinkers. The appendix of this essay lists literary
and filmic works that may be useful for a course like this. Organizing a graduate
or advanced undergraduate course focused on the nineteenth century around
Leigh Mercer's valuable study *Urbanism and Urbanity: The Spanish Bourgeois
Novel and Contemporary Customs, 1845–1925* is another way to incorporate
La Tribuna. In this course instructors could use mid-nineteenth-century *fol-
letines* ("serial sagas") and serialized novels, such as *La gaviota* (1849; "The Sea
Gull") by Cecilia Bohl de Faber (Fernán Caballero); other realist works studied

by Mercer, such as Benito Pérez Galdós's *La desheredada* (1881; "The Disinherited Lady") or Blasco Ibáñez's *Arroz y tartana* (1894; "Rice and Wagon"); and conclude the course with a modernist or Generation of 1898 novel, such as Miguel de Unamuno's *Nada menos que todo un hombre* (1916; "Every Inch a Man") or Pío Baroja's *La busca* (1904; "The Quest"). Such a course, in which "novels from each of these three literary moments in modernity chart the shape of the bourgeois city from initiation and inclusion to exclusion, and ultimately to its decadent moment of necessary reinvention," outlines how these artistic models engage in varying ways with bourgeois modes of urbanity in a trajectory from the mid-nineteenth century to the beginning of the twentieth (Mercer 17). Another useful text for faculty and students who read Spanish is Edward Baker's book, *Materiales para escribir Madrid: Literatura y espacio urbano de Moratín a Galdós* ("Materials for Writing Madrid: Literature and Urban Space from Moratín to Galdós"), especially chapters 4 and 5, which focus on the end of the nineteenth century and guide readers through literary strategies informed by narrated urban spatiality (83–145).

In approaching *La Tribuna* from an urban studies perspective, we understand the urban spaces in the novel as sites of performativity in which a locale's physical space only tells part of the story—the social interactions that take place there tell another. The French philosopher Henri Lefebvre posits that a city is "a space which is fashioned, shaped and invested by social activities during a finite historical period" (*Production* 73). Leigh Mercer, who grounds her work in Lefebvre's ideas, likewise posits that public space is a performative realm "in which the Spanish middle class enacted and displayed, first, its coming of age and, later, its own decline into decadence" (5). Mercer's *Urbanism and Urbanity* is an accessible text that most advanced undergraduate and graduate students should find insightful; its introduction is particularly useful for establishing the theoretical basis for readings (1–19). Another helpful text is Collin McKinney's chapter "Mapping the City" from his book *Mapping the Social Body: Urbanisation, the Gaze, and the Novels of Galdós* (15–46). Likewise, the introduction to Jen Jack Gieseking and William Mangold's *The People, Place, and Space Reader* (xix–xxxiv) and Lefebvre's short chapter in this same reader, which contains excerpts from *The Production of Space* (1991), are suitable readings for most graduate students. Benjamin Fraser's introduction to his study *Henri Lefebvre and the Spanish Urban Experience: Reading the Mobile City* is a useful and accessible summary of the spatial theories of Lefebvre and some of his disciples, such as the geographer David Harvey (1–38). Fraser underscores the dialectical nature of these theorists' work while also giving some background on Lefebvre's life and his place within philosophical movements of the twentieth century.

In *La Tribuna* each part of the city of Marineda is initially linked to the social class that populates it: the streets of the Ciudad Vieja are home to the nobility; the promenades, cafés, and theaters of the commercial neighborhood La Pescadería are the meeting places of the bourgeoisie. The southern neighborhood, where Amparo lives, is a poor, working-class area whose inhabitants live in dirty, meager conditions that contrast markedly with the comfort and opulence of the Sobrado family home. The slums of the Cementerio are the marginal areas surrounding the city. The tobacco factory where Amparo works is also organized according to a specific sociospatial distribution. Mapping the city is an exercise that allows students to acquire an understanding of the dynamics of the novel's spatial spheres and of the complexities of nineteenth-century society.[1] In class, this exercise can be easily facilitated with the help of two charts from the introduction to Benito Varela Jácome's edition of the novel (45–46).

Of all the urban locations frequented by Amparo, the tobacco factory is the most important because it is where she develops her identity. This working space, popularly known as "La Granera" ("The Granary") because it provides protection and nourishment, is where Amparo grows as a worker and a person. It is here that she forms strong bonds with other women and reads aloud to them in an attempt to inform them about the tumultuous political situation of the time. Nevertheless, Amparo also develops part of her identity as she explores different parts of the city on her own, particularly at the beginning of the novel. Amparo stands apart as a unique female character in many ways because her lower social standing affords her a certain level of freedom to roam the city streets, a freedom that a bourgeois or aristocratic woman would not have had because of the strict codes of female behavior that women of these classes were expected to follow. Students could be assigned a few excerpts from Rosa María Capel Martínez's "Life and Work in the Tobacco Factories: Female Industrial Workers in the Early Twentieth Century" to gain insight into working conditions in Spain's tobacco factories. Because the factories were populated primarily by female laborers, they were likely environments for raising workers' awareness of women's rights. Instructors should point out that the factory is a gendered space where women can act more openly than in other spaces, despite its status as a state institution.

At this point, instructors could shift their focus to the different types of labor in the factory and its structural organization. The *cigarreras* (tobacco workers) carry out their work in various areas of the factory, according to their responsibilities and status. Though it makes a product mainly for consumption by men, the factory employs about four thousand women: female labor is cheap and female hands are skillful and agile. Amparo adapts well to industrial labor, and her good performance provides her with opportunities to advance and earn more money: "en las yemas de los dedos tenía el medio de acrecentar sus rentas" ("in the tips of her fingers she had the means to increase her income"; 95).[2]

Amparo's labor performance is complemented by her reading of articles from the press about the liberal uprisings in the country. Amparo is fairly ignorant of the political events surrounding the ratification of the republic, but her ability to read helps her to stand out among her peers and gain status inside the factory. As a result the young *cigarrera* ascends to an upper floor where the working conditions are much better. The insightful book by Araceli Tinajero about the history of cigar factories, *El Lector: A History of the Cigar Factory Reader*, is essential reading for instructors and students alike.

Although working women in the late nineteenth century had to endure many external pressures, the factory's gendered space offered them a certain amount of autonomy and the possibility of partial emancipation, at least within its walls. Christina Dupláa posits that the hybrid, heterogeneous factory space blurs the supposedly well-defined divisions between working activity and domestic life: "La fábrica/hogar es el espacio materno que ejerce una función protectora con sus hijas/cigarreras, las cuales se relacionan entre sí bajo formas solidarias que sobrepasan el marco del corporativismo profesional y de clase social" ("The factory/home is a maternal space that serves a protective function with its daughters/*cigarreras*, who relate to one another based on a solidarity that moves well beyond the framework of professional corporatism and social class"; 195). The community of relatively independent young women workers provides crucial support when Amparo falls prey to the seducing *señorito*. When describing the representation of female laborers, Geraldine Scanlon suggests that "as a recurrent literary image, a community of women is a rebuke to the conventional ideal of a solitary woman living for and through men, attaining citizenship in the community of adulthood through masculine approval alone" ("Class" 143).

The blurring of public and private space inside the factory works as a metaphor for a female collectivity that stands apart from the patriarchal model of separate female and male spaces promoted by the liberal bourgeois project. The tobacco workers' autonomy differs from the submission and detachment that defines the societal role of bourgeois women, whose most important commodity is their appearance. Likewise, the gendered space of the women's floors of the factory contrasts with the masculine space of the street and promenades where bourgeois women display themselves individually, following a strict urban code (Mercer 67).

After focusing on the factory and the main character's working life, students are encouraged to discuss other spaces in the city visited by Amparo. As a companion to this discussion, instructors could assign the chapter "Walking in the City" from Michel de Certeau's *The Practice of Everyday Life* (91–110). Amparo, an avid walker, experiences various urban spaces (including the factory) and attempts to make them her own. In Amparo's performance in areas outside the factory she subverts the established bourgeois spatial order: for example, her strolling through the streets of the Ciudad Vieja leads to her encounter with her future noble suitor, Baltasar Sobrado. The young woman enjoys walking through the promenade, which, in Mercer's terms, serves as a public forum that brings together the working class, bourgeoisie, and aristocracy, which are normally socially segregated in urban space (92). Indeed, a good companion reading to this discussion is chapter 2 of Mercer's monograph, which outlines the urban codes associated with the promenade and the boutique (61–104). Mercer proposes that urban spaces are both geographical and behavioral configurations. The city is the stage where the working-class protagonist attempts to move up the social ladder, echoing values of the republic itself. But she is ultimately unsuccessful because she fails to adhere to bourgeois behavioral standards, as Mercer has posited: "the protagonist is incapable of mastering the promenade's urban codes of conduct that might enhance her social standing. As the novel shows, the established bourgeoisie of the late nineteenth century has grown ever more dismissive of the low-born social climbers as it fiercely guards its own ritualistic territory" (95).

Jo Labanyi asserts that Galdós's novels, contemporary to Pardo Bazán's, are "concerned with appearances not in the sense that they are false, but because . . . modern city life is based on visual display" (*Gender* 111). Exhibition in public spaces such as the promenade was common in nineteenth-century urban environments, especially for middle-class women. Though Amparo is a lower-class woman living in a sordid and marginal environment, she has an innate desire for independence and an instinctive talent for rising above her social status. As a child, her rebelliousness urged her to wander through the public spaces of the Ciudad Vieja; later, as an attractive young woman, she catches the attention of the young Baltasar Sobrado while strolling on the Las Filas promenade. She even gains access to the aristocratic domestic space of the Sobrado family residence to sing Christmas carols. The *habanera* melody (a song from Havana, Cuba) interpreted by Josefina García, the bourgeois young lady who will eventually become engaged to Baltasar, supersedes the poor children's popular carolling led by Amparo, a clear premonition of the doomed future relationship between Amparo and Baltasar. In class, students could be encouraged to explore how the music parallels Amparo's performance, which is also echoed in this historical moment by the short-lived republic.

The novel underscores how female conduct differs according to social status. In particular, the superficial, frivolous behaviour of bourgeois women is juxtaposed with the solidarity and generosity among the women working in the tobacco factory. The ostentatious manners of bourgeois women who "iban casi en orden hierático" ("went almost in ritualistic order"; 98) are compared to the spontaneity of working-class women. Such contrasts in female behavior according to social class help students understand the industrial space of the factory: in the factory the lower-class workers have their own behavioral code that values solidarity above all else. The irony is that Amparo's self-liberating impulses as well as her political liberalism, while strengthened inside the tobacco factory, are destined to fail in a mixed public space; public patriarchal space cannot offer her welfare and sustenance because it is governed by a male power structure entwined with state and class inequities. According to Dupláa, the street and the state are two domains in which Amparo is powerless (194). Her transformation, growth, and emancipation will depend on—and only be valid in—a space adapted to her gender and class. And even the female-dominated work space cannot ensure her success, because no Spanish space existed outside male authority. The exaggerated description of the factory building's majesty and dominating presence establishes that the factory belongs to the state. In order to help students understand how expectations for women's behavior differed in the lower and middle classes during this period in Spain, instructors are encouraged to assign the two corresponding sections of Pardo Bazán's 1889 essay "La mujer española" ("The Women of Spain"; Pardo Bazán, "La mujer" 99–116).[3] Additionally, Catherine Jagoe's *Ambiguous Angels: Gender in the Novels of Galdós* is a useful resource for background information on class and behavior expectations in nineteenth-century Spain.

Joseba Gabilondo addresses the importance of the performative, as opposed to the literary, in cultural settings that include the subaltern woman in nineteenth-century Spain. By not looking at subalternity in literary terms and by privileging speaking over writing, Gabilondo asserts that the subaltern does speak, although performatively ("Subaltern" 90–92). Amparo's romantic adventure takes place exclusively on the outskirts of Marineda. Although she stands out because of her natural beauty and talent, her lower-class status is an impediment to her social ascent. Amparo manages to briefly date a man of a higher class, but he will not be seen in public bourgeois spaces with her. Instead, their precarious romance takes place in the meadowlands, a liminal space outside the city. The young woman's removal to a marginal location mirrors female displacement and exclusion in the late nineteenth century. In their relationship, Sobrado suppresses Amparo, and she cannot perform her duties at the factory well. When she is abandoned by Sobrado while she is pregnant with his child, Amparo is able to "speak" performatively (Gabilondo, "Subaltern" 90–92). She enters another space emblematic of the bourgeois public sphere, the theater, an institutional space of performance and exhibition (Mercer 23). In this space, however, it is not Amparo who is on display. The *cigarrera* sets her gaze on Josefina García, who is seated next to Sobrado and is officially engaged to him. Despite her shame, Amparo's humiliation and her anger toward her former lover and his girlfriend move her to action. Upon leaving the theater, the cigar factory worker performs two actions that transcend the status quo of class boundaries. First, she paints a red cross on Sobrado's front door to protest her displacement from the urban bourgeois setting. Second, her maternity, the outcome of class mixing, affirms her agency and represents the birth of a new nation, a fitting contrast to the sterility of patriarchal power.

The urban setting in *La Tribuna* is the stage where the lower-class protagonist performs her attempt at social mobility, which is a metaphor for the republic's ascendency. Despite Amparo's displacement from the bourgeois domain, her performative acts define her identity. The first chapters of the novel clearly show that various places in the city are linked to particular social classes, but Amparo's presence in locales that belong to the bourgeoisie shows her desire to break the restrictive social barriers that separate her class from others and also highlights the dialectical nature of these spaces. In line with Lefebvre's emphasis on the performativity of urban spaces, the young *cigarrera*'s performance in urban spaces demonstrates that space is a social product that "is made, not given" (Arias 31).

NOTES

[1] Other studies dedicated to the use of space in *La Tribuna* are Álvarez Méndez; and Thion Soriano-Mollá, "Realismo." The 2007 volume of the journal *La Tribuna: Cadernos de estudios da Casa Museo Emilia Pardo Bazán* also has a special section devoted to this novel.

2 All translations are our own. This praise of the laborer's work ethic contrasts well with the late-nineteenth-century disdain of productivity by the bourgeoisie, which sought to establish itself as the new aristocracy (Mercer 89). In the novel Pardo Bazán extols bourgeois progress based on commerce and industriousness while also showing the decline of that progress.

3 For an English version of this essay, see Pardo Bazán, "Women."

APPENDIX
Additional Texts for Urban Cartographies Course

LITERARY TEXTS
La plaza del diamante, by Mercè Rodoreda (1962)
Los misterios de Madrid, by Antonio Muñoz Molina (1992)
Okupada, by Care Santos (1997)
Madrid/Barcelona, edited by Jorge Carrión (2009)

FILMS
Metropolis, directed by Fritz Lang (1927)
La colmena, directed by Mario Camus (1982)
¿Qué he hecho yo para merecer esto?, directed by Pedro Almodóvar (1984)
Barrio, directed by Fernando León de Aranoa (1998)
En construcción, directed by José Luis Guerín (2001)

Pardo Bazán and
the Images of an Era

Alicia Cerezo

> The kinds of nets we know how to weave determine the
> kind of nets we cast. These nets, in turn, determine the
> kinds of fish we catch.
> — Elliot Eisner, *Cognition and Curriculum* (1982)

Teaching literature within the context of visual culture offers not only a multidisciplinary approach, and thus a better contextualization of the texts, but also a path to understanding the texts through the prism of visual methodologies. In other words, with this approach students benefit from visualizing the texts in order to better interpret them. Numerous scholars have advocated the integration of the arts in the classroom (Eisner; Bresler), emphasizing the cognitive importance of engaging with works of art in an aesthetic experience that could not be achieved by other means. Another benefit to this approach is that cultural studies seek to avoid imposing a hierarchy among different art forms. Such a horizontal approach to cultural expression allows students to explore how cultural products dialogue with one another. Students live in an image-saturated world, so they are especially receptive to classroom techniques that allow the visualization of textual materials and the contextualization of texts within the visual culture of the historical period studied. This essay applies this approach to teaching Pardo Bazán's texts. My examples come primarily from the short story "El indulto" (1883; "The Pardon") and the novel *La Tribuna* (1883; "The Tribune"). I propose a variety of comparisons and contrasts that will make students aware of formal aspects of the texts and images—perspective, distance, tone, composition of elements, and so on—and the ways in which these aspects contribute to the creation of social and cultural meanings in the texts.

In "El indulto," the washerwoman Antonia fears that her imprisoned husband, who killed her mother, may receive a pardon from the king of Spain on the occasion of the king's marriage.[1] When Antonia accused him of the murder, he threatened to kill her in revenge. Despite rumors that the husband had died, Antonia later discovers that he did indeed receive a pardon. After returning home, he abuses her in front of their child; in the morning, he realizes she is lying in bed motionless and runs away cowardly. The woman's son alerts the neighbors of his mother's condition, and the doctor is called. After an unsuccessful bleeding, the doctor can only certify that she died "de muerte natural" (127; "of natural causes"). However, it is obvious that there is nothing natural about the way her blood froze: she was literally scared to death.

The intensity of graphic details in this short text invites reading it as a picture or even as a film: the description of Antonia's appearance and mental state, the harshness of her job, her husband's way of eating after his return, and his cruel abuse. For example, the study of this short story alongside the 1894 painting *¡Aún dicen que el pescado es caro!* ("And They Still Say That the Fish Is Expensive!"), by the Valencian painter Joaquín Sorolla y Bastida (1863–1923), introduces students to realist art that focuses on the lower social classes. Although Sorolla is better known as a key figure of the impressionist movement in Spain, the style and compositions of some of his first paintings align more with social realism. For example, the tiny detail of the lantern in this painting shows the movement of the boat on the water, its instability reflecting the sailors' insecurity. The painting focuses on an injured sailor in a fishing boat being helped by two other men, giving attention to the injured man much in the same way that Pardo Bazán describes Antonia. In the story and in the painting, the tragic destinies of the washerwoman and the sailor appear to be predetermined, connecting these works to realism and deterministic naturalism.[2]

Although this kind of comparison contextualizes Pardo Bazán's story within a broader social and aesthetic framework, certain details in the story bring together written and visual culture from a formal perspective. In particular, questions of perspective and distance, which affect both literature and painting, can be brought to students' attention. The distance between the painting's title and its content underscores the distance between the sailor, who indeed pays a high price (his life), and people who complain about the cost of the fish—that is, people who can afford to have others provide fish for them.[3] Sorolla foregrounds the sailor; only the title suggests the comments of the affluent buyers, providing an additonal shade of meaning. After they read Pardo Bazán's story, students can be asked to imagine it as a painting, organizing its components and commentary about different social classes into backgrounds and foregrounds. Pardo Bazán has foregrounded Antonia and her community, while the king is left in the background—present, but mostly out of sight. The fact that the narrator names the laundress but does not name the king individualizes Antonia and moves her closer to the reader in a gesture that recalls Diego Velázquez's famous play on perspectives in *Las meninas* (1656).

The distance between Antonia and the king is clearly posed in the text: "No creería de seguro el rey, cuando vestido de capitán general y con el pecho cargado de condecoraciones daba la mano ante el ara a una princesa, que aquel acto solemne *costaba* amarguras sin cuenta a una pobre asistenta, en *lejana* capital de provincia" ("Surely the king would not believe, when dressed as a captain general with his chest full of medals about to marry a princess, that this solemn act would *cause* a poor maid unimaginable grief, in a *faraway* provincial capital"; 123; my emphasis).[4] The text impels us to see the gulf between Antonia and the monarch just as Sorolla's title claims the distance between the sailors and the buyers of fish. At a primary level, Antonia and the king are situated in physical places and social classes distant from one another. But on another level, readers picture how the fatal connection between the two characters transcends the physical and social distances: specifically, how the liberation of the criminal ordered by the king, a supposedly magnanimous gesture, has caused Antonia's tragic fate. Like Sorolla's sailor, Antonia pays a high price: first *amarguras* (suffering) and then death.

Showing students nineteenth-century portraits and historical paintings in which the nobility and other key historical figures are unquestionably the main characters can illustrate how the less-favored members of society are unrepresented in certain discourses. The portraits of King Alfonso XII and of his wife, María Cristina de Habsburgo — painted, respectively, by Federico de Madrazo in 1886 and by Raimundo de Madrazo y Garreta in 1887 — make good examples and are contemporary to Pardo Bazán's story. In the paintings, both in the Prado, the king and his wife are painted along with signs of power and nobility, such as a lion and medals; there is no indication of their subjects, the common people. In the same way, history paintings — even if they occasionally portray common people, as in *Fusilamiento de Torrijos* ("The Execution of Torrijos"), painted in 1888 by Antoni Gisbert — present a main figure that participates in a historical event considered worthy of treatment, in this case the uprising led by General Torrijos against the absolutist King Fernando VII. History paintings don't treat the everyday life of people like Antonia and the anonymous fisherman.

Pardo Bazán's works may also be studied alongside more popular visual culture, in particular the miscellaneous illustrated magazines that proliferated during the last third of the nineteenth century. Thanks to revolutionary reproduction techniques, such as engravings, photogravures, and photography, these magazines exposed readers and viewers to new combinations of texts and images that visually constructed gender roles. Works by Lou Charnon-Deutsch, such as *Fictions of the Feminine in the Nineteenth-Century Spanish Press* and *Hold That Pose: Visual Culture in the Late-Nineteenth-Century Spanish Periodical*, are invaluable sources of ideas for the analysis of Spanish visual culture in popular magazines. *Hemeroteca Digital*, part of the Biblioteca Nacional de España's Web site, is a helpful and user-friendly resource for students and instructors that allows searches by keyword, date, and name of publication. Studying contemporary popular images can be productive when teaching Pardo Bazán's novel *La Tribuna* (1883), whose main character, Amparo, is a *cigarrera*, a tobacco factory worker, a common figure in late-nineteenth-century Spanish magazines. Studying textual and visual representations of the *cigarrera* figure side by side helps students understand the concept of a cultural construct. Contemplating several media, students can explore a variety of images and learn to recognize contradictions in those images, which teaches students the instability of representation.

A lack of homogeneity in representations of the *cigarrera* figure signals that the figure may be described in many different ways. In *La Tribuna*, Amparo, a working-class character, is presented as a naive young woman who nevertheless possesses agency — while she does not succeed in subverting social conventions, she challenges the status quo in the public and private female spheres in Marineda's tobacco factory. Amparo is a developed character, whereas most visual representations of female tobacco workers tend to be one-dimensional. Sometimes they are sexualized and objectified women whose bodies do not show the toll of labor; they are presented as beautiful landmarks that tourists should not miss. In other contexts they appear as mischievously irrational women capable of provoking a riot by protesting their unfair labor conditions. Rarely are they characterized in a less ideologically charged way. The variety of popular representations of tobacco workers exemplifies Mieke Bal's comments about realism. According to Bal, realism is erroneously understood to mean that art can be seen as a document. However, Bal posits that "realism is not a project of approaching reality but of promoting ways of reading as the only possible ones" (397). The popular images of *cigarreras* do not so much reflect a reality as construct possibilities. Two magazine engravings, for example, present *cigarreras* as classic costumbrista types (Balaca; Díaz Huertas, *La cigarrera*). Along with their textual counterparts, the images smooth over a diverse group of people and present them as essential, eternal symbols that stand for all female tobacco workers. Students should notice the ways in which Amparo, by contrast, is a much more developed, multidimensional *cigarrera*. If time permits, a class discussion of the differences between costumbrista sketches of everyday life and realism could follow. Students should be able to understand the difference between *costumbrism* representing the *cigarrera* as a type and realism representing Amparo as individualized woman with a unique story, who happens to be a tobacco factory worker.

Two images, published in *Blanco y negro*, are particularly useful for contrasting the literary representation of the tobacco worker with mass-produced visual illustrations of this figure and for understanding the ideologies of the two types of portrayals (García y Ramos; Díaz Huertas, *El motín*). Both depict workers at the entrance of Seville's tobacco factory, but their differences are overwhelming. While the first image, *Salida de las cigarreras de la fábrica de tabacos de Sevilla* ("The Departure of the Workers from the Tobacco Factory in Seville"), presents the workers as elegant and beautiful women, the second, *El motín de las cigarreras* ("The Tobacco Workers' Riot"), published a year later with a note about a strike that took place shortly before its publication, presents them as ugly, irrational, and uncontrollable revolutionaries. Both images are accompanied by short but highly significant texts. The first one explains that whereas in other countries female workers normally end the day quietly and head home for some rest, in Seville, female laborers leave the factory well-dressed, happy, and ready to please the men they are going to meet after work. The *cigarreras* are defined by their desire to look good and are presented as one of the city's attractions. The idealization of these women contrasts with the way they are presented in the second illustrated fragment, which represents them as revolutionary, violent, and unattractive. The text explains that their revolutionary attempts are useless. Amparo, who is sometimes depicted in the novel as an attractive woman but other times as a tired and socially aware worker, corresponds to neither of these one-dimensional characterizations of the *cigarrera*.

Comparing the *Blanco y negro* images with Amparo can demonstrate to students the one-sidedness of the images. The main character of *La Tribuna* suffers the consequences of her job in body and soul. Because tobacco workers are paid for the number of cigars rolled daily, Amparo's neck and fingers hurt from long shifts of manual labor (92). The alienating effect of mechanical labor also leaves her feeling mentally drained. Exhaustion prevents Amparo from being like the happy and beautiful women shown in *Salida de las cigarreras*, whose bodies are not affected by their work. *La Tribuna* includes two episodes in which Amparo successfully leads a strike and demands fair pay (237–47, 248–52), a demonstration of her agency that would be impossible for the archetypical women pictured in *Salida*. But Amparo is not like the irrational women portrayed in *El motín de las cigarreras*, nor is she like a pouty little girl, which is how *El motín's* accompanying article describes the tobacco workers as a way to minimize the rebellion. While the image emphasizes the ugliest aspects of the workers and the text summarizes the unproductive uprising carried out by women who probably lost part of their salaries, *La Tribuna* stresses the fact that the workers were heard and were paid their "haberes íntegros" ("whole wages"; 248).

If our goal as instructors is the contextualized production of knowledge, or situated knowledge, our classes will benefit from pairing visual texts and various perspectives with texts by Pardo Bazán. By enriching classes with images from the visual culture of her time, instructors help students to read texts critically and therefore understand them more fully. Moreover, showing the relations between different cultural productions will enable students to appreciate their rhetorical and contextual subtleties. Finally, this approach will expand the students' own dialogue with works of art, which enhances their aesthetic and intellectual experience and, as Elliott Eisner writes, helps them catch as many fish as possible with the best possible nets (49).

NOTES

[1] I cite the story in Paredes Núñez's edition of Pardo Bazán, *Cuentos completos*, 1: 122–27.

[2] Later paintings, like *La carga* (1902; "The Load"), by Ramón Casas, have the same approach toward the lower classes as in "El indulto." In *La carga*, the lower classes are not made up of individualized persons but are presented as a mass proletariat that protests poor working conditions in factories.

[3] In his book about popular Valencian sayings, José Soler Carnicer states that the title of the painting refers to the pronouncement by the grandmother of a dead sailor at the end of Vicente Blasco Ibáñez's novel *Flor de Mayo* (1895): "¡Que viniesen allí todas las zorras que regateaban al comprar en la Pescadería! ¿Aún les parecía caro el pescado? ¡A duro debía costar la libra!" ("All the bitches who used to bargain every time they bought in the fish shop should go there! Did they really think that the fish was expensive? A pound should cost five cents!"; qtd. in Carnicer 61–62). W. J. T. Mitchell's short article "Word and Image" can help students understand the interaction of words and images.

[4] Translations are my own.

Teaching Pardo Bazán's Travel Writing

Javier Torre

If I could choose a profession, or better, a perpetual
task, this is what I would be: a relentless traveler
throughout Spain. I wouldn't go to the pagodas in India,
I wouldn't traverse the Russian steppe, I wouldn't jog
through Constantinopolis and the Bosphorus. I'm more
interested in Spain than in the rest of the world, for each
corner of Spain is a world in itself.

—Pardo Bazán, *Viajes por España*

Emilia Pardo Bazán penned numerous travel accounts that were widely read
in her lifetime. Between 1873 and 1902 she traveled extensively through Spain
and parts of Europe and wrote about her travels, offering a fresh perspective on
a myriad of social, political, artistic, cultural, and religious matters. Her travel
accounts were first published in magazines such as *El imparcial, Nuevo teatro
crítico*, and *La ilustración artística* and later as books titled *De mi tierra* (1888;
"About My Land"), *Mi romería* (1888; "My Pilgrimage"), *Al pie de la Torre Eiffel* (1889; "At the Foot of the Eiffel Tower"), *Por Francia y por Alemania* (1889;
"Through France and Germany"), *Cuarenta días en la exposición* (1900; "Forty
Days in the Exhibition"), *Por la España pintoresca* (1896; "Through Picturesque
Spain"), and *Por la Europa católica* (1902; "Through Catholic Europe"). Her
travel writing is entertaining, descriptive, reflective, and, overall, a fundamental
way to understand the society of her times as well as her opinions—expressed
in passing or through long digressions—on numerous topics. It is certainly surprising that these travel accounts were only rescued for contemporary Spanish
readers with the edition by Tonina Paba published in 2006 (Pardo Bazán, *Viajes
por España* and *Viajes por Europa*), from which I quote in this essay.

In my advanced undergraduate literature class, Travel Narratives, I teach
some of the more emblematic travel accounts by Pardo Bazán. I have taught
this class in Spanish for Spanish majors and in English as a first-year seminar.[1]
In both classes I offer an overview of the evolution of travel narratives written by Spaniards and by foreigners who traveled to Spain, discussing different
styles and trends in travel writing published in the nineteenth and twentieth
centuries. My goals are for students to learn from first-person accounts what
traveling through Spain must have been like a century or more ago and compare
it to the experience that some students have had studying abroad in Spain; to
learn about Spain's social situation at the turn of the twentieth century and the
intellectual debates in which Pardo Bazán actively participated; and to develop
the critical skills necessary to recognize and analyze cultural stereotypes in the
writings of foreign travelers in Spain and those of Spanish writers in the nineteenth century.

Our first readings are mostly from Romantic writers who imprinted in their writings strongly subjective interpretations of the places they visited. During the nineteenth century, Spain was an exotic destination for French (Prosper Mérimée, Théophile Gautier, Alexandre Dumas, Victor Hugo), British (George Borrow), American (Washington Irving), and Argentine writers (Domingo Faustino Sarmiento). I contrast their orientalized and stereotyped images—in his preface to *Les orientales* Victor Hugo writes that "l'Espagne c'est encore l'Orient; l'Espagne est à demi africaine, l'Afrique est à demi asiatique" (88; "Spain is still the Orient; Spain is half African, Africa is half Asian")—with subsequent travel writing accounts produced by Spaniards, whose depictions of Spain take different paths. I distinguish themes in travel writing and essays written by Spaniards that differ from those written by foreigners: mainly the rejection of the stereotyped and simplified view of their country but also the acknowledgment of problems in the industry, economy, and social mores of Spain, particularly after the crisis of 1898, as in writings by Miguel de Unamuno, Ángel Ganivet, and José Martínez Ruiz (Azorín). We finish up the quarter by reading travel literature produced decades later during Francisco Franco's dictatorship (1939–75).

The course also offers an overview of the historical, political, and economic evolution of the country and how local and foreign travelers have reflected on these changes and on the essence of Spanish identity over time. Pardo Bazán is a fundamental figure in the structure of the course. Her travel writing encapsulates, often in a few pages, the anxieties, frustrations, and expectations of the Spanish intellectuals of her time.

How to Read a Travel Book

In this course I train students to read travel books as fiction. Travel writing is textually constructed as an artifact: the travel writer selects landscapes to describe, puts circumstances in a specific order, emphasizes feelings, and delineates with precision certain characters while eliminating others, all for the purpose of expressing a specific perception of the place visited.

I provide students with a list of questions with which they can critically approach any travel account that attempts to portray the people, culture, and life in a given place. Some of the questions are structural—Are there flashbacks, flash-forwards? Is the third or the first person used? What is the narrative structure? Is the work a letter, a personal journal, an article for the press?— but I'm more interested in questions of cultural identity and perceptions of the other. My questions include the following:

> How do travelers characterize themselves? Do they describe themselves physically, ideologically? For what purpose? What is the reason for their trip?
>
> How do travelers portray other travelers and tourists? Do they identify themselves with others or distinguish themselves from them? Why?

How are the locals portrayed? Do travelers distinguish the individual personalities of local characters or are these characters taken as representative of their group? Do travelers show empathy or disdain toward them? Does the local other have a voice in the narration?

What mode of transportation do travelers use? Do travelers reflect on the advantages of one mode of transportation over others? What are the ideological implications of using any particular mode of transportation?

What is the landscape like? Do travelers link the landscape to the character of the inhabitants? Are there traces of environmental determinism in this linkage?

With what different racial, ethnic, or cultural groups do travelers identify? Do they establish, either openly or tacitly, any sort of hierarchies? If so, where is their group located within this hierarchy?

Do travelers comment on gender differences or describe the situation of women? Do travelers sympathize with women?

Do travelers use dichotomies—past/present, rural/urban, old/young, lazy/active—to compare the local culture with their own culture? Why?

Do travelers mention other books or travelers? What is the relation between the texts? Do travelers subscribe to what previous authors wrote, follow their path, or offer a different perspective?

These questions are aimed at increasing students' critical-thinking skills and their ability to reflect on cultural interactions.

Romantic Travelers in Spain

Before reading Pardo Bazán's travel writing, students read selected passages from Washington Irving's *Tales of the Alhambra* (1829)—in particular the chapters "El viaje," "La habitación del autor," "El balcón," and "La Alhambra a la luz de la luna"—that perfectly represent how the tendency to exoticize and orientalize Spain was encumbered in the fragrance of noble savagery and romance. We study paragraphs such as this one: "Give a Spaniard the shade in summer, and the sun in winter; a little bread, garlic, oil, and garbances, an old brown cloak and a guitar, and let the world roll on as it pleases" (86). This and similar descriptions have been analyzed by Pere Gifra Adroher.

As a counterpoint, we read *Viajes por Europa, Africa y América* (1847; "Travels through Europe, Africa, and America") by the Argentinean writer Domingo Faustino Sarmiento, who, rejecting the Romantic paradigm for interpreting Spain, depicts a gloomy image of a backward country paralyzed by ignorance and brutal primitivism: "[noto] la falta de todo accidente que indique el menor cambio debido a los progresos de las artes o las ciencias modernas. Opino porque se colonice la España" ("[I notice] the lack of any signal indicating change due to advances in the modern arts and sciences. I believe Spain must be colonized"; 166).[2]

Students also watch all or part of the opera *Carmen* by Georges Bizet to better understand the stereotype of the sensuous, exotic, and passionate Spanish woman, which José Colmeiro has analyzed. Students are presented with more examples of the Romantic literary construction of Spain as a preindustrial, rural, and exotic society populated by temperamental and picturesque people by reading some of the most inflammatory quotations and clichéd descriptions of Spain by well-known Romantic writers, like the statement usually attributed to Alexandre Dumas that Africa begins in the Pyrenees. We also analyze some orientalist paintings by Eugène Delacroix and Théodore Géricault on Spanish topics so that students have the opportunity to comment on these cultural texts.

Pardo Bazán's Travel Writing

Students are now well prepared to read Pardo Bazán within the relevant cultural and literary contexts. The author offers critical, sometimes poignant comments on social and cultural norms of the places she visits. She pays special attention to literature, art, and landscapes. She provides moving descriptions of certain regions, including her native Galicia in northern Spain, a region whose landscape contrasts with the aridity of southern Spain. She travels all over Spain, visiting remote rural churches and chapels with the intention of describing these artistic treasures for her readers. Her travel writing contains many intertextual references, as she frequently refers to other writers who are associated with a particular location. Nevertheless, as much as she is drawn to highbrow matters of art and culture, she is also interested in industry, economy, and development. In that sense she is a visionary with a practical view. She writes during an early stage of the growth of tourism in Spain, and she is committed to improving travel opportunities for the benefit of Spaniards and foreign tourists alike. She doesn't shy away from recommending improvements to the nascent tourist industry and to the poor service provided by many lodges: a good hotel is simply one without bedbugs. One of her other basic demands is that trains arrive on time. Students get a sense of what it was like to travel through Spain a hundred years ago and many can compare these experiences to traveling in Spain today. A valuable writing exercise for students who have already visited Spain is to compare their experience to Pardo Bazán's. For this class I consistently use one of Pardo Bazán's travel essays, "El viaje por España" ("Traveling through Spain"; *Viajes por España* 141–61) and a selection of readings from her book *Por la Europa católica* (*Viajes por Europa* 587–667), which synthesize her position on matters such as reasons for traveling, tourism, the image of Spain, and the so-called problem of Spain.

"El viaje por España" (1895)

"El viaje por España," published in *La España moderna* in 1895, is a twenty-page essay that reflects on the value as well as the inconveniences of traveling through Spain. It is dedicated "a los extranjeros que acometen la empresa de recorrer nuestra patria, sin arrendrarse ante las contradictorias y tal vez alarmantes noticias esparcidas en los relatos de los exploradores que ya dieron felice cima a la hazaña" ("to the foreign travelers who decide to travel through Spain, not getting intimidated by the contradictory and even scary news spread by the travel accounts of previous explorers"; *Viajes por España* 141).

Pardo Bazán is faced with a challenge: on the one hand, the essay necessarily has to agree with some of the criticism of Spanish culture (lack of initiative, slowness, poor hygiene and even worse service in some hotels and trains) because she feels it her duty to denounce these failures as a way to potentially improve society; on the other hand, she wishes to defend Spain from some of those attacks, arguing that Spain's extraordinary diversity and industry cannot be reduced to a handful of clichés, and certainly not to those that regularly defined southern Spain. She argues that Spaniards' response to progress changes from place to place and that it's a common mistake of foreign visitors to generalize and simplify.

Through guided questions, class conversation, and writing assignments on this essay, students learn to recognize the following:

> The dialogue with and intertextual references to Romantic travelers in Spain and also to Spanish texts (such as *Don Quijote*).
>
> Foreign stereotypes about Spain (the slower pace in Andalucía and other areas, which Pardo Bazán dismisses by defending northern Spain's industrial activity, particularly in Catalonia and Biscay).
>
> Pardo Bazán's own racial and national prejudices against Jews and North Africans: "Cuando España recuenta sus cualidades y sus defectos, propendo . . . a atribuir las primeras a la sangre ibera y eúskara, y los segundos a la semítica y beréber" ("When Spain lists its qualities and its defects I tend to attribute . . . the qualities to its Iberian and Basque blood, and the defects to its Semitic and Berber blood line"; *Viajes por España* 159). (In a graduate class, this could be linked directly to the intellectual dispute between the historians Américo Castro and Claudio Sánchez Albornoz about the three cultures of Spain [Surtz et al.]). Her prejudices against other countries, such as Portugal, Romania, Greece, and Turkey, should also be noted (141).
>
> What is praised as good and functional in Spain, what can and should be defended. Pardo Bazán defends traveling in Spain as safe for women, particularly in rural Spain, where hospitality and courtesy are much more alive than in the large cities.
>
> Pardo Bazán's recommendations for improving Spain's tourism infrastructure (trains, hotels, meals, etc.).
>
> Pardo Bazán's advocacy for modes of transportation other than trains, which could make possible travel to remote towns with rich historical and artistic legacies.

Por la Europa católica *(1902)*

The second travel account by Pardo Bazán that I use in my class comes from her book *Por la Europa católica* (1902). She travels to Belgium "movida por el deseo de ver cómo funcionaba una nación donde los católicos ocupan el poder desde hace diecisiete años . . . una nación que figura entre las más adelantadas, y que es católica, al menos en gran parte, con un catolicismo activo, coherente, vivaz, sin letras muertas" ("moved by the desire to see how a nation where Catholics have been in power for the last seventeen years works . . . a nation that is located among the most modern and still is Catholic, at least in part, with an active, coherent and vivacious Catholicism"; *Viajes por Europa* 589).

Why does Pardo Bazán posit the incompatibility of Catholicism and modernity? Perhaps because Spain's decay as a nation was attributed to its fanatical defense of Catholic orthodoxy, which was believed to produce the obscurantism, ignorance, and backwardness described in the most critical Romantic narratives. Her trip to Belgium aims to prove that Catholicism and modernity were not antagonistic. She sees industrialized, modern, and Catholic Belgium as a model for Spain.

If "El viaje por España" dialogues with Romantic foreign travelers in Spain, this essay dialogues with her fellow Spaniards—particularly with the intellectuals associated with the *Regeneracionismo* ("Regenerationism") movement and the Institución Libre de Enseñanza, a movement dedicated to educational reform—from Ramón de Mesonero Romanos, Rafael Altamira, and Julian Sainz del Río to Unamuno, Pío Baroja, Ganivet, and Azorín. But how could Spain become modern and European? Pardo Bazán tries to answer that question on her European quest. In class we read the chapters titled "Desde el tren" and "Hacia la frontera" (*Viajes por Europa* 591–94, 595–98), the second of which opens with an emphatic and highly emblematic command: "¡Europeicémonos!" ("Let's become Europeans!"; 595).

I make a point to contrast Spaniards traveling abroad with foreigners traveling to Spain. While European Romantic writers, who came mostly from industrialized European centers, traveled to Spain in search of oriental ruins with medieval flavor, inhospitable landscapes, rural characters, and picturesque *casticismo* ("authenticity"), Spanish writers searched in Europe for modern, industrial, successful models for their plans to revive their country. In this class we read Pardo Bazán's article in this key. Students also read selected travel essays by Pardo Bazán's Spanish contemporaries, such as the introduction of Mesonero Romanos's *Escenas y tipos matritenses* ("Street Scenes and Typical People of Madrid"), Ganivet's *Cartas finlandesas* ("Letters from Finland"; in particular the chapter on women), and Azorín's *Los pueblos* ("The Villages"; especially the essays "El hidalgo" ["The Hidalgo"], "La decadencia" ["Decadence"], "Los ferrocarriles" ["The Trains"], and "Ventas, posadas y Fondas" ["Hotels, Hostels, and Guest Houses"]). My aim is for students, by answering the guiding questions listed at the beginning of this essay, to recognize Pardo Bazán's adscription to the mentioned group of writers. For example, she relies on the typical fin de siècle tendency to refer to Spain's problems in medical terms: "Tomadle el pulso a España—ahora parece que lo ha recobrado, que pulso hay, aunque desatento y febril" ("Take the pulse of Spain—it now seems like it has recovered it, although it is irregular and feverish"; *Viajes por Europa* 596).

Several other travel writings by Pardo Bazán make excellent readings for students. In "Francia! Aquel París" ("France! That Paris"; *Viajes por Europa* 133–45), she offers interesting comparisons between Spain and France that allow students to see what France meant for the Spanish imaginary of the time. "Diversiones; gente rara" ("Diversions; Weird People"; *Viajes por Europa* 385–97) is one of several articles in which she describes her visit to the 1889 World Exposition in Paris. It includes prejudiced descriptions of people and races from other continents. She also offers interesting opinions about the United States, with reflections on characters such as Buffalo Bill, whom she compares to El Cid Campeador. "Notitas portuguesas" ("Portuguese Notes"; *Viajes por Europa* 661–67) deals with cultural differences and similarities between Portugal and Spain. In "Castilla: Fondas y posadas" ("Castile: Guest Houses and Inns"; *Viajes por España* 319–22) she criticizes the poor quality of hotels and service in Madrid. She describes different types of travels and travelers and lists the traits of a good traveler. Finally, "Las chinches; Viajar en automóvil" ("Bedbugs; Traveling by Car"; *Viajes por España* 415–22), written in 1915, is one of Pardo Bazán's last travel essays. The author reflects upon the advantages of traveling in Spain by car, a new invention at the time, and offers recommendations for improving tourism in Spain.

By reading Pardo Bazán's travel writing students get an understanding of the challenges faced by Spain at the turn of the twentieth century. Furthermore, students comprehend how the aesthetic and ideological frames employed by foreign and local travelers filter their perceptions and generate startlingly different views of Spain. Pardo Bazán is usually studied as a feminist who also introduced the naturalist movement to the Spanish literary public in the late nineteenth century. The readings for my class reframe the Galician author as an intellectual of the twentieth century who was completely engaged in contemporary discussions about Spanish identity and the future of the nation.

NOTES

[1] Pardo Bazán's travel writing has not been published in English. For my class I use an unpublished translation by Professor Lee Chambers. Jennifer J. Wood's book on Spanish women travelers includes a chapter on Pardo Bazán's travel writing and translates several fragments.

[2] Translations are my own.

Teaching Cultural Difference through Translation: Pardo Bazán's *Insolación*

Jennifer Smith

To help students overcome their initial reluctance to read a nineteenth-century text, I suggest they approach the work as a search for answers to questions personally relevant to them. In teaching the works of Emilia Pardo Bazán, for example, I have found that her concern with gender issues speaks to many students, no matter their linguistic or cultural background. Yet I also stress that an informed reading involves appreciating how the text differs from their lives and experiences. For this reason I encourage them to look for elements of the text they identify with as well as for those that are foreign to them. While studying the historical context of a work and the biography of its author can foster understanding of such cultural differences between a text and a reader's own experience, I have found that asking students to translate specific passages that are less accessible to them can effectively highlight details that otherwise may be overlooked. My own experience bears this out: not until I had to grapple with translating certain passages from *Insolación* (1889; "Sunstroke") did I realize not only how difficult they were for me to render into English but also how much of the text's richness I had missed by glossing over certain cultural and linguistic elements. Based on this realization and the benefits I gained from the process, I now have my students translate passages of *Insolación* into English in a class on Spanish realism and naturalism that combines undergraduate and graduate students. My students are a mix of native English speakers from the United States and native Spanish speakers from Latin America. For all my students, Pardo Bazán's work is foreign temporally, culturally, and, to greater or lesser degrees, linguistically.

For translation exercises I choose passages that deal with issues of social class, regional identities, and ethnicities, since they are inextricably tied to the time and place of the work, not readily comprehended by students, consistently represented across Pardo Bazán's works, and currently studied by contemporary critics.[1] Before considering how to translate specific passages, we discuss some of the ways translation can elucidate cultural difference. I begin by introducing students to the concepts of domestication and foreignization from Lawrence Venuti's book *The Translator's Invisibility: A History of Translation*. Domestication aims to make a text conform to the target language and the target culture, whereas foreignization seeks to underscore the temporal and cultural differences between the source text and the translation (15). I give some examples of domestication—the decision to have African Americans speak with Cuban accents in the Spanish dubbing of the film *Gone with the Wind* (Gubern and Vernon 378) and John Rutherford's decision to translate *cocido* as "chick-pea stew" in his translation of *La Regenta* ("The Regent's Wife") (Rutherford 165–66).

Examples of foreignization include the retention of certain features or words of the Spanish language. Rutherford, for example, explains that he tried to preserve the unique linguistic and cultural references of *La Regenta* by retaining the Spanish names of characters, streets, and places; Leopoldo Alas's use of the historical past tense (common in Spanish but unusual in English); as well as the author's somewhat convoluted syntax (166–67). Discussing such interpretive decisions makes students more aware of how their translations could either emphasize the foreignness of the text or appropriate the text into their own culture. I tell them that while domestication is the more common translation practice, as most readers prefer to have the unfamiliar made familiar to make the reading easier, Venuti denounces domestication as a form of violence that erases the unique culture of the original work (14).

Following the discussion of approaches to translation, I introduce the historical context of the novel. *Insolación*, like many of Pardo Bazán's novels and short stories, is populated with characters from a variety of socioeconomic, regional, and ethnic backgrounds, and markers of these categories are inscribed in the language the characters speak. I begin with a discussion of social class in Spain at the end of the nineteenth century, stressing that despite the progressive dismantling of the old regime, mainly through the disentailment of Church and aristocratic lands (Carr, "Liberalism" 208–09), Spain lagged behind other European nations in terms of industrialization (Bahamonde and Martínez 471). While this meant that Spain remained primarily an agricultural society, the aristocracy now had to share power with a small but growing middle class (455–56). This situation is reflected in *Insolación*: while the lower middle class is almost completely absent, the ruling class comprises titled aristocracy (the protagonist, Asís de Taboada, Marchioness de Andrade; the Duchess of Sahagún), untitled aristocracy (Gabriel Pardo de la Lage), and a member of the upper bourgeoisie (Diego Pacheco). Because the novel has an urban setting, the lower classes are represented not by rural peasantry but by *chulos* (working-class people of eighteenth- and nineteenth-century Madrid), *cigarreras* (tobacco workers), domestic help, and gypsies.

Chulos are typical of Madrid and represent the idea of cultural authenticity, of the real Spain. They are defined largely by social class and are signaled in the novel by their attire and speech. Showing students images of *chulos* and their characteristic dress is helpful, as Pardo Bazán's conception of a *chulo* is foreign to most students who are not from Spain. Joaquina Balmaseda's "La chula madrileña" and Pardo Bazán's sketch of the *chula* in "La mujer española" (108–11), although stereotypical portrayals, are useful for understanding what the *chula* represented in the cultural imagination of the time. Since the *chulos* do not speak for themselves in *Insolación* as much as the *cigarreras* and gypsies do, there are only a few passages to work with: the scene where the *chulos* yell out *piropos* (catcalls) to Asís in front of the Cibeles fountain, the brief scene where Pacheco asks a *chulo* on the street for the whereabouts of a restaurant, and the scene where a *chula* enters the *merendero* (open-air restaurant) at the fair to try to sell the couple flowers (41, 55–56, 63–64). In the first example students can contrast the *chulos'* speech with that of Asís, who narrates this section; in the other two examples students could try their hand at representing the character of the Andalusian Pacheco who, although a gentleman, speaks with a regional dialect.

The *cigarreras* can be treated similarly. While *chulos* are specifically associated with Madrid, the *cigarrera* figure transcends regions. Many *chulas* also worked as *cigarreras* (Balmaseda 261), but the *cigarrera* was by no means unique to Madrid. The Spanish government nationalized tobacco manufacturing in the late eighteenth century, and by 1914 there were ten national tobacco factories in Spain, the first and most famous being the one in Seville (Shubert 39–40).[2] The overwhelming majority of tobacco factory workers were women, and the *cigarreras* became famous for their outspokenness, flirtatiousness, and political activism (O'Connor 152–53), a stereotype that was most famously popularized in Prosper Merimée's *Carmen* (1845) and later, in 1875, in Henri Meilhac and Georges Bizet's operatic adaptation of Merimée's work of the same name (Shubert 39–40). I point out to students that in Merimée and in the opera Carmen is both a gypsy and a *cigarrera*. The *cigarrera*, because she might also be a *chula* and a gypsy, was a figure who crossed ethnic and socioeconomic categories. Like *chulos*, *cigarreras* are defined by their thick accents and uncouth yet spontaneous and quaint behavior. Contemporary illustrations and photographs as well as Pardo Bazán's sketch of the *cigarrera* ("La cigarrera") can help students visualize these women. Students work with the scenes where the *cigarreras* comment on Diego and Asís soon after their arrival at the *fonda* in Las Ventas, the scene where la señá Donata asks Diego to help get one of her granddaughters a job at the factory, and the scene where the *cigarreras* watch Pacheco and Asís leave, speculating on their relationship (139–50).

Students also work with the scenes in chapters five and six in which gypsy characters are presented. There is a lengthy passage with the first gypsy fortune-teller and another with the *gitanilla* (little gypsy girl) who places a curse on the waitress who chases her away. I give students additional background about the Spanish Roma. Drawing largely on Lou Charnon-Deutsch's book *The Spanish Gypsy: A History of a European Obsession* (2004), I explain that in Pardo Bazán's time, although linguistic evidence had already linked the origins of the Roma to India, many in Spain continued to insist on their Egyptian origins (7–9). Indeed, in *Insolación* the intra- and homodiegetic narrator refers to the gypsy women as "egipcias" (Egyptian women) (*Insolación* 60).[3] I also discuss the contradictory portrayals of gypsies at the time as both Romantic symbols of nonconformity, passion, and nature and as the poor, uncivilized other, naturally inclined toward theft and trickery.

I structure these activities by dividing the class into groups and assigning the same passage to each group. The class uses my edition of the book, which includes English glosses of particularly difficult words and phrases. I remind students that if they choose a foreignized translation, footnotes might be necessary to explain unknown terms. For a domesticated translation, students might want to consider what social stereotypes in American culture, from the late nineteenth century or the present, could represent a cultural equivalent for certain characters. Students also must decide how these characters will speak: for example, will their accents be transcribed phonetically, as Pardo Bazán did? I give examples of what a domesticated translation might look like: for the *chula*, perhaps a woman in a pink-collar profession such as waitressing or a blue-collar profession such as manufacturing; for Pacheco, a Southern gentleman; and for Asís, a woman with a British accent.

After the groups produce their translations, they share them with the class and we compare them with both the original Spanish and with Amparo Loring's 1907 translation, *Midsummer Madness*.[4] The following examples, from the scene of the violent exchange between the *gitanilla* and the waitress at the *merendero* (*Insolación* 67; *Midsummer Madness* 57–58), are useful points of comparison for the class to discuss:

> "¿Hase visto hato de pindongas?" ("How dare you come here, you gad-about baggage?")
>
> "¿No dejarán comer en paz a las personas decentes?" ("Can't decent folks eat their victuals in peace?")
>
> "¿Conque las barre uno por un lado y se cuelan por otro? ¿Y cómo habrá entrado aquí semejante calamidá, digo yo?" ("Snakes nest of gypsies! Sweep one away, and another drops on your head. How did this abomination get in, I wonder?")
>
> "Pues si no te largas más pronto que la luz, bofetá como la que te arrimo no la has visto tú en tu vía" ("Make tracks like lightning, or you'll get such a crack as you never felt in all your life!").
>
> "Te doy un recorrío al cuerpo, que no te queda lengua pa contarlo" ("I'll dress you down so that you'll have no tongue left to tell of it!")
>
> La chiquilla huyó más lista que un cohete; pero no habrían transcurrido dos segundos, cuando vimos entreabrirse la lona que nos protegía las espaldas, y por la rendija del lienzo asomó una jeta que parecía la del mismo enemigo, unos dientes que rechinaban, un puño cerrado, negro como una bola de bronce, y la gitanilla berreó. . . . (The gypsy darted off like a rocket. But two seconds later the canvas behind me parted, and we saw a foaming mouth, bristling with sharp teeth, and a bronzed fist which the gypsy shook as she bellowed. . . .)
>
> "Arrastrá, condená, tía cochina, que malos retortijones te arranquen las tripas, y malos mengues te jagan picaíllo e los jígados, y malas culebras te piquen, y remardita tiña te pegue con er moño pa que te quedes pelá como tu ifunta agüela. . . ." ("Jade! Castaway! She-devil!" [We are obliged to soften the language.] "May poisonous adders sting you! May your hair drop out till you are as bald as your carrion grandmother!")

Next, I pose the following questions to prompt the students to analyze their own and Loring's translations:

> How did you and Loring translate colloquial words and passages?
>
> How did you approach archaic usages (e.g., *hase*) and phonetic transcriptions of character dialects?
>
> Do the translations feel Spanish or American?
>
> Do the translations sound contemporary or from the turn of the century?
>
> What aspects of Loring's translation make it sound foreign to a present-day American reader?
>
> Where did you and Loring change the syntax or sentence order? Why and to what effect?
>
> Where did you and Loring eliminate words or sentences? Why and to what effect?
>
> How is Loring's translation different from your own?
>
> What works well and what does not work well in your and Loring's translations?

It's also interesting for the class to discuss Loring's translation of the title — *Midsummer Madness* for *Insolación* — and the replacement of Pardo Bazán's dedication to José Lázaro Galdiano with the translator's dedication to the Marquis of Casa-Loring.

Another aspect of this exercise is translating cultural phenomena that are particular to the late nineteenth century. Among many possibilities in the novel, three make especially good examples: *sainete*, Abanico, and Worth. A *sainete* is a short, comic, one-act play featuring characters from the lower classes. This entertainment was initially staged between the acts of longer plays and, in the late nineteenth century, in combination with other one-act plays in the so-called *teatros por horas* (theater by the hour). The *sainete* brings to mind a certain representation of an authentic yet farcical Spain that the popular classes represent — such a representation is an important theme in the novel. Loring translates "sainete de don Ramón de la Cruz" (38) as a "burlesque by Ramón de la Cruz" (18) and "más divertida que en un sainete" (64) as "all this entertained me more than a play" (55). For each instance, I ask students what Loring's translation preserves from the original, what is lost, and how they would translate the passage. The second example, Abanico, is mentioned by the waitress who calls the gypsies thieves after the second gyspy woman leaves the *merendero*: "Y está la romería plagada de estas tunantas, embusteronas. Lástima de Abanico" (63). Abanico is a reference to Madrid's Cárcel Modelo, the main prison in the capital during the late nineteenth and early twentieth centuries. Modeled on Jeremy Bentham's Panopticon, it acquired its nickname because it was shaped like a fan (*abanico*).[5] Loring omits any reference to the prison and translates this passage as "The Fair is overrun with that kind of vermin, more's the pity" (53). Students can be asked to discuss what is lost by the translation's omission of this specificity. Finally, the novel makes a reference to the famous nineteenth-century English tailor Charles Frederick Worth (85), the so-called father of haute couture. Worth was well known in Loring's day, so Loring simply maintains the original (80). The reference, however, would be lost on many readers today. Students can be asked how they would translate this—would they substitute something more contemporary like Versace?

Returning to Venuti's argument that the domestication approach to translation is a form of linguistic and cultural violence, my final question asks students how much of the original culture and language was lost in their translations and why these elements were sacrificed. Building on Walter Benjamin's assertion that the "basic error" of the translator "is that he preserves the state in which his own language happens to be instead of allowing his language to be powerfully affected by the foreign tongue" (82), I conclude by encouraging students to think about how preserving the foreign elements of *Insolación* could add to the richness of the English language and English-speaking cultures.

NOTES

I would like to express my gratitude to Joyce Tolliver, who took the time to brainstorm with me and generously shared her translation-theory materials. References to *Insolación* refer to my 2011 edition.

[1] Recent studies on *Insolación* have focused largely on questions of national identity, social class, and race. See Amann; Heneghan, "Fashion"; Pereira-Muro, "Parecía"; Smith, "Cultural Capital"; Smith, "Gypsy's Curse"; Tsuchiya, *Marginal Subjects* 136–61.

[2] The factory in Madrid opened in 1809 under the rule of Joseph Bonaparte and employed between 3,000 and 5,000 people, almost all of whom were women (Vallejo Fernández Cela 137), while the factory in A Coruña, Galicia, which Pardo Bazán visited to do research for her novel *La Tribuna*, opened in 1804 and by 1886 was employing between 3,500 and 4,000 women (Aira).

[3] See also Pardo Bazán's short story "Maldición gitana" ("Gypsy Curse"; *Cuentos completos* 1: 318–21).

[4] As far as I have been able to ascertain, this is the only English translation of *Insolación*.

[5] See the note by Ermitas Penas Varela in the 2001 Cátedra edition of *Insolación* (128n49).

NOTES ON CONTRIBUTORS

Maryellen Bieder is professor emerita of Spanish at Indiana University, Bloomington. She has written extensively on Pardo Bazán and Concepción Gimeno de Flaquer as well as on Carmen de Burgos. Her current research is on women's networks, including Pardo Bazán's literary friendships. Previously she published widely on contemporary Spanish- and Catalan-language writers, including Juan Goytisolo, Mercè Rodoreda, Manuel Vázquez Montalbán, Carme Riera, and Marina Mayoral. She has edited, with Roberta Johnson, *Spanish Women Writers and Spain's Civil War* and coedited the nineteenth-century chapter of *A New History of Iberian Feminisms*. She also published *Narrative Perspective in the Post–Civil War Novels of Francisco Ayala*.

Alicia Cerezo is assistant professor at the University of Wisconsin, Madison. She teaches nineteenth- and twentieth-century Peninsular literature and culture. She has published articles on the visual and textual representations of women in illustrated periodicals, sketches of everyday life, and turn-of-the-century novels; on spiritualism; on *costumbrismo*, including its manifestations in contemporary television; and on silent film. Her publications have appeared in *Revista de estudios hispánicos, Letras femeninas, Journal of Spanish Cultural Studies, Decimonónica, Journal of Hispanic Modernism*, and *Hispanófila*. She edited, with Ryan Davis, *Modernity and Epistemology in Nineteenth-Century Spain: Fringe Discourses*. She is also the author of *Cada espíritu es un libro: Espiritismo, ciencia y sociedad en el fin de siglo*.

Lou Charnon-Deutsch is professor emerita of Hispanic languages and literature at Stony Brook University. She specializes in nineteenth-century Spanish narrative and visual culture. Her books include *Hold That Pose: Visual Culture in the Nineteenth Century Spanish Press, The Spanish Gypsy: A History of a European Obsession, Fictions of the Feminine in the Nineteenth-Century Spanish Press, Narratives of Desire: Nineteenth-Century Spanish Fiction by Women, Culture and Gender in Nineteenth-Century Spain* (edited with Jo Labanyi), and *Gender and Representation: Women in Spanish Realist Fiction*. She has served on the editorial boards of *Hispanic Research Journal, Letras femeninas, Revista de estudios hispánicos, Journal of Spanish Cultural Studies, Decimonónica*, and *La Tribuna*.

Isabel Clúa is lecturer in the Department of Spanish and Latin American Literature at the Universidad de Sevilla, where she teaches Spanish literature and cultural studies. She is a member of the research group Creació i pensament de les dones and reseacher at the Centre Dona i Literatura, both at the Universitat de Barcelona. Her work focuses on mechanisms of gender construction and identity in European fin de siècle culture; she also investigates contemporary popular culture from the perspective of feminist cultural studies. Since 2011 she is codirector of the peer-reviewed journal *Lectora: Revista de dones i textualitat*.

Denise DuPont is professor of Spanish in the Department of World Languages and Literatures at Southern Methodist University. She is a specialist in nineteenth-century Spanish literature and the author of *Writing Teresa: The Saint from Ávila at the fin-de-siglo* and *Realism as Resistance: Romanticism and Authorship in Galdós, Clarín, and*

Baroja. She is completing a Master of Theological Studies degree at the Perkins School of Theology at Southern Methodist University. Her latest book, *Whole Faith: The Catholic Ideal of Emilia Pardo Bazán*, is forthcoming from the Catholic University of America Press.

Zachary Erwin is assistant professor of Spanish at Monmouth College in Illinois. His research focuses primarily on representations of masculinity in nineteenth-century Spanish realism, especially in Pardo Bazán's novels. His other interests include late-twentieth-century Spanish narrative and poetry; Galician language, literature, and culture; and nineteenth-century Spanish theater. Before joining the faculty at Monmouth College, Zachary held visiting positions at Swarthmore College and the University of Texas, Austin. He earned his BA in Spanish from Emory University and his MA and PhD in Romance studies from Duke University.

Hazel Gold, associate professor of Spanish at Emory University, is the author of *The Reframing of Realism: Galdós and the Discourses of Nineteenth-Century Realism*; chapters in edited volumes including *Intertextual Pursuits: Literary Mediations in Modern Spanish Narrative* and *La literatura de Emilia Pardo Bazán*; and articles published in *Revista hispánica moderna*, *Hispanic Review*, *Journal of Spanish Cultural Studies*, and *España contemporánea*, among others. She is vice president of the Sociedad de Literatura Española del Siglo XIX and a past president of the Asociación Internacional de Galdosistas and of the Ibero-American Society for Eighteenth-Century Studies. Her current book project examines epistolary discourse and the postal system in the modern Spanish state.

Francisca González Arias received her doctoral degree from Harvard University. Her dissertation highlights Pardo Bazán's intertextual dialogues with Benito Pérez Galdós, Émile Zola, Gustave Flaubert, and the Goncourt brothers. Another area of her research is contemporary Spanish-speaking women writers. In addition to her interest in the field of Galician studies, she specializes in translation studies and has translated into English authors such as Soledad Puértolas and Cristina Rivera Garza. She lives in Cambridge, Massachusetts.

María Luisa Guardiola is professor of Spanish at Swarthmore College. Her research and teaching interests focus on Spanish literature of the last three centuries, with an emphasis on nineteenth- and twentieth-century women writers. She is the author of *La temática de García Gutiérrez: Índice y estudio (la mujer)* and editor of critical editions of Antonio García Gutiérrez's *El trovador* and Juan Valera's *Pepita Jiménez*. Recent articles and book chapters have explored nineteenth-century Spanish and Catalonian literature by Pardo Bazán and Caterina Albert, respectively. She also has worked on the literary production of Carmen Martín Gaite and Carme Riera, among others.

Rebecca Ingram is associate professor of Spanish in the Department of Languages, Cultures, and Literatures and affiliated faculty to the program in women's and gender studies at the University of San Diego. She received her PhD in Romance studies from Duke University. Her research focuses on Peninsular cultural studies, in particular food cultural studies, and examines how prominent writers and intellectuals from the early twentieth century negotiated their anxieties about Spain's modernization through culinary and gastronomical writing. Recent articles have appeared in the *Bulletin of Spanish Studies*, the *Bulletin of Hispanic Studies*, and *Cincinnati Romance Review*.

Susan M. McKenna is associate professor of Spanish at the University of Delaware, where she teaches courses in Spanish language, literature, and culture. She is the author of *Crafting the Female Subject: Narrative Innovation in the Short Fiction of Emilia Pardo Bazán* and of articles on Pardo Bazán, Juan Valera, Benito Pérez Galdós, Sor Juana Inés de la Cruz, and Miguel de Cervantes. Her current research focuses on the American playwright and author Barrie Stavis and his relation to the Spanish Civil War.

Helena Miguélez-Carballeira is senior lecturer in Hispanic studies at Bangor University in the United Kingdom. She is the author of *Galicia, a Sentimental Nation: Gender, Culture, and Politics*, which has been translated into Portuguese. She is the editor of *A Companion to Galician Culture* and has published works on contemporary Spain, women's writing, and translation studies. She directs the Centre for Galician Studies in Wales.

Lisa Nalbone is associate professor at the University of Central Florida. Her research focuses on women's writing in late-nineteenth- and twentieth-century Spain. She is the author of *The Novels of Carmen Conde: An Expression of Feminine Subjectivity* and the coeditor of *Intersections of Race, Class, Gender, and Nation in* Fin-de-siècle *Spanish Literature and Culture*. Her research engages with sociocultural representations of femininity in writings of the Civil War and postwar periods. Another research focus is the relation between modernity and gender in late-nineteenth- and early-twentieth-century Spanish literature, in particular social constructs, identity, and political conventions during the transition to modernity. Her current line of inquiry explores censorship in Francoist Spain in relation to late-nineteenth to mid-twentieth-century prose.

Carmen Pereira-Muro is associate professor of Spanish in the Department of Classical and Modern Languages and Literatures at Texas Tech University. She specializes in eighteenth- and nineteenth-century Peninsular literature, with a focus on the interrelated questions of gender and national identity. Her book *Género, nación y literatura: Emilia Pardo Bazán en la literatura gallega y española* studies these issues in the textual production from and around Pardo Bazán. Pereira-Muro has published essays in the areas of eighteenth- and nineteenth-century Peninsular studies, Galician studies, and on the interaction of literature and the arts. She is also the author of *Culturas de España*.

Dale J. Pratt is professor of Spanish and comparative literature at Brigham Young University, where he teaches introductory literature courses as well as graduate seminars on *Don Quixote*, Miguel de Unamuno, Benito Pérez Galdós, Spanish science fiction, and literature and science. He studies Spanish realism, protohumans and posthumans, and the Spanish Golden Age. His publications include *Signs of Science: Literature, Science, and Spanish Modernity since 1868* and articles on Pardo Bazán, Leopoldo Alas's *La Regenta*, the *comedia*, and the narratology of time travel stories. His most current publications include *España poshumana* (with Juan Carlos Martín) and *Los Soñadores: La ficción sobre la prehistoria ibérica y sus autores*.

Íñigo Sánchez-Llama is professor of Spanish at Purdue University. He is the current series editor of Purdue Studies in Romance Literatures (PSRL) and a member of the editorial board of *Siglo diecinueve*. He has published a book on Isabelline women writers; articles in *Hispanic Review, Romance Quarterly, Hispanic Research Journal, Revista de estudios hispánicos, Hispania, Hispanófila, Letras peninsulares, Revista hispánica moderna, Revista canadiense de estudios hispánicos, La Tribuna, Siglo diecinueve,* and

Boletín galego de literatura; and critical editions of Isabelline women's writing, of Benito Pérez Galdós's novels, and of Pardo Bazán's criticism. He is currently working on a book on representations of modernity in Spanish essays between the 1850s and 1931.

Jennifer Smith is associate professor of Spanish at Southern Illinois University, Carbondale. She specializes in late-nineteenth- and early-twentieth-century Spanish literature and culture. Her current research focuses on the role of science and medicine in the construction of female gender identities and how women writers contested scientific determinism by making use of Spain's rich mystical tradition. In addition to a bilingual edition of Pardo Bazán's *Insolación* and a coedited volume titled *Intersections of Race, Class, Gender, and Nation in* Fin-de-siècle *Spanish Literature and Culture,* she has published articles in journals such as *Revista canadiense de estudios hispánicos, Revista de estudios hispánicos,* and *Anales de la literatura española contemporánea.*

Erika M. Sutherland is associate professor of Spanish at Muhlenberg College in Pennsylvania. She received her PhD in Spanish literature from the University of Pennsylvania, with a dissertation on domestic violence in the nineteenth-century novel. Her current research is on the representation of the female body and gender-based violence in literary and medical texts. She is also developing pedagogies for language, culture, and literature courses. She is coeditor of *(Con)textos femeninos,* a forthcoming critical anthology of Spanish women writers.

Joyce Tolliver is a specialist in modern Spanish literature and culture, with a particular focus on discourse and gender. Her books include *Cigar Smoke and Violet Water: Gendered Discourse in the Stories of Emilia Pardo Bazán; "El encaje roto" y otros cuentos; "Torn Lace" and Other Stories;* and *Disciplines on the Line: Feminist Research on Spanish, Latin American, and U.S. Spanish Women.* Her more recent work focuses on Spain and the Philippines at the end of the Spanish empire. She is associate professor of Spanish, affiliate faculty in gender and women's studies and in translation studies, and director of the Center for Translation Studies at the University of Illinois, Urbana-Champaign.

Javier Torre is associate professor of Spanish literature at the University of Denver. He has published numerous articles on Spanish travel narratives in various academic venues. He is the editor of a special issue of the *Nueva revista de literatura* on contemporary Spanish travel writing in the global era. His current project is an annotated edition of the *Journal of the Expedition Domínguez-Escalante,* the eighteenth-century journey of two priests through the American Southwest.

Harriet Turner is the Harold E. Spencer Professor of Modern Languages and Literatures at the University of Nebraska, Lincoln. Her teaching and research focus is on nineteenth-century Spain and comparative studies on the poetics of realism. Her publications include *Galdós, Fortunata y Jacinta; Textos y contextos de Galdós; Toward a Poetics of Realism / Hacia una poética del realism;* and *The Cambridge Companion to the Spanish Novel.* In 2007 she received the Encomienda de la Orden de Isabel la Católica, a knighthood conferred by King Juan Carlos I of Spain, and was inducted as a corresponding member of the Real Academia de Bellas Artes y Ciencias Históricas de Toledo.

Margot Versteeg is professor of Spanish at the University of Kansas. A native of the Netherlands, Versteeg has published numerous articles on nineteenth- and early-twentieth-century literature and culture and is the author of *De fusiladores y morcilleros: El discur-*

so cómico del género chico, 1870–1910 and *Jornaleros de la pluma: Hacia la (re)definición del papel del escritor periodista en la revista Madrid Cómico*. Her recently completed book, *Propuestas para (re)construir una nación: El teatro de Emilia Pardo Bazán*, focuses on Pardo Bazán's theatrical production.

Susan Walter is associate professor in the Department of Languages and Literatures at the University of Denver, where she teaches courses on Spanish literature, film, culture, and language. Her main research interests include nineteenth- and early-twentieth-century Spanish narrative, women's writing, film, narratology, and representations of gender. Her essays have appeared in academic journals including *Decimonónica*, *Letras peninsulares*, *Hispania*, and *Romance Notes*. Her first monograph, *From the Outside Looking In: Narrative Frames and Narrative Spaces in the Short Fiction of Emilia Pardo Bazán*, analyzes the intersections of gender and narrative design in Pardo Bazán's short stories.

Linda M. Willem is the Betty Blades Lofton Professor of Spanish at Butler University, where she received the College of LAS Teaching Excellence Award. She specializes in nineteenth-century Spanish literature and contemporary Spanish film. She is a four-time recipient of National Endowment for the Humanities awards for college teachers and has served two terms as secretary-treasurer of the Asociación Internacional de Galdosistas. Her publications include *Galdós's Segunda Manera*, *Carlos Saura: Interviews*, classroom editions of Spanish literature, and over thirty articles in such venues as *Letras Peninsulares*, *MLN*, *Hispania*, and *Literature/Film Quarterly*. Her current project examines radical twenty-first-century adaptations of nineteenth-century Spanish novels.

SURVEY RESPONDENTS

Debra Andrist, *Sam Houston State University*
José I. Badenes, *Loyola Marymount University*
Maryellen Bieder, *Indiana University, Bloomington*
Christine Blackshaw, *Mount Saint Mary's University*
Walter Borenstein, *State University of New York, New Paltz*
Sara Brenneis, *Amherst College*
Guada M. Cabedo-Timmons, *Western Illinois University*
Alicia Cerezo, *University of Wisconsin, Madison*
Isabel Clúa, *Universidad de Sevilla, Spain*
Maria Dolores Costa, *California State University, Los Angeles*
Ryan Davis, *Illinois State University, Normal*
Kathleen Doyle, *Rhodes College*
Maryjane Dunn, *Henderson State University*
Bárbara P. Esquival-Heinemann, *Winthrop University*
Zachary Erwin, *Monmouth College*
Kathryn Everly, *Syracuse University*
Liana Ewald, *San Diego State University*
Guiomar C. Fages, *Barcelona, Spain*
Álvaro Fernández, *Queens College, City University of New York*
Hazel Gold, *Emory University*
Irene Gómez Castellano, *University of North Carolina, Chapel Hill*
Vicente Gomis-Izquierdo, *Saint Vincent College*
Francisca González Arias, *Boston University*
Olga Guadalupe, *University of Pennsylvania*
Valerie Hegstrom, *Brigham Young University*
Rebecca Ingram, *University of San Diego*
Catherine Jaffe, *Texas State University*
Zoé Jiménez-Corretjer, *University of Puerto Rico, Humacao*
Leslie M. Kaiura, *University of Alabama, Huntsville*
Mary Kempen, *Ohio Northern University*
Travis Landry, *Kenyon College*
Gloria Elsa Li, *Santa Clara University*
Lynne Flora Margolies, *Manchester University*
Ellen Mayock, *Washington and Lee University*
Susan M. McKenna, *University of Delaware*
Eloy E. Merino, *Northern Illinois University*
Stephen Miller, *Texas A&M University*
W. Michael Mudrovic, *Skidmore College*
Sara Muñoz, *Dartmouth College*
Lisa Nalbone, *University of Central Florida*
Paul Nelson, *Louisiana Tech University*
Pepa Novell, *Queen's University, Canada*
Jeffrey Oxford, *University of Wisconsin, Milwaukee*

Mehl A. Penrose, *University of Maryland*
Carmen Pereira-Muro, *Texas Tech University*
José M. Pereiro-Otero, *Temple University*
Pedro Pérez del Solar, *University of Texas, El Paso*
Pamela Phillips, *University of Puerto Rico, Río Piedras*
Randolph Pope, *University of Virginia*
Dale J. Pratt, *Brigham Young University*
Anton Pujol, *University of North Carolina, Charlotte*
Elizabeth Rhodes, *Boston College*
José María Rodríguez García, *Duke University*
Olga Sendra Ferrer, *Swarthmore College*
Sarah Sierra, *Virginia Polytechnic Institute and State University*
Robert Simon, *Kennesaw State University*
Jennifer Smith, *Southern Illinois University, Carbondale*
Elizabeth Smith Rousselle, *Xavier University of Louisiana*
Anda Stefanovici, *Petru Maior University of Tg. Mures, Romania*
Erika M. Sutherland, *Muhlenberg College*
Maureen Tobin Stanley, *University of Minnesota, Duluth*
Harriet Turner, *University of Nebraska, Lincoln*
Linda M. Willem, *Butler University*

WORKS CITED

Acosta, Eva. *Emilia Pardo Bazán: La luz en la batalla: Biografía.* Lumen, 2007.

Aira, María J. "Una tabacalera de prestigio nacional." *La opinión* [A Coruña, Spain], 1 Mar. 2009, www.laopinioncoruna.es/economia/2009/03/01/tabacalera-prestigio-nacional/264717.html.

Alas, Leopoldo (Clarín). *Solos.* 1881. Fernando Fe, 1891.

Aldaraca, Bridget. *El ángel del hogar: Galdós and the Ideology of Domesticity in Spain.* U of North Carolina P, 1991.

———. "El ángel del hogar: The Cult of Domesticity in Nineteenth-Century Spain." *Theory and Practice of Feminist Criticism,* edited by Gabriela Mora and Karen S. Van Hooft, Bilingual Press, 1982, pp. 62–87.

Altamira, Rafael. "El realismo y la literatura contemporánea." *La ilustración ibérica* [Barcelona], vol. 4, no. 189, 14 Aug. 1886, p. 515. *Hemeroteca Digital de la Biblioteca Nacional de España,* hemerotecadigital.bne.es/issue.vm?id=0001344195.

Álvarez Junco, José. *Mater dolorosa: La idea de España en el siglo XIX.* Taurus Ediciones, 2001.

———. "Rural and Urban Popular Cultures." Graham and Labanyi, pp. 82–90.

Álvarez Méndez, Natalia. "La dimensión espacial narrativa: *La Tribuna* de Emilia Pardo Bazán." *La Tribuna: Cadernos de estudios da Casa Museo Emilia Pardo Bazán,* no. 5, 2007, pp. 121–48.

Amago, Samuel. "The Form and Function of Homosocial Desire in *La madre naturaleza.*" *Romance Quarterly,* vol. 48, no. 1, 2001, pp. 54–63.

Amann, Elizabeth. "Nature and Nation in Emilia Pardo Bazán's *Insolación.*" *Bulletin of Spanish Studies,* vol. 85, no. 2, 2008, pp. 175–92.

Amorós, Celia. *La gran diferencia y sus pequeñas consecuencias para las luchas de las mujeres.* Cátedra, 2005.

Anderson, Lara. *Cooking Up the Nation: Spanish Culinary Texts and Culinary Nationalization in the Late Nineteenth and Early Twentieth Century.* Tamesis Books, 2013.

Appadurai, Arjun. "How to Make a National Cuisine: Cookbooks in Contemporary India." *Comparative Studies in Society and History,* vol. 30, no. 1, 1988, pp. 3–24.

Arenal, Concepción. *La mujer del porvenir.* 1869. Edited by Vicente de Santiago Mulas, Castalia, 1993.

Arias, Santa. "Rethinking Space: An Outsider's View of the Spatial Turn." *GeoJournal,* vol. 75, 2010, pp. 29–41.

Armstrong, Nancy. *Fiction in the Age of Photography: The Legacy of British Realism.* Harvard UP, 1999.

Auerbach, Erich. *Mimesis: The Representation of Reality in Western Literature.* Translated by Willard R. Trask, Princeton UP, 1953.

Avakian, Arlene, and Barbara Haber, editors. *From Betty Crocker to Feminist Food Studies: Critical Perspectives on Women and Food*. U of Massachusetts P, 2005.

Badenhausen, Richard. "Fear and Trembling in Literature of the Fantastic: Edgar Allan Poe's 'The Black Cat.'" *Studies in Short Fiction*, vol. 29, no. 4, 1992, pp. 487–98.

Bahamonde, Ángel, and Jesús A. Martínez. *Historia de España, Siglo XIX*. Cátedra, 1994.

Baker, Edward. *Materiales para escribir Madrid: Literatura y espacio urbano de Moratín a Galdós*. Siglo Veintiuno Editores, 1991.

Bakhtin, Mikhail M. *The Dialogic Imagination: Four Essays*. Edited by Michael Holquist, translated by Caryl Emerson and Holquist, U of Texas P, 1981.

———. *Problems of Dostoevsky's Poetics*. Edited and translated by Caryl Emerson, U of Minnesota P, 1984.

Bal, Mieke. "His Master's Eye." *Modernity and the Hegemony of Vision*, edited by David Michael Levin, U of California P, 1993, pp. 379–404.

Balaca, Ricardo. *La cigarrera*. *La ilustración española y americana*, 22 Dec. 1881, p. 304.

Balfour, Sebastian. *The End of the Spanish Empire, 1898–1923*. Clarendon Press, 1997.

Balmaseda, Joaquina. "La chula madrileña." Sáez de Melgar, pp. 260–75.

Baquero Goyanes, Mariano. *La novela naturalista española: Emilia Pardo Bazán*. Secretariado de la Universidad de Murcia, 1986.

Barrio. Directed by Fernando León de Aranoa, produced by Elías Querejeta, 1998.

Barroso, Fernando. *El naturalismo en la Pardo Bazán*. Plaza Mayor, 1973.

Barthes, Roland. "L'effet de réel." *Communications*, vol. 11, 1968, pp. 84–89.

———. "The Reality Effect." *The Rustle of Language*, translated by Richard Howard, U of California P, 1989, pp. 141–48.

Baumslag, Naomi, and Dia L. Michels. *Milk, Money, and Madness: The Culture and Politics of Breastfeeding*. Bergin and Garvey, 1995.

Beauvoir, Simone de. *Le deuxième sexe*. 1949. Gallimard, 1986.

Becker, George J., editor. *Documents of Modern Literary Realism*. Princeton UP, 1963.

Bédarida, François. *A Social History of England, 1851–1990*. Translated by A. S. Forster and Jeffrey Hodgkinson, Routledge, 2005.

Benjamin, Walter. "The Task of the Translator: An Introduction to the Translation of Baudelaire's *Tableaux Parisiennes*." Translated by Harry Zohn. *The Translation Studies Reader*, edited by Lawrence Venuti, 2nd ed., Routledge, 2004, pp. 75–83.

Bhabha, Homi K. *The Location of Culture*. 2nd ed., Routledge, 2007.

Bieder, Maryellen. "Between Genre and Gender: Emilia Pardo Bazán and *Los pazos de Ulloa*." *In the Feminine Mode: Essays on Hispanic Women Writers*. Edited by Noël Valis and Carol Maier, Associated UP, 1990, pp. 131–45.

———. "Divina y perversa: La mujer decadente en *Dulce dueño* de Emilia Pardo Bazán." *Perversas y divinas: La representación de la mujer en las literaturas hispánicas;*

El fin de siglo y/o el fin de milenio actual, edited by Carme Riera et al., Universitat Autónoma de Barcelona, 2002, pp. 8–19.

———. "Emilia Pardo Bazán and Gabriela Cunninghame Graham: A Literary and Personal Friendship." *Bulletin of Spanish Studies*, vol. 89, no. 5, July 2012, pp. 725–49.

———. "Emilia Pardo Bazán and Literary Women: Women Reading Women's Writing in Late-Nineteenth-Century Spain." *Revista hispánica moderna*, vol. 46, 1993, pp. 19–33.

———. "Emilia Pardo Bazán: Veintiuna cartas a Gabriela Cunninghame Graham." *Siglo diecinueve*, vol. 18, 2012, pp. 29–64.

———. "Plotting Gender / Replotting the Reader: Strategies of Subversion in Stories by Emilia Pardo Bazán." *Indiana Journal of Hispanic Literatures*, vol. 2, no. 1, Fall 1993, pp. 137–55.

Blanco, Alda. *Cultura y conciencia imperial en la España del siglo XIX*. Universitat de Valencia, 2012.

Bonet, Laureano, editor. *Benito Pérez Galdós: Ensayos de crítica literaria*. Ediciones Península, 1972.

"Books by Pardo Bazán, Emilia, condesa de." *Project Gutenberg*, www.gutenberg.org /ebooks/author/6152.

Borda Crespo, María Isabel. "El modernismo de Emilia Pardo Bazán: Hacia una aproximación didáctica." *La Tribuna: Cadernos de estudios da Casa Museo Emilia Pardo Bazán*, no. 3, 2005, pp. 155–72.

Bordwell, David, et al. *Film Art: An Introduction*. 11th ed., McGraw-Hill, 2017.

Botrel, Jean-François. "A Contribution to a 'Historical History' of Literature." *Journal of European Studies*, vol. 21, 1991, pp. 55–66.

———. *Libros, prensa y lectura en la España del siglo XIX*. Pirámide, 1993.

———. "Narrativa y lectura del pueblo en España del siglo XIX." *Cuadernos hispanoamericanos*, no. 516, June 1993, pp. 69–91.

Bourdieu, Pierre. *Distinction: A Social Critique of the Judgment of Taste*. Harvard UP, 1984.

Boyd, Anne E. *Writing for the Immortality: Women and the Emergence of High Literary Culture in America*. Johns Hopkins UP, 2004.

Braidotti, Rosi. *Nomadic Subjects: Embodiment and Sexual Difference in Contemporary Feminist Theory*. Columbia UP, 1994.

Bravo-Villasante, Carmen. *Emilia Pardo Bazán: Vida y obra*. Revista de Occidente, 1962.

Bresler, Liora. "Toward Connectedness: Aesthetically Based Research." *Studies in Art Education*, vol. 48, no. 1, 2006, pp. 52–69.

Bretz, Mary Lee. "Emilia Pardo Bazán on John Stuart Mill: Towards a Redefinition of the Essay." *Hispanic Journal*, vol. 9, no. 2, Spring 1988, pp. 81–88.

———. "The Theater of Emilia Pardo Bazán and Concha Espina." *Estreno*, vol. 10, no. 2, 1984, pp. 43–45.

Brooks, Peter. *The Melodramatic Imagination: Balzac, Henry James, Melodrama, and the Mode of Excess*. Yale UP, 1976.

———. *Realist Vision*. Yale UP, 2005.

Brown, Donald Fowler. *The Catholic Naturalism of Pardo Bazán*. 2nd ed., U of North Carolina P, 1971.

Butler, Judith. *Gender Trouble: Feminism and the Subversion of Identity*. Routledge, 1990.

El Caballero Audaz (José María Carretero Novillo). "Nuestras visitas: La condesa de Pardo Bazán." *La esfera*, no. 7, 14 Feb. 1914, pp. 8–9.

Cagiao Vila, Pilar. *Muller e emigración*. Xunta de Galicia, 1991.

Campbell, Hugh, et al. "Masculinity and Rural Life: An Introduction." *Country Boys: Masculinity and Rural Life*, edited by Campbell et al., Penn State UP, 2006, pp. 1–22.

Cantalupo, Barbara, editor. *Poe's Pervasive Influence*. Lehigh UP, 2012.

Capel Martínez, Rosa María. "Life and Work in the Tobacco Factories: Female Industrial Workers in the Early Twentieth Century." Enders and Radcliff, pp. 131–50.

Carasa, Pedro. "La Restauración Monárquica." *Historia de España, Siglo XX: 1875–1939*, edited by Ángel Bahamonde, Cátedra, 2005.

Carballal Miñán, Patricia. "'Rabeno' de Emilia Pardo Bazán: Mito y reflexión didáctica sobre la violencia sexual." *Proceedings of the Tenth World Congress of the International Association for Semiotic Studies*, Universidade da Coruña, 2012, pp. 1559–68.

Carlson, Marvin. *The Haunted Stage: The Theater as Memory Machine*. U of Michigan P, 2008.

Carr, Raymond. "Liberalism and Reaction." *Spain: A History*, edited by Carr, Oxford UP, 2000, pp. 205–42.

———. *Modern Spain, 1875–1980*. Oxford UP, 1980.

Carrión, Jorge, editor. *Madrid/Barcelona: Literatura y ciudad, 1995–2010*. Iberoamericana/Vervuert, 2009.

Cartagena Calderón, José R. *Masculinidades en obras: El drama de la hombría en la España imperial*. Juan de la Cuesta, 2008.

Casas, Ramón. *La carga*. 1902. *Museo Nacional del Prado*, www.museodelprado.es /aprende/enciclopedia/voz/casas-y-carbo-ramon/97c000f5-7bb7-499b-bca5-17f 991c33b9b.

Castelao, Manuel. *A escaleira desigual:* La condesa rebelde: *Unidade didáctica*. Presidencia, 2012.

Castro, Rosalía de. *Cantares gallegos*. 1863. *Obras completas*, edited by Victoriano García Martí, Aguilar, 1972, pp. 257–389.

Cate-Arries, Francie. "Murderous Impulses and Moral Ambiguity: Emilia Pardo Bazán's Crime Stories." *Romance Quarterly*, vol. 39, no. 2, 1992, pp. 205–10.

Cejador y Frauca, Julio. *Historia de la lengua y literatura castellana*. Vol. 9, Tipografía de la revista de archivos, bibliotecas y museos, 1918.

Certeau, Michel de. *The Practice of Everyday Life*. Translated by Steven F. Rendall, U of California P, 1984.

Certeau, Michel de, et al. *The Practice of Everyday Life, Volume 2: Living and Cooking*. Translated by Timothy J. Tomasik, U of Minnesota P, 1998.

Charnon-Deutsch, Lou. "El discurso de la higiene física y moral en la narrativa femenina." *La mujer de letras o la letraherida: Discursos y representaciones sobre la mujer escritora en el siglo XIX*, edited by Pura Fernández and Marie-Linda Ortega, Consejo Superior de Investigaciones Científicas, 2008, pp. 177–88.

———. *Fictions of the Feminine in the Nineteenth-Century Spanish Press*. Penn State UP, 2000.

———. *Hold That Pose: Visual Culture in the Late-Nineteenth-Century Spanish Periodical*. Penn State UP, 2008.

———. *Narratives of Desire: Nineteenth-Century Spanish Fiction by Women*. Penn State UP, 1994.

———. *The Spanish Gypsy: A History of a European Obsession*. Penn State UP, 2004.

———. "Tenía corazón: *Dulce dueño* de Emilia Pardo Bazán." *Arbor: Revista de ciencia, pensamiento y cultura*, no. 719, 2006, pp. 325–36.

Charques Gámez, Rocío. "El descubrimiento de América en el *Nuevo teatro crítico* de Emilia Pardo Bazán." González Herrán et al., *Actas del III Simposio*, pp. 349–66.

———. *Emilia Pardo Bazán y su* Nuevo teatro crítico. Fundación Universitaria Española, 2012.

Chatfield-Taylor, H. C. *The Land of the Castanet: Spanish Sketches*. Herbert S. Stone, 1896.

Chekhov, Anton. "Before the Wedding." Chekhov, *Complete Early Short Stories*, pp. 26–28.

———. "The Chemist's Wife." *Project Gutenberg*, www.gutenberg.org/cache/epub/13505/pg13505-images.html.

———. *The Complete Early Short Stories of Anton Chekhov: "He and She" and Other Stories*. Translated by Peter Sekirin, Megapolis, 2001. Vol. 1 (1880–82).

———. "The Husband." *Project Gutenberg*, www.gutenberg.org/files/13415/13415-h/13415-h.htm#THE_HUSBAND.

———. "Wedding American Style." Chekhov, *Complete Early Short Stories*, pp. 29–30.

———. "The Wife." *Project Gutenberg*, www.gutenberg.org/files/1883/1883-h/1883-h.htm.

Cixous, Hélène. *Le rire de la Méduse et autres ironies*. 1975. Galilée, 2010.

Clémessy, Nelly. *Emilia Pardo Bazán como novelista*. Fundación Universitaria Española, 1982. 2 vols.

Clúa, Isabel. "Los secretos de las damas muertas: Dos reelaboraciones de lo fantástico en la obra de Emilia Pardo Bazán." *Cuadernos de investigación filológica*, vol. 26, 2000, pp. 125–35.

Colmeiro, José. "Exorcising Exoticism: Carmen and the Construction of Oriental Spain." *Comparative Literature*, vol. 54, no. 2, Spring 2002, pp. 127–44.

La colmena. Directed by Mario Camus, produced by José Luis Dibildos, 1982.

Coloma, Luis. *Pequeñeces*. 1890. Edited by Rubén Benítez, Cátedra, 1999.

Comte, Auguste. *Catéchisme positiviste*. 1852. Temple de l'Humanité, 1957.

Connell, R. W. *Masculinities*. 2nd ed., U of California P, 1995.

Cook, Teresa A. *El feminismo en la novela de la Condesa de Pardo Bazán*. Diputación Provincial, 1976.

Copeland, Eva Maria. "Empire, Nation, and the *Indiano* in Galdós's *Tormento* and *La loca de la casa*." *Hispanic Review*, vol. 80, no. 2, 2012, pp. 221–42.

"Core Competencies for Entering Medical Students." *Association of American Medical Colleges*, www.staging.aamc.org/initiatives/admissionsinitiative/competencies/.

Coronado, Carolina. *Poesías*. Edited by Noël Valis, Castalia, 1991.

Courtad, James C., et al., editors. *Intrigras: Advanced Spanish through Literature and Film*. Vista Higher Learning, 2012.

Crawley, LaVera M. "Literature and the Irony of Medical Science." Hawkins and McEntyre, pp. 316–26.

Cruz, Jesús. *Gentlemen, Bourgeois, and Revolutionaries: Political Change and Cultural Persistence among the Spanish Dominant Groups, 1750–1850*. Cambridge UP, 1996.

———. *The Rise of Middle-Class Culture in Nineteenth-Century Spain*. Louisiana State UP, 2011.

Darwin, Charles. *The Origin of Species*. 6th ed., Prometheus Books, 1991.

Davis, Ryan A., and Alicia Cerezo, editors. *Modernity and Epistemology in Nineteenth-Century Spain: Fringe Discourses*. Rowman and Littlefield, 2016.

DeCoster, Cyrus. "Pardo Bazán and Her Contemporaries." *Anales galdosianos*, vol. 19, 1984, pp. 123–31.

Dendle, Brian. "The Racial Theories of Emilia Pardo Bazán." *Hispanic Review*, vol. 38, no. 1, 1970, pp. 17–31.

Díaz Huertas, Carlos Ángel. *La cigarrera*. *La ilustración ibérica*, 25 July 1891, p. 472.

———. *El motín de las cigarreras*. *Blanco y negro*, no. 248, 1 Feb. 1896. *ABC Hemeroteca*, hemeroteca.abc.es/nav/Navigate.exe/hemeroteca/madrid/blanco.y.negro/1896/02/01/014.html.

Diego, Patricia. *La ficción en la pequeña pantalla: Cincuenta años de series en España*. Ediciones Universidad de Navarra, 2010.

Dijkstra, Bram. *Idols of Perversity: Fantasies of Feminine Evil in Fin-de-Siècle Culture*. Oxford UP, 1986.

Dupláa, Christina. "'Identidad sexuada' y 'conciencia de clase' en los espacios de mujeres de *La Tribuna*." *Letras femeninas*, vol. 22, nos. 1–2, 1996, pp. 189–201.

DuPont, Denise. "Cabezas cortadas, 'imágenes de vestir' y manos femeninas: Emilia Pardo Bazán y el decadentismo español." *Revista internacional d'humanitats*, vol. 26, 2012, pp. 65–78.

———. "Decadence, Women Writers, and Literary History in Emilia Pardo Bazan's Late Criticism." *MLN*, vol. 117, no. 2, 2002, pp. 343–64.

———. *Writing Teresa: The Saint from Ávila at the Fin-de-siglo*. Bucknell UP, 2011.

Echegaray, José. *El gran galeoto*. Imprenta de José Rodríguez, 1881.

Eiselely, Loren. *Darwin's Century: Evolution and the Men Who Discovered It*. Anchor Books, 1961.

Eisner, Elliot. *Cognition and Curriculum*. Longman, 1982.

"Emilia Pardo Bazán." *Biblioteca Virtual Miguel de Cervantes*, www.cervantesvirtual .com/portales/pardo_bazan/.

"Emilia Pardo Bazán: Cuentos: Textos digitales completos." *Biblioteca Digital Ciudad Seva*, ciudadseva.com/autor/emilia-pardo-bazan/cuentos/.

Emilia Pardo Bazán: La condesa rebelde. Directed by María Ignacia Ceballos, Zenit Televisión, 2011.

Encinas, S. G. "La mujer comparada con el hombre II: Caracteres físico-anotómicos que distinguen á la mujer del hombre." *Revista europea*, vol. 9, May 1875, pp. 365–69.

En construcción. Directed by José Luis Guerín, produced by Jordi Balló, 2001.

Enders, Victoria Lorée, and Pamela Beth Radcliff, editors. *Constructing Spanish Womanhood: Female Identity in Modern Spain*. State U of New York P, 1999.

Entwistle, Joanne. *The Fashioned Body: Fashion, Dress and Modern Social Theory*. Polity Press, 2000.

Erwin, Zachary. "Fantasies of Masculinity in Emilia Pardo Bazán's *Memorias de un solterón*." *Revista de estudios hispánicos*, vol. 46, no. 3, 2012, pp. 547–68.

Espronceda, José. "El pastor clasiquino." 1835. *Artículo literario y narrativa breve del romanticismo español*, edited by María José Alonso Seoane et al., Castalia, 2004, pp. 151–53.

———. *Poesías líricas y fragmentos épicos*. Edited by Robert Marrast, Castalia, 1987.

Estampas de la guerra de la independencia. Calcografía Nacional, 1996.

Ezama Gil, Angeles. "La fusión de las artes en *Dulce dueño* de Emilia Pardo Bazán." *La Tribuna: Cadernos de estudios da Casa Museo Emilia Pardo Bazán*, no. 5, 2007, pp. 171–206.

Fages, Guiomar. "En busca de una tipología maternal: (Re)considerando la mujer-madre en la España de los siglos XIX y XX." 2007. U of Nebraska, Lincoln, PhD dissertation. *Digital Commons@University of Nebraska–Lincoln*, docplayer.es /30892243-En-busca-de-una-tipologia-maternal-re-considerando-la-mujer-madre -en-la-espana-de-los-siglos-xix-y-xx.html.

Fanon, Franz. *The Wretched of the Earth*. Penguin Books, 2001.

Faus Sevilla, Pilar. *Emilia Pardo Bazán: Su época, su vida, su obra*. Fundación Pedro Barrié de la Maza, 2003. 2 vols.

Feal, Carlos. "Psicoanálisis: 'Cómo se construye (y desconstruye) una identidad masculina: *Morriña* de Pardo Bazán y *Nada menos que todo un hombre* de Unamuno.'" *El hispanismo en los Estados Unidos: Discursos críticos/prácticos textuales*, edited by José Manuel del Pino and Francisco La Rubia Prado, Visor, 1999, pp. 71–89.

Feeny, Thomas. "Maupassant's 'Lui?' and Pardo Bazán's 'La calavera': A Possible Case of Influence." *South Atlantic Bulletin*, vol. 41, no. 4, 1976, pp. 44–47.

Fellowes, Julian, creator. "Original UK Version Episode 2." *Downton Abbey*, season 1, Public Broadcasting Service, 26 Oct. 2010. *Amazon Video*, a.co/5iJ9RSn.

Felski, Rita. *The Gender of Modernity*. Harvard UP, 1995.

Fernández Cubas, Cristina. *Emilia Pardo Bazán*. Omega, 2001.

Ferrer del Río, Antonio. "El indiano." *Los españoles pintados por sí mismos*, edited by José Gaspar Maristany and José Roig Oliveras, Gaspar y Roig, 1851, pp. 16–20.

Fontana, Josep. *La época del liberalismo*. Marcial Pons, 2007. Vol. 6 of *Historia de España*.

Forth, Christopher E. *Masculinity in the Modern West: Gender, Civilization, and the Body*. Palgrave Macmillan, 2008.

Fraser, Benjamin. *Henri Lefebvre and the Spanish Urban Experience: Reading the Mobile City*. Bucknell UP, 2011.

Freire López, Ana María, editor. *Estudios sobre la obra de Emilia Pardo Bazán: Actas de las jornadas conmemorativas de los 150 años de su nacimiento*. Fundación Pedro Barrié de la Maza, 2003.

Freud, Sigmund. *The Question of Lay Analysis: The Standard Edition of the Complete Psychological Works of Sigmund Freud*. Vol. 20, Hogarth Press, 1926.

———. *The Uncanny*. Translated by David McLintock, introduced by Hugh Haughton, Penguin Books, 2003.

Furst, Lilian R. *All Is True: The Claims and Strategies of Realist Fiction*. Duke UP, 1995.

———, editor. *Realism*. Longman, 1992.

Gabilondo, Joseba. "The Subaltern Cannot Speak but Performs: Women's Public and Literary Cultures in Nineteenth-Century Spain." *Hispanic Research Journal*, vol. 5, no. 1, 2003, pp. 73–95.

———. "Towards a Postnational Theory of Galician Literature: On Pardo Bazán's Transnational and Translational Position." *Bulletin of Hispanic Studies*, vol. 86, no. 2, 2009, pp. 249–69.

Ganivet, Ángel. *Cartas finlandesas: Hombres del norte*. Biblioteca Virtual Miguel de Cervantes, 1999. *Biblioteca Virtual Miguel de Cervantes*, www.cervantesvirtual.com/obra-visor/cartas-finlandesas-hombres-del-norte--0/html/.

García Castañeda, Salvador. "El teatro de Emilia Pardo Bazán: Estado de la cuestión." González Herrán, *Estudios*, pp. 113–45.

García y Ramos, José. *Salida de las cigarreras de la fábrica de tabacos de Sevilla. Blanco y negro*, no. 200, 2 Mar. 1895. *ABC Hemeroteca*, hemeroteca.abc.es/nav/Navigate.exe/hemeroteca/madrid/blanco.y.negro/1895/03/02/008.html.

Gasior, Bonnie. "The Economy of the Feminine in Emilia Pardo Bazan's 'Las medias rojas.'" *Hispania*, vol. 90, no. 4, 2007, pp. 747–54.

Gemie, Sharif. *Galicia: A Concise History*. U of Wales P, 2006.

Giddings, Robert, and Keith Selby. *The Classic Serial on Television and Radio*. Palgrave Macmillan, 2001.

Gies, David. *The Cambridge Companion to Modern Spanish Culture*. Cambridge UP, 1999.

Gieseking, Jen Jack, and William Mangold, editors. *The People, Place, and Space Reader*. Routledge, 2014.

Gifra Adroher, Pere. *Between History and Romance: Travel Writing on Spain in the Early Nineteenth-Century United States*. Fairleigh Dickinson UP, 2000.

Giles, Mary E. "Feminism and the Feminine in Emilia Pardo Bazan's Novels." *Hispania*, vol. 63, no. 2, 1980, pp. 356–67.

Gisbert, Antoni. *Fusilamiento de Torrijos y sus compañeros en las playas de Málaga*. 1888. *Museo Nacional del Prado*, www.museodelprado.es/coleccion/obra-de-arte /fusilamiento-de-torrijos-y-sus-compaeros-en-las/43e96694-c05c-4ce8-84a2-5d 246f20f879?.

Gold, Hazel. *The Reframing of Realism: Galdós and the Discourses of the Nineteenth-Century Spanish Novel*. Duke UP, 1993.

Gómez de Avellaneda, Gertrudis. "La mujer." *Antología de la prensa periódica isabelina escrita por mujeres, 1843–1894*, edited by Íñigo Sánchez-Llama, Universidad de Cádiz, 2001, pp. 81–89.

Gómez-Ferrer Morant, Guadalupe. "Emilia Pardo Bazán en el ocaso del siglo XIX." *Cuadernos de historia contemporánea*, vol. 20, 1998, pp. 129–50.

———. *Vida, literatura e historia en la España de la Restauración*. Universidad Complutense de Madrid, 2008.

González, Isidro. *El retorno de los judíos*. Editorial Nerea, 1991.

González Arias, Francisca. "La poética de Galicia en los cuentos de Emilia Pardo Bazán." González Herrán, *Estudios*, pp. 147–69.

———. *Portrait of a Woman as Artist: Emilia Pardo Bazán and the Modern Novel in France and Spain*. Garland Publishing, 1992.

González Herrán, José Manuel. "Ediciones y estudios sobre la obra literaria de Emilia Pardo Bazán: Estado de la cuestión, 1921–2003." *La Tribuna: Cadernos de estudios da Casa Museo Emilia Pardo Bazán*, no. 1, 2003, pp. 19–46.

———. "Emilia Pardo Bazán ante el 98, 1896–1905." *El camino hacia el 98: Los escritores de la Restauración y la crisis del fin de siglo*, edited by Leonardo Romero Tobar, Visor, 1998, pp. 139–53.

———. "Estudio introductorio." Pardo Bazán, *La cuestión* [González Herrán], pp. 7–108.

———, editor. *Estudios sobre Emilia Pardo Bazán: In Memoriam Maurice Hemingway*. Universidade de Santiago–Consorcio de Santiago, 1997.

González Herrán, et al., editors. *Actas del I Simposio Emilia Pardo Bazán: El estado de la cuestión*. Real Academia Galega, 2005.

———, editors. *Actas del II Simposio Emilia Pardo Bazán: Los cuentos*. Real Academia Galega, 2006.

———, editors. *Actas del III Simposio Emilia Pardo Bazán: El periodismo*. Real Academia Galega, 2007.

———, editors. *Actas del IV Simposio Emilia Pardo Bazán y las artes del espectáculo*. Real Academia Galega, 2008.

———, editors. *La literatura de Emilia Pardo Bazán*. Real Academia Galega, 2009.

González López, Emilio. *Emilia Pardo Bazán: Novelista de Galicia*. Hispanic Institute in the United States, 1944.

González-Millán, Xoán. "E. Pardo Bazán y su imagen del 'Rexurdimento' cultural gallego en la *Revista de Galicia*." *La Tribuna: Cadernos de estudios da Casa Museo Emilia Pardo Bazán*, no. 2, 2004, pp. 35–62.

González Turmo, Isabel. *Comida de rico, comida de pobre: Los hábitos alimenticios en el Occidente andaluz (Siglo XX)*. Universidad de Sevilla, 1997.

Goode, Joshua. *Impurity of Blood: Defining Race in Spain, 1870–1930*. Louisiana State UP, 2009.

Goody, Jack. *The Domestication of the Savage Mind*. Cambridge UP, 1977.

Graham, Helen, and Jo Labanyi, editors. *Spanish Cultural Studies: An Introduction*. Oxford UP, 1995.

Gregerson, Halfdan. *Ibsen and Spain: A Study in Comparative Drama*. Harvard UP, 1936.

Grossberg, Lawrence. *Cultural Studies in the Future Tense*. Duke UP, 2010.

Grupo de Investigación *La Tribuna*. "La trágica muerte de Joaquina Mosquera Ribera, abuela de doña Emilia." *La Tribuna: Cadernos de estudios da Casa Museo Emilia Pardo Bazán*, no. 8, 2010–11, pp. 15–59.

Gubern, Román, and Kathleen M. Vernon. "Soundtrack." *A Companion to Spanish Cinema*, edited by Jo Labanyi, e-book, Wiley-Blackwell, 2013, pp. 370–88.

Gumplowicz, Ludwig. *La lucha de razas*. La España Moderna, [after 1883].

Haidt, Rebecca. *Embodying Enlightenment: Reading the Body in Eighteenth-Century Spanish Literature and Culture*, Palgrave Macmillan, 1998.

Hannaford, Ivan. *Race: The History of an Idea in the West*. Johns Hopkins UP, 1996.

Hanson, Helen. *Hollywood Heroines: Women in Film Noir and the Female Gothic Film*. Palgrave Macmillan, 2007.

Harpring, Mark. "Homoeroticism and Gender Role Confusion in Pardo Bazán's *Memorias de un solterón*." *Hispanic Research Journal*, vol. 7, no. 3, 2006, pp. 195–210.

Hawkins, Anne Hunsaker, and Marilyn Chandler McEntyre, editors. *Teaching Literature and Medicine*. Modern Language Association of America, 2000.

Helstosky, Carol. *Garlic and Oil: Food and Politics in Italy*. Berg, 2004.

Hemingway, Maurice. "Emilia Pardo Bazán: Narrative Strategies and the Critique of Naturalism." *Naturalism in the European Novel: New Critical Perspectives*, edited by Brian Nelson, Berg, 1992, pp. 135–50.

———. *Emilia Pardo Bazán: The Making of a Novelist*. Cambridge UP, 1983.

Heneghan, Dorota K. "Fashion and Femininity in Emilia Pardo Bazán's *Insolación*." *Hispanic Review*, vol. 80, no. 1, 2012, pp. 63–84.

———. *Striking Their Modern Pose: Fashion, Gender, and Modernity in Galdós, Pardo Bazán, and Picón*. Purdue UP, 2015.

Henn, David. "Reflections on the War of 1898 in Pardo Bazán's Fiction and Travel Chronicles." *Modern Language Review*, vol. 94, no. 2, 1999, pp. 415–25.

Heydl-Cortínez, Cecilia, editor. *Cartas de las condesa en el* Diario de la Marina, *La Habana, 1909–1915*. Pliegos, 2002.

Hirsh, Sharon. *Symbolism and Modern Urban Society*. Cambridge UP, 2004.

Hollows, Joan. *Feminism, Femininity and Popular Culture*. Manchester UP, 2000.

Hooper, Kirsty. "Girl, Interrupted: The Distinctive History of Galician Women's Narrative." *Romance Studies*, vol. 21, no. 2, 2003, pp. 101–14.

———. *A Stranger in My Own Land: Sofía Casanova, a Spanish Writer in the European Fin de Siècle*. Vanderbilt UP, 2008.

Hugo, Victor. *Oeuvres poétiques complètes*. Éditions Bernard Valiquette, 1944.

Hutcheon, Linda. *A Theory of Adaptation*. Routledge, 2006.

Huyssen, Andreas. *After the Great Divide: Modernism, Mass Culture, and Postmodernism*. Indiana UP, 1986.

El indulto. Directed by José Luis Sáenz de Heredia, Suevia Films, 1960.

Ingram, Rebecca. "Popular Tradition and Bourgeois Elegance in Emilia Pardo Bazán's *Cocina española*." *Bulletin of Hispanic Studies*, vol. 91, no. 3, 2014, pp. 261–74.

Irving, Washington. *Tales of the Alhambra*. Putman, 1895.

"Islas filipinas." *La ilustración artística*, no. 778, 23 Nov. 1896, pp. 785, 800. *Hemeroteca Digital de la Biblioteca Nacional de España*, hemerotecadigital.bne.es/issue.vm?id=0001531283.

Jagoe, Catherine. *Ambiguous Angels: Gender in the Novels of Galdós*. U of California P, 1994.

———. "Disinheriting the Feminine: Galdós and the Rise of the Realist Novel in Spain." *Revista de estudios hispánicos*, vol. 27, 1993, pp. 225–48.

———. "La enseñanza femenina en la España decimonónica." Jagoe et al., pp. 105–45.

———. "Sexo y género en la medicina del siglo XIX." Jagoe et al., pp. 305–39.

Jagoe, Catherine, et al., editors. *La mujer en los discursos de género: Textos y contextos en el siglo XIX*. Icaria, 1998.

Jagoe, Catherine, and Cristina Enríquez de Salamanca. "Introducción." Jagoe et al., pp. 13–19.

Jameson, Fredric. *The Antinomies of Realism*. Verso, 2013.

———. "Beyond the Cave: Demystifying the Ideology of Modernism." *Bulletin of the Midwest Modern Language Association*, vol. 8, no. 1, 1975, pp. 1–20.

———. "The Ideology of the Text." *Salmagundi*, vols. 31–32, 1975, pp. 204–46.

Jones, Virginia Pompei. "Teaching Elements of Literature through Art: Romanticism, Realism, and Culture." *Pedagogy*, vol. 7, no. 2, 2007, pp. 264–70.

Jurecic, Ann. *Illness as Narrative*. U of Pittsburgh P, 2012.

Kazin, Alfred. "Literary Realism." *New York Review of Books*, 1 June 1963, www.nybooks.com/articles/archives/1963/jun/01/literary-realism.

Kelley, Heidi, and Ken Betsalel. "Teaching Galicia in Appalachia: Lessons from Anthropology, Ethnographic Poetry, Documentary Photography, and Political Theory." (Re)Mapping Galician Studies in North America Conference, 2 May 2014, U of Wisconsin, Milwaukee.

Kirby, Harry L., Jr. "Pardo Bazán, Darwinism, and *La madre naturaleza*." *Hispania*, vol. 47, 1964, pp. 733–37.

Kirkpatrick, Susan. "Gender and Modernist Discourse: Emilia Pardo Bazán's *Dulce dueño.*" *Modernism and Its Margins: Reinscribing Cultural Modernity from Spain and Latin America,* edited by A. L. Geist and J. B. Monleón, Garland Reference Library of the Humanities, 1999, pp. 69–82.

———. *Mujer, modernismo y vanguardia en España, 1898–1931.* Cátedra, 2003.

Korsmeyer, Carolyn. *Gender and Aesthetics: An Introduction.* Routledge, 2004.

Krauel, Javier. *Imperial Emotions: Cultural Responses to Myths of Empire in Fin-de-Siècle Spain.* Liverpool UP, 2013.

Kristeva, Julia. *Histoires d'amour.* Denoël, 1985.

Kronik, John. "Entre la ética y la estética: Pardo Bazán ante el decadentismo francés." *Estudios sobre* Los pazos de Ulloa, edited by Marina Mayoral, Cátedra, 1999, pp. 163–74.

Labanyi, Jo. "El diálogo de *La madre naturaleza* con Rousseau." González Herrán et al., *La literatura,* pp. 401–10.

———. *Gender and Modernization in the Spanish Realist Novel.* Oxford UP, 2000.

———. "Relocating Difference: Cultural History and Modernity in Late-Nineteenth-Century Spain." *Spain beyond Spain: Modernity, Literary History, and National Identity,* edited by Brad Epps and Luis Fernández Cifuentes, Bucknell UP, 2005, pp. 168–88.

———. *Spanish Literature: A Very Short Introduction.* Oxford UP, 2010.

Landry, Travis. *Subversive Seduction: Darwin, Sexual Selection, and the Spanish Novel.* U of Washington P, 2012.

Laqueur, Thomas. *Making Sex: Body and Gender from the Greeks to Freud.* Harvard UP, 1990.

———. "Orgasm, Generation, and the Politics of Reproductive Biology." *The Making of the Modern Body: Sexuality and Society in the Nineteenth Century,* edited by Catherine Gallagher and Laqueur, U of California P, 1987, pp. 1–41.

Larra, Mariano José de. "La fonda nueva." *Artículos,* by Larra, Cátedra, 1999, pp. 234–40.

Larson, Susan, and Eva Woods, editors. *Visualizing Spanish Modernity.* Berg, 2005.

Lauretis, Teresa de. *Technologies of Gender: Essays on Theory, Film, and Fiction.* Indiana UP, 1987.

Lefebvre, Henri. *The Production of Space.* Translated by Donald Nicholson-Smith, Wiley-Blackwell, 1991.

———. "The Production of Space." Gieseking and Mangold, pp. 289–93.

Leonardi, Susan. "Recipes for Reading: Pasta Salad, Lobster à la Riseholme, Key Lime Pie." *PMLA,* vol. 104, no. 3, 1989, pp. 340–47.

Levin, Amy, and Phoebe Stein Davis. "'Good Readers Make Good Doctors': Community Readings and the Health of the Community." *PMLA,* vol. 125, no. 2, 2010, pp. 426–37.

Llácer Llorca, Eusebio, et al., editors. *A Twenty-First-Century Retrospective View about Edgar Allan Poe.* Peter Lang, 2011.

Llinares García, Mar. "Antropoloxía da muller en Galicia: Balance provisorio e perspectivas de futuro." *A muller na historia de Galicia,* edited by Xavier Castro and Jesús de Juan, Deputación Provincial de Ourense, 1995, pp. 7–19.

Lombroso, Cesare. *Criminal Man.* 1876. Translated by Mary Gibson and Nicole Hahn Rafter, Duke UP, 2006.

López-Morillas, Juan. *The Krausist Movement and Ideological Change in Spain, 1854–1874.* Translated by Frances M. López-Morillas, Cambridge UP, 1981.

López Sández, María. *Paisaxe e nación.* Galaxia, 2008.

Madrazo, Federico de. *Retrato de Alfonso XII.* 1886. *Museo Nacional del Prado,* www .museodelprado.es/coleccion/obra-de-arte/alfonso-xii/02f0ce8a-7e8e-426d-9e68 -d916c391f31b?.

Madrazo y Garreta, Raimundo de. *Retrato de María Cristina de Habsburgo-Lorena.* 1887. *Museo Nacional del Prado,* www.museodelprado.es/coleccion/obra-de-arte/maria -cristina-de-habsburgo-lorena/d24681fc-80a2-4812-92da-a92dd038b40c?.

Mangraner y Marinas, Julio. "Historia clínica: Tuberculosis pulmonar en una mujer de 16 años." *Instituto de Historia de la Medicina y de la Ciencia,* Universitat de València, hicido.uv.es/Expo_medicina/Patologia_XIX/texto_magraner.html. Originally published in Mangraner y Marinas's *Programa de las lecciones de clínica médica adaptado a los casos habidos en ella por el profesor de la misma . . . Curso 1881 a 1882,* Valencia, 1882, pp. 57–64.

Martínez Ruiz, José (Azorín). *Los pueblos: La Andalucía trágica y otros artículos.* Castalia, 2000.

Mata y Fontanet, Pedro. *Tratado de medicina y cirugía legal.* Vol. 1, 3rd ed., Bailly-Bailliere, 1857.

Maupassant, Guy de. "Le Horla." *East of the Web Short Stories,* 2017, eastoftheweb .com/short-stories/UBooks/Horl.shtml.

———. "The Terror" ["Lui?"]. *The University of Adelaide eBooks@Adelaide,* ebooks .adelaide.edu.au/m/maupassant/guy/m45s/part81.html.

May, Charles E. *Edgar Allan Poe: A Study of the Short Fiction.* Twayne, 1991.

McKenna, Susan M. *Crafting the Female Subject: Narrative Innovation in the Short Fiction of Emilia Pardo Bazán.* Catholic U of America P, 2009.

McKevitt, Kerry Ann. "O espazo simbólico: Pardo Bazán, Valle-Inclán e os pazos galegos señoriais." *Bradomín,* vol. 1, 2006, pp. 67–77.

McKinney, Collin. *Mapping the Social Body: Urbanisation, the Gaze, and the Novels of Galdós.* U of North Carolina P, 2010.

Medina, Raquel. "Dulce esclava, dulce histérica: La representación de la mujer en *Dulce dueño* de Emilia Pardo Bazán." *Revista hispánica moderna,* vol. 51, 1998, pp. 291–303.

Méndez, Lourdes. *"Cousas de Mulleres": Campesinas, poder y vida cotidiana (Lugo, 1940–1980).* Anthropos, 1988.

Menéndez Pelayo, Marcelino. Prologue. 1882. *San Francisco de Asís (siglo XIII),* by Emilia Pardo Bazán, Editorial Porrúa, 1982, pp. ix–xv.

Mercer, Leigh. *Urbanism and Urbanity: The Spanish Bourgeois Novel and Contemporary Customs, 1845–1925.* Bucknell UP, 2013.

Mesonero Romanos, Ramón de. *Escenas y tipos matritenses. Biblioteca Virtual Miguel de Cervantes,* 2000, www.cervantesvirtual.com/obra-visor/escenas-y-tipos -matritenses--0/html/.

Metropolis. Directed by Fritz Lang, distributed by UFA, 1927.

Michelet, Jules. *Introduction a l'histoire universelle.* 1830. Hachette, 1843.

Miguélez-Carballeira, Helena. *Galicia, a Sentimental Nation: Gender, Culture and Politics.* U of Wales P, 2013.

Miller, Martha LaFollette. "Mythical Conceptualizations of Galicia in Murguía and Pardo Bazán: Aspects of Rosalian Context." *Actas do segundo congreso de estudios galegos,* edited by Antonio Carreño, Galaxia, 1988, pp. 267–76.

Mitchell, Sally. *Daily Life in Victorian England.* 2nd ed., Greenwood Press, 2009.

Mitchell, W. J. T. "Word and Image." *Critical Terms for Art History,* edited by Robert S. Nelson and Richard Shiff, U of Chicago P, 1996, pp. 47–57.

Moi, Toril. *"What Is a Woman?" and Other Essays.* Oxford UP, 1999.

Monlau, Pedro Felipe. *Higiene del matrimonio ó el libro de los casados en el cual se dan las reglas e instrucciones necesarias para conservar la salud de los esposos, asegurar la paz conyugal y educar bien a la familia. HathiTrust Digital Library,* babel.hathitrust.org/cgi/pt?id=ucm.5322558049;view=1up;seq=7.

Moreno, María Paz. *De la página al plato: El libro de cocina en España.* Trea, 2012.

Morris, Pamela. *Realism.* Routledge, 2003.

Mosse, George L. *The Image of Man: The Creation of Modern Masculinity.* Oxford UP, 1996.

Muñoz Molina, Antonio. *Los misterios de Madrid.* Seix Barral, 2007.

Nadal, Jordi. *El fracaso de la revolución industrial en España, 1814–1913.* Ariel, 1975.

Nash, Mary. *Mujer, familia y trabajo en España, 1875–1936.* Anthropos, 1983.

———. "The Rise of the Women's Movement in Nineteenth-Century Spain." *Women's Emancipation Movements in the Nineteenth Century: A European Perspective,* edited by Sylvia Paletschek and Bianka Pietrow-Ennker, Stanford UP, 2004, pp. 243–62.

Nelken, Margarita. *Las escritoras españolas.* Labor, 1930.

Nordau, Max. *Degeneration.* 1892. Introduced by George L. Mosse, H. Fertig, 1968.

Nunemaker, J. Horace. "Emilia Pardo Bazán as a Dramatist." *Modern Language Quarterly,* vol. 6, no. 2, 1945, pp. 161–66.

Núñez de Arce, Gaspar. *Discurso leído en el Ateneo Científico y Literario de Madrid con motivo de la apertura de sus cátedras [Discurso sobre la poesía].* Sucesores de Rivadeneyra, 1887.

Núñez Rey, Concepción. *Carmen de Burgos "Colombine" en la Edad de Plata de la literatura española.* Fundación José Manuel Lara, 2005.

O'Connor, D. J. "Representations of Women Workers: Tobacco Strikers in the 1890s." Enders and Radcliff, pp. 151–72.

Olivio Jiménez, José. *Antología crítica de la poesía modernista hispanoamericana.* Hiperión, 1994.

"1.300 millones de pesetas en películas para RTVE." *ABC de Sevilla,* 3 Aug. 1979, p. 6.

Opera en Marineda. Directed by Pilar Miró, Televisión Española, 1974.

Ordóñez, Elizabeth J. "Mapping Modernity: The *Fin de Siècle* Travels of Emilia Pardo Bazán." *Hispanic Research Journal,* vol. 5, no. 1, 2004, pp. 15–25.

Ortega y Gasset, José. "El mito del hombre allende la técnica." Ortega y Gasset, *Obras completas*, vol. 9, Alianza, 1997, pp. 617–24. 12 vols.

Otis, Laura. *Organic Memory: History and the Body in the Late Nineteenth and Early Twentieth Centuries*. U of Nebraska P, 1994.

———. "Science and Signification in the Early Writings of Emilia Pardo Bazán." *Revista de estudios hispánicos*, vol. 29, 1995, pp. 73–106.

Pardo Bazán, Emilia. "La adopción." *Blanco y negro*, no. 20, 29 Jan. 1910. *ABC Hemeroteca*, hemeroteca.abc.es/nav/Navigate.exe/hemeroteca/madrid/blanco.y.negro/1910/01/29/020.html.

———. *Al pie de la torre Eiffel*. *Biblioteca Virtual Miguel de Cervantes*, www.cervantes virtual.com/portales/pardo_bazan/obra_libros_viajes.

———. *Al pie de la torre Eiffel (Crónicas de la Exposición)*. España Editorial, 1889.

———. *The Angular Stone*. Translated by Mary J. Serrano, Cassell, 1892.

———. "Apuntes autobiográficos." *Los pazos de Ulloa*. Daniel Cortezo, 1886, pp. 15–92.

———. "Apuntes autobiográficos." 1886. Pardo Bazán, *Obras completas* [Sainz de Robles and Kirby], vol. 3, pp. 698–732.

———. "Asfixia." *La ilustración artística*, no. 903, 17 Apr. 1899, p. 129.

———. "El *Cancionero popular gallego*." Pardo Bazán, *Obras completas* [Sainz de Robles and Kirby], vol. 3, pp. 902–12.

———. "La ciencia amena." *La revista compostelana*, vol. 3–14, 1876–77, pp. 17–18, 25–27, 41–43, 49–51, 57–59, 65–67, 73–75, 81–83, 89–91, 97–99, 105–07.

———. "La cigarrera." Sáez de Melgar, pp. 796–802.

———. *El cisne de Vilamorta*. Alicante, 2002. *Biblioteca Virtual Miguel de Cervantes*, www.cervantesvirtual.com/obra-visor/el-cisne-de-vilamorta--0/html/ffa05e78-82b1-11df-acc7-002185ce6064_2.html#I_1_.

———. *El cisne de Vilamorta*. Simancas Ediciones, 2006.

———. *Cocina española antigua y moderna*. Iano Books, 2009.

———. "Confesión política." Pardo Bazán, *Viajes por Europa*, pp. 109–14.

———. "Conversación entre Emilia Pardo Bazán y el caballero audaz." Pardo Bazán, *La mujer española*, p. 330.

———. *Una cristiana*. Simancas Ediciones, 2006.

———. *Cuentos completos*. Edited by Juan Paredes Núñez, Fundación Barrié de la Maza, 1990. 4 vols.

———. *Cuentos de la patria*. Pardo Bazán, *Obras completas* [Sainz de Robles and Kirby], vol. 1, pp. 1513–33.

———. *Cuentos de Marineda*. Pardo Bazán, *Obras completas* [Sainz de Robles and Kirby], vol. 1, pp. 1063–119.

———. *La cuestión palpitante*. Edited by Carmen Bravo-Villasante, 2nd ed., Anaya, 1970.

———. *La cuestión palpitante*. Edited by José Manuel González Herrán, Antropos, 1989.

———. "Las cuevas de Altamira." *La época*, vol. 15, no. 985, 19 Nov. 1894, pp. 1–2.

———. *De mi tierra*. Agustín Avrial, 1893.

————. *De siglo a siglo: Crónicas periodísticas de Emilia Pardo Bazán.* Edited by María Luisa Pérez Bernardo, Pliegos, 2014.

————. *De siglo a siglo, 1896–1901.* Pardo Bazán, *Obras completas,* vol. 24, Administración, 1902.

————. *Un destripador de antaño y otros cuentos.* Alianza, 2009.

————. "Días nublados." *La ilustración artística,* no. 778, 23 Nov. 1896, p. 786. *Hemeroteca Digital de la Biblioteca Nacional de España,* hemerotecadigital.bne.es /issue.vm?id=0001531283.

————. "Discurso pronunciado en los Juegos Florales de Orense." Pardo Bazán, *Obra crítica,* pp. 305–39.

————. *Doña Milagros.* Pardo Bazán, *Obras completas* [Villanueva and González Herrán], vol. 3, pp. 571–776.

————. *Dulce dueño.* Edited by Marina Mayoral, Castalia, 1989.

————. "La educación del hombre y la de la mujer." *Nuevo teatro crítico,* vol. 2, no. 22, Oct. 1892, pp. 14–82.

————. *"El encaje roto" y otros cuentos.* Translated by María Cristina Urruela, edited and introduced by Joyce Tolliver, Modern Language Association of America, 1996.

————. *En las cavernas.* Pardo Bazán, *Obras completas* [Sainz de Robles and Kirby], vol. 2, pp. 1195–218.

————. "La España de ayer y la de hoy: La muerte de una leyenda." 1899. Pardo Bazán, *Obra crítica,* pp. 267–304.

————. "La España remota." *Nuevo teatro crítico,* vol. 1, no. 3, Mar. 1891, pp. 75–81. *Biblioteca Virtual Miguel de Cervantes,* www.cervantesvirtual.com/obra-visor /nuevo-teatro-critico--27/html/.

————. *A Galician Girl's Romance.* Translated by Mary J. Serrano, Mershon, 1900.

————. "La gallega." *El Folk-lore Gallego, Biblioteca de las tradiciones populares españolas,* edited by Antonio Machado y Álvarez, vol. 4, Alejandro Guichot, 1884, pp. 164–72.

————. *Historias y cuentos de Galicia.* Pardo Bazán, *Obras completas* [Sainz de Robles and Kirby], vol. 1, pp. 1304–81.

————. *Homesickness.* Translated by Mary J. Serrano, Cassell, 1891.

————. *The House of Ulloa.* Translated by Lucía Graves and Paul O'Prey, Penguin Classics, 2013.

————. *Insolación.* Edited by Ermitas Penas Varela, Cátedra, 2001.

————. *Insolación.* Edited by Jennifer Smith, European Masterpieces / Cervantes, 2011.

————. Letter to Blanca de los Ríos. 13 Sept. 1902. Biblioteca Nacional, Madrid, Manuscritos.

————. Letter to Blanca de los Ríos. [1905]. Biblioteca Nacional, Madrid, Manuscritos.

————. *El lirismo en la poesía francesa.* Pueyo, 1923.

————. *La literatura francesa moderna.* Renacimiento, 1910–14. 3 vols.

————. *La madre naturaleza.* Edited by Ignacio Javier López, Cátedra, 2007.

————. "Marineda." *De mi tierra,* by Pardo Bazán, Edicións Xerais de Galicia, 1984, pp. 265–87.

————. *Memorias de un solterón*. Edited by María de los Ángeles Ayala, Cátedra, 2004.

————. *Midsummer Madness*. 1907. Translated by Amparo Loring, reprint, Fredonia Books, 2004.

————. "Mi libro de Cocina: La cocina española antigua, la Biblioteca de la Mujer y otros asuntos feministas." Heydl-Cortínez, pp. 220–26. Originally published in *El diario de la marina*, 30 June 1913.

————. *"Miquiño mío": Cartas a Galdós*. Edited by Isabel Parreño and Juan Manuel Hernández, Turner, 2013.

————. *Mi romería*. *Universidad Autónoma de Nueva León Biblioteca Digital*, cdigital.dgb.uanl.mx/la/1020027925/1020027925.PDF.

————. *Morriña*. Edited by Ermitas Penas Varela, Cátedra, 2007.

————. *Mother Nature*. Translated by Walter Borenstein, Bucknell UP, 2010.

————. "La mujer española." Pardo Bazán, *La mujer*, pp. 83–116.

————. *La mujer española y otros escritos*. Edited by Guadalupe Gómez-Ferrer, Cátedra, 1999.

————. *"Náufragas" y otros cuentos*. Edited by Linda M. Willem, Cervantes, 2010.

————. *La nueva cuestión palpitante*. Pardo Bazán, *Obras completas* [Sainz de Robles and Kirby], vol. 3, pp. 1157–95.

————. *La nueva cuestión palpitante*. *La cuestión palpitante; La revolución y la novela en Rusia; La nueva cuestión palpitante*, introduced by Laura Silvestri and Carlos Dorado, Bercimuel, 2009, pp. 385–440.

————. *Obra crítica, 1888–1908*. Edited by Íñigo Sánchez-Llama, Cátedra, 2010.

————. *Obras completas*. Edited by Federico Carlos Sainz de Robles and Harry L. Kirby, Jr., Aguilar, 1957–73. 3 vols.

————. *Obras completas*. Edited by Darío Villanueva and José Manuel González Herrán, Fundación José Antonio de Castro, 1999–2011. 12 vols.

————. "El país de las castañuelas." Pardo Bazán, *De siglo a siglo, 1896–1901*, pp. 47–53. Originally published in *La época*, no. 49, 5 Jan. 1897, p. 1.

————. *Pascual López: Autobiografía de un estudiante de medicina*. Pardo Bazán, *Obras completas* [Sainz de Robles and Kirby], vol. 2, pp. 11–99.

————. *Los pazos de Ulloa*. Edited by María de los Ángeles Ayala, Cátedra, 1997.

————. *La piedra angular*. 1891. Simancas Ediciones, 2006.

————. "Por España." *Sud-exprés: Cuentos actuales*. *Obras completas*, vol. 36, Administración, 1909, pp. 142–48.

————. "Por España." *Biblioteca Virtual Miguel de Cervantes*, www.cervantesvirtual.com/obra-visor/por-espana--0/html/ffb4a18a-82b1-11df-acc7-002185ce6064_2.html#I_0_.

————. "Progreso: Cuestión de razas." *La ilustración artística*, vol. 19, no. 964, 1900, p. 394.

———. *La prueba*. La España editorial, 1890.

———. *La quimera*. Edited by Marina Mayoral, Cátedra, 1991.

———. "Realidad: Drama de don Benito Pérez Galdós." *Nuevo teatro crítico*, vol. 2, no. 16, Apr. 1892, pp. 19–69. *Biblioteca Virtual Miguel de Cervantes*, www .cervantesvirtual.com/obra-visor/nuevo-teatro-critico--29/html/029579ce-82b2 -11df-acc7-002185ce6064_22.html.

———. *Reflexiones científicas contra el darwinismo*. Pardo Bazán, *Obras completas* [Sainz de Robles and Kirby], vol. 3, pp. 537–70.

———. "Restorán." *El imparcial*, 10 June 1901. *Biblioteca Virtual Miguel de Cervantes*, www.cervantesvirtual.com/obra-visor-din/restoran--0/html/.

———. *Retratos y apuntes literarios*. Administración, [1908].

———. *La revolución y la novela en Rusia: Lecturas en el Ateneo de Madrid*. Imprenta M. Tello, 1887.

———. *La sirena negra*. 1908. Simancas Ediciones, 2006.

———. "Sobre la huelga, la filología de la cocina, el Diccionario de la Academia." Heydl-Cortínez, pp. 143–49. Originally published in *El diario de la marina*, 22 Oct. 1911.

———. *The Swan of Villamorta*. Translated by Mary J. Serrano, Cassell, 1891.

———. *Teatro completo*. Edited by Montserrat Ribao Pereira, Ediciones Akal, 2010.

———. *"Torn Lace" and Other Stories*. Translated by María Cristina Urruela, introduced by Joyce Tolliver, Modern Language Association of America, 1996.

———. *La Tribuna*. Edited by Benito Varela Jácome, Cátedra, 2006.

———. *The Tribune of the People*. Translated by Walter Borenstein, Bucknell UP, 1999.

———. *Verdad*. Pardo Bazán, *Teatro*, pp. 103–67.

———. *El vestido de boda*. Pardo Bazán, *Teatro*, pp. 79–87.

———. *Un viaje de novios*. Edited by Marisa Sotelo Vázquez, Alianza, 2003

———. "El viaje de novios de Mr. Bigpig." *El liberal*, 27 Dec. 1896, pp. 1–2. *Hemeroteca Digital de la Biblioteca Nacional de España*, hemerotecadigital.bne.es/issue .vm?id=0001263172.

———. *Viajes por España*. Edited by Tonina Paba, Bercimuel, 2006.

———. *Viajes por Europa*. Edited by Tonina Paba, Bercimuel, 2006.

———. *La vida contemporánea*. Edited and introduced by Carlos Dorado, Madrid Ayuntamiento, 2005.

———. "Vides y rosas." Pardo Bazán, *Obras completas* [Sainz de Robles and Kirby], vol. 3, pp. 895–901.

———. *A Wedding Trip*. Translated by Mary J. Serrano, Cassell, 1891.

———. "The Women of Spain." *Fortnightly Review*, vol. 51, 1889, pp. 879–904.

Pardo de Figueroa, Mariano (Thebussem). *La mesa moderna: Cartas sobre el comedor y la cocina cambiadas entre el doctor Thebussem y un cocinero de S.M.* Parsifal Ediciones, 1888.

Paredes Núñez, Juan. *Los cuentos de Emilia Pardo Bazán*. Universidad de Granada, 1979.

———. "Paralelos de lo fantástico decadentista: Un caso de proyección de Maupassant en España." *Hispania*, vol. 56, no. 3, 1973, pp. 587–92.

———. *La realidad gallega en los cuentos de Emilia Pardo Bazán, 1851–1921*. Ediciós do Castro, 1983.

Parkhurst Ferguson, Priscilla. *Accounting for Taste: The Triumph of French Cuisine*. U of Chicago P, 2006.

Patiño Eirín, Cristina. *Poética de la novela en la obra crítica de Emilia Pardo Bazán*. Universidade de Santiago, 1998.

Pattison, Walter. *Emilia Pardo Bazán*. Twayne, 1971.

Los pazos de Ulloa. Directed by Gonzalo Suárez, produced by Vicente Andrés Gómez, Televisión Española, 1984. *RTVE*, www.rtve.es/television/pazos-ulloa/.

"*Los pazos de Ulloa:* Entrevista a Gonzalo Suárez." *RTVE*, 8 Apr. 2009, www.rtve .es/alacarta/videos/los-pazos-de-ulloa/pazos-ulloa-entrevista-gonzalo-suarez /477104/.

"*Los pazos de Ulloa:* Presentación oficial en A Coruña." *RTVE*, 19 Mar. 2009, www .rtve.es/alacarta/videos/los-pazos-de-ulloa/pazos-ulloa-presentacion-oficial-serie -coruna/456673/.

Pereira-Muro, Carmen. *Género, nación y literatura: Emilia Pardo Bazán en la literatura gallega y española*. Purdue UP, 2013.

———. "Maravillosas supercherías: Género sexual y nacionalismo en los 'Apuntes autobiográficos' de Pardo Bazán y *Trafalgar* de Galdós." *Hispanic Review*, vol. 78, no. 1, Winter 2010, pp. 71–100.

———. "'Parecía efecto escénico, coro de zarzuela bufa': La zarzuela como intertexto y alegoría nacional en *Insolación* de Emilia Pardo Bazán." *Studi ispanici*, no. 37, 2012, pp. 165–80.

Pérez, Janet. "Naturalism and Gothic: Pardo Bazán's Transmogrifications of the Genre in *Los pazos de Ulloa*." *Studies in Honor of Donald W. Bleznick*, edited by Delia V. Galván et al., Juan de la Cuesta, 1995, pp. 143–56.

———. "Subversion of Victorian Values and Ideal Types: Pardo Bazán and the *Ángel del Hogar*." *Hispanófila*, no. 113, 1995, pp. 31–43.

Pérez Galdós, Benito. *La desheredada*. Edited by Germán Gullón, Cátedra, 2000.

———. *Montes de Oca*. Biblioteca Virtual Miguel de Cervantes, 2001. *Biblioteca Virtual Miguel de Cervantes*, www.cervantesvirtual.com/obra-visor/montes-de-oca --0/html/.

———. "Observaciones sobre la novela contemporánea en España." Bonet, pp. 105–20.

———. *O'Donnell*. Biblioteca Virtual Miguel de Cervantes, 2001. *Biblioteca Virtual Miguel de Cervantes*, www.cervantesvirtual.com/obra-visor/odonnell--0 /html/.

———. *Realidad: Drama en cinco actos y en prosa: Arreglo de la novela del mismo titulo*. La Guirnalda, 1892. *Biblioteca Virtual Miguel de Cervantes*, www.cervan tesvirtual.com/obra-visor/realidad-drama-en-cinco-actos-y-en-prosa--0/html/.

———. "La sociedad presente como materia novelable." Bonet, pp. 157–65.

———. *Tormento*. Edited by Teresa Barjau and Joaquim Parellada, Crítica, 2007.

Picón, Jacinto Octavio. "Estreno de *Realidad*." *El Correo*, 16 Mar. 1892, p. 22.

Pilcher, Jeffrey. *¡Que vivan los tamales! Food and the Making of Mexican Identity*. U of New Mexico P, 1998.

Pitt, Richard N., and Steven Tepper. *Double Majors: Influences, Identities, and Impacts*. The Curb Center for Art, Enterprise, and Public Policy / Vanderbilt UP, 2013. Prepared for the Teagle Foundation.

Poe, Edgar Allan. "The Black Cat." *Poe Stories*, poestories.com/read/blackcat.

———. "Imp of the Perverse." *Complete Poems and Stories by Edgar Allan Poe*. Doubleday, 1984, pp. 271–91.

———. "Ligeia." *Complete Poems and Stories by Edgar Allan Poe*. Doubleday, 1966, pp. 97–107.

———. "Review of *Twice Told Tales*." *Short Story Theories*, edited by Charles E. May, Ohio UP, 1976, pp. 45–51.

Powell, Eilene Jamie. *Hurts So Good: Representations of Sadomasochism in Spanish Novels, 1883–2012*. 2016. U of California, Los Angeles, PhD dissertation.

Pratt, Dale J. "Sex, Science, and the Origins of Culture in Emilia Pardo Bazán." *Mujer, sexo y poder en la literatura femenina iberoamericana del S. XIX*, edited by Joanna Courteau, Universitas Castellae, 1999, pp. 39–49.

———. *Signs of Science: Literature, Science, and Spanish Modernity since 1868*. Purdue UP, 2001.

Puga y Parga, Manuel María (Picadillo). *La cocina práctica*. Galí, 1981.

Purves, Mark Richard. "Marriage in the Short Stories of Chekhov." *Comparative Literature and Culture*, vol. 16, no. 3, 2014, doi:10.7771/1481-4374.2454.

¿Qué he hecho yo para merecer esto? Directed by Pedro Almodóvar, Kaktus Producciones cinematográficas / Tesauro, 1984.

Quesada Novás, Ángeles. *El amor en los cuentos de Emilia Pardo Bazán*. Publicaciones de la Universidad de Alicante, 2005.

———. "Los cuentos de Emilia Pardo Bazán en el aula." González Herrán et al., *Actas del II Simposio*, pp. 59–87.

Rabinowitz, Peter. "Reading Beginnings and Endings." *Narrative Dynamics: Essays on Time, Plot, Closure, and Frames*, edited by Brian Richardson, Ohio State UP, 2002, pp. 300–13.

Ragan, Robin. "Another Look at Nucha's Hysteria: Pardo Bazán's Response to the Medical Field of Late-Nineteenth-Century Spain." *Letras femeninas*, vol. 30, no. 1, 2004, pp. 141–54.

Revilla, Manuel de la. *Críticas*. Imprenta de Timoteo Arnáiz, 1884–85. 2 vols.

———. *Obras*. Imprenta de Víctor Sáiz, 1883.

Ribao Pereira, Montserrat. "Estudio preliminar." Pardo Bazán, *Teatro*, pp. 7–57.

Ringrose, David R. *Madrid and the Spanish Economy, 1560–1850*. U of California P, 1983.

———. *Spain, Europe, and the "Spanish Miracle," 1700–1900*. Cambridge UP, 1998.

Ríos-Font, Wadda. *Rewriting Melodrama: The Hidden Paradigm in Modern Spanish Theater*. Bucknell UP, 1997.

Rodoreda, Mercè. *La plaza del Diamante*. Translated by Enrique Sordo, Edhasa, 1999.

Rodríguez, Adna Rosa. *La cuestión feminista en los ensayos de Emilia Pardo Bazán*. Ediciós do Castro, 1991.

Rodríguez, Francisco. "Análise da literatura española feita por galegos: Dª Emilia, como exemplo." *O ensino*, no. 7, 1985, pp. 50–57.

Romero, Eugenia R. "The Other Galicia: Construction of National Identity through Absence." *Contemporary Galician Cultural Studies: Between the Local and the Global*, edited by Kirsty Hooper and Manuel Puga Moruxa, Modern Language Association of America, 2011.

Romero Tobar, Leonardo, coordinator. *Historia de la literatura española: Siglo XIX*. Vol. 2, Espasa Calpe, 1998.

Rosaldo, Renato. *Culture and Truth: The Remaking of Social Analysis*. Beacon Press, 1989.

Roseman, Sharon. "Celebrating Silenced Words: The 'Reimagining' of a Feminist Nation in Late-Twentieth-Century Galicia." *Feminist Studies*, vol. 23, no. 1, 1997, pp. 43–71.

———. "Reivindicando el paisaje gallego: Asociaciones rurales y políticas de desarrollo." *Galicia and Terranova and Labrador: Comparative Studies on Economic, Political and Socio-cultural Processes*, edited by Xaquín Rodríguez Campos and Xosé Santos Solla, Universidade de Santiago de Compostela, 2006, pp. 93–106.

Rowold, Katharina. *The Educated Woman: Minds, Bodies, and Women's Higher Education in Britain, Germany, and Spain, 1865–1914*. Routledge, 2010.

Ruibal, Euloxio R. "Unha conferencia inédita de Emilia Pardo Bazán sobre os problemas de Galicia." *Boletín galego de literatura*, no. 29, 2003, pp. 147–66.

Ruiz-Ocaña Dueñas, Eduardo. *La obra periodística de Emilia Pardo Bazán en* La ilustración artística *de Barcelona, 1895–1916*. Fundación Universitaria Española, 2004.

Rutherford, John. "Teoría y práctica de la traducción literaria: *La Regenta* al inglés." *Actas XI Congreso Aedean: Translation across Cultures; La traducción entre el mundo hispánico y anglosajón: Relaciones lingüísticas, culturales y literarias*, edited by J. C. Santoyo, Universidad de León, 1989, pp. 159–72.

Sáez de Melgar, Faustina. *Las mujeres españolas, americanas y lusitanas pintadas por sí mismas*. Vol. 1, Establecimiento Tipográfico-Editorial de Juan Pons, [1881].

Said, Edward. *Orientalism*. Penguin Books, 2003.

Salaün, Serge, and Carlos Serrano, editors. *1900 en España*. Espasa-Calpe, 1991.

Sánchez-Llama, Íñigo. *Galería de escritoras isabelinas: La prensa periódica entre 1833 y 1895*. Cátedra, 2000.

Santos, Care. *Okupada*. Alba Editorial, 1997.

Sarmiento, Domingo Faustino. *Viajes en Europa, Africa y América: 1845–1847*, edited by Javier Fernández, Fondo de Cultura Económica, 1993.

Scanlon, Geraldine. "Class and Gender in Pardo Bazán's *La Tribuna*." *Bulletin of Hispanic Studies*, vol. 67, no. 2, 1990, pp. 137–49.

———. *La polémica feminista en la España contemporánea, 1868–1974*. Translated by Rafael Mazarrasa, Ediciones Akal, 1986.

Scari, Robert M. *Bibliografía descriptiva de estudios críticos sobre la obra de Emilia Pardo Bazán*. Ediciones Albatros Hispanofila, 1982.

Schiavo, Leda, and Ángela Mañueco Ruiz. "El teatro de Emilia Pardo Bazán: Documentos inéditos." *Homenaje a R. Martínez López*, edited by Kathleen N. March, Edicións do Castro, 1990, pp. 55–67.

Schmidt-Nowara, Christopher. *The Conquest of History*. U of Pittsburgh P, 2006.

Scholes, Robert. *Structural Fabulation: An Essay on Fiction of the Future*. U of Notre Dame P, 1975.

Schwartz, Vanessa, and Jeannene Przyblyski, editors. *The Nineteenth-Century Visual Culture Reader*. Routledge, 2004.

Segal, Lynne. "Back to the Boys? Temptations of the Good Gender Theorist." *Textual Practice*, vol. 15, no. 2, 2001, pp. 231–50.

Segarra, Marta. "Crítica feminista y escritura femenina en Francia." *Teoría y crítica en la literatura francesa del siglo XX: Estudios sobre crítica feminista, postestructuralismo y psicoanálisis*, edited by Blanca Acinas López, Universidad de Burgos, 2000, pp. 79–108.

Shields, David. *Reality Hunger: A Manifesto*. Alfred A. Knopf, 2010.

Showalter, Elaine. *Sexual Anarchy: Gender and Culture at the Fin de Siècle*. Viking Books, 1990.

Shubert, Adrian. *A Social History of Modern Spain*. Routledge, 2003.

Shubert, Adrian, and José Álvarez Junco, editors. *Spanish History since 1808*. Arnold, 2000.

Sieburth, Stephanie. *Inventing High and Low: Literature, Mass Culture, and Uneven Modernity in Spain*. Duke UP, 1994.

Sileno. "La Inevitable en Paris." *Gedeón*, vol. 6, no. 249, 29 Aug. 1900, cover.

Silva, José Asunción. *De sobremesa*. Alcalá Grupo Editorial, 2009.

Silverman, Kaja. "Fragments of a Fashionable Discourse." *Studies in Entertainment: Critical Approaches to Mass Culture*, edited by Tania Modleski, Indiana UP, 1986, pp. 139–54.

Sinúes de Marco, María del Pilar. *La dama elegante: Manual práctico y completísimo del buen tono y del buen orden doméstico*. Librería de A. de San Martín, 1880.

La sirena negra. Directed by Carlos Serrano de Osma, Producciones Boga, 1947.

Smith, Jennifer. "Cultural Capital and Social Class in Emilia Pardo Bazán's 'La mujer española' and *Insolación*." *Anales de la literatura española contemporánea*, vol. 41, no. 1, 2016, pp. 143–68.

———. "The Gypsy's Curse: Race and Impurity of Blood in Pardo Bazán." *Revista canadiense de estudios hispánicos*, vol. 39, no. 2, 2015, pp. 459–82.

———. "The Wet Nurse and the Subversion of the *Ángel del Hogar* in Medical and Literary Texts from Nineteenth-Century Spain." *Hispanic Journal*, vol. 31, no. 1, 2010, pp. 39–52.

———. "Women, Mysticism, and Alternative Technologies of the Self in Selected Writings of Emilia Pardo Bazán." *Revista de estudios hispánicos*, vol. 45, no. 1, 2011, pp. 155–75.

Smith, Jennifer, and Lisa Nalbone, editors. *Intersections of Race, Class, Gender, and Nation in Fin-de-siècle Spanish Literature and Culture*. Routledge, 2017.

Smith Rousselle, Elizabeth. *Gender and Modernity in Spanish Literature, 1789–1920*. Palgrave Macmillan, 2014.

Sociedad del Folk-Lore Gallego. *Cuestionario*. Ricardo Fé, 1885.

Soler Carnicer, José. *Valencia pintoresca y tradicional: Personajes, hechos y dichos populares*. Vol. 1, Carena, 1997.

Sorolla y Bastida, Joaquín. *¡Aún dicen que el pescado es caro!* 1894. *Museo Nacional del Prado*, www.museodelprado.es/coleccion/obra-de-arte/aun-dicen-que-el-pescado-es-caro/a4fcf4c7-4d54-4e50-9255-25b44f0e0416.

Spicer-Escalante, J. P., and Lara Anderson, editors. *Au natural: (Re)reading Hispanic Naturalism*. Cambridge Scholars Publishing, 2010.

Spivak, Gayatri. "Can the Subaltern Speak?" *Marxism and the Interpretation of Culture*, edited by Cary Nelson and Lawrence Grossberg, Macmillan, 1988, pp. 271–313.

Surtz, Ronald, et al., editors. *Américo Castro: The Impact of His Thought*. Hispanic Seminary of Medieval Studies, 1988.

Thion Soriano-Mollá, Dolores. "Amistades literarias: Doce cartas de Emilia Pardo Bazán a Isaac Pavlosvky [sic]." *La Tribuna: Cadernos de estudios da Casa Museo Emilia Pardo Bazán*, no. 1, 2003, pp. 97–147.

———. "Realismo y espacio urbano: Notas sobre *La Tribuna* de Emilia Pardo Bazán." *Anales de literatura española*, no. 24, 2012, pp. 195–213.

Tinajero, Araceli. *El Lector: A History of the Cigar Factory Worker*. U of Texas P, 2010.

Todorov, Tzvetan. *The Fantastic: A Structural Approach to a Literary Genre.* Translated by Richard Howard, Case Western Reserve UP, 1973.

Tolliver, Joyce. *Cigar Smoke and Violet Water: Gendered Discourse in the Stories of Emilia Pardo Bazán*. Bucknell UP, 1998.

———. "Framing Colonial Manliness, Domesticity, and Empire in 'Página suelta' and 'Oscuramente.'" *Revista de estudios hispánicos*, vol. 46, no. 1, 2012, pp. 3–24.

———. "Over Her Bloodless Body: Gender, Race, and the Spanish Colonial Fetish in Pardo Bazán." *Revista canadiense de estudios hispánicos*, no. 34, vol. 2, 2010, pp. 285–301.

Tortella Casares, Gabriel. *The Development of Modern Spain: An Economic History of the Nineteenth and Twentieth Centuries*. Translated by Valerie J. Herr, Harvard UP, 2000.

Tosh, John. *Manliness and Masculinities in Nineteenth-Century Britain: Essays on Gender, Family, and Empire*. Pearson Longman, 2005.

Tsuchiya, Akiko. "Género y orientalismo en *Insolación* de Emilia Pardo Bazán." González Herrán et al., *La literatura*, pp. 771–79.

——. *Marginal Subjects: Gender and Deviance in Fin-de-Siècle Spain*. U of Toronto P, 2011.

Tuñón de Lara, Manuel. *Estudios sobre el siglo XIX español*. 8th ed., Editorial Siglo XXI, 1984.

Turner, Harriet. "The Realist Novel." *The Cambridge Companion to the Spanish Novel: From 1600 to the Present*, edited by Turner and Adelaida López de Martínez, Cambridge UP, 2003, pp. 81–101.

Unamuno, Miguel de. "¡Adentro!" *Tres ensayos: ¡Adentro!, La ideocracia, La fe*, edited by B. Rodriguez Serrar, Imprenta de A. Marzo, 1900, pp. 5–22.

Underwood, John. *Hablando de cine: Conversación avanzada*. McGraw-Hill, 2003.

Urry, John. *The Tourist Gaze*. Sage, 2002.

Valera, Juan. *El arte de la novela*. Edited by Adolfo Sotelo Vázquez, Lumen, 1996.

——. *Crítica literaria, 1864–1871*. Imprenta Alemana, 1909.

——. *Discursos académicos*. Imprenta Alemana, 1905. 2 vols.

——. *Estudios críticos sobre literatura, política y costumbres de nuestros días*. 1864. Francisco Álvarez, 1884. 3 vols.

——. *Pepita Jiménez*. 1874. Edited by Adolfo Sotelo, SGEL, 1983.

Vales Vía, José-Domingo. "Doña Emilia Pardo-Bazán y su efímero título nobiliario." *Anuario brigantino*, no. 28, 2005, anuariobrigantino.betanzos.net/Ab2005PDF /2005%20265-276%20JDomingo%20Condesa.pdf.

Valis, Noël. "Confession and the Body in Emilia Pardo Bazán's *Insolación*." *Reading the Nineteenth-Century Spanish Novel: Selected Essays*, by Valis, Juan de la Cuesta, 2005, pp. 235–56.

——. *The Culture of* Cursilería: *Bad Taste, Kitsch, and Class in Modern Spain*. Duke UP, 2002.

——. "The Female Figure and Writing in *Fin de Siglo* Spain." *Romance Quarterly*, vol. 36, no. 3, 1989, pp. 369–81.

——. "Figura femenina y escritura en la España finisecular." *¿Qué es el modernismo? Nueva encuesta, nuevas lecturas*, edited by Richard Cardwell and Bernard Mc-Guirk, Society of Spanish and Spanish-American Studies, 1993, pp. 103–25.

——. "'Tell It Slant': Defamiliarizing Spanish Realism." *Romance Studies*, vol. 30, nos. 3–4, 2012, pp. 193–99.

Vallejo Fernández Cela, Sergio. "La cigarreras de la Fábrica Nacional de Tabacos de Madrid." *Capas populares y conflictividad social: Población, abastecimientos y crisis de subsistencias; Cultura y mentalidades*, edited by Luis E. Otero Carvajal and Ángel Bahamonde, Comunidad de Madrid, Consejería de Cultura, Revista Alforz Cidur, 1986, pp. 135–49. Vol. 2 of *Madrid en la sociedad del siglo XIX*.

Vázquez Montalbán, Manuel. *Contra los gourmets*. Mondadori, 2001.

Velasco Souto, Carlos F. *A sociedade galega da Restauración na obra literaria de Pardo Bazán, 1875–1900*. Artes Gráficas Portela, 1987.

Velázquez, Diego. *Las meninas*. 1656. *Museo Nacional del Prado*, www.museodelprado .es/coleccion/obra-de-arte/las-meninas/9fdc7800-9ade-48b0-ab8b-edee94ea877f?.

Venuti, Lawrence. *The Translator's Invisibility: A History of Translation*. 2nd ed., Routledge, 2008.

Versteeg, Margot A. "'Una mujer como las demás': El deseo de maternidad en cinco cuentos de Emilia Pardo Bazán." *Journal of Iberian and Latin American Studies*, vol. 14, no. 1, 2008, pp. 39–50.

———. *Propuestas para (re)construir una nación: El teatro de Emilia Pardo Bazán.* Purdue UP, forthcoming.

Un viaje de novios. Directed by Gonzalo P. Delgrás. Ediciones cinematográficas Cumbre, 1947.

Vida y obra literaria de Emilia Pardo Bazán. Directed by Ricardo Groizard Moreno, written by Ana María Freire López and Margarita Almela Boix, UNED / CEMAV, 2006. *Biblioteca Virtual Miguel de Cervantes*, www.cervantesvirtual.com/portales /pardo_bazan/documentales_emilia_pardo_bazan/.

"Videoteca." *Biblioteca Virtual Miguel de Cervantes*, Fundación Biblioteca Virtual Miguel de Cervantes, www.cervantesvirtual.com/portales/pardo_bazan/videoteca/.

Villiers de l'Isle-Adam, Auguste. "Véra." *Contes cruels: Oeuvres complètes.* Vol. 1, Gallimard, 1986, pp. 554–61.

Walter, Susan. *From the Outside Looking In: Narrative Frames and Narrative Spaces in the Short Stories of Emilia Pardo Bazán.* Juan de la Cuesta, 2010.

Wilson, Elizabeth. *Adorned in Dreams: Fashion and Modernity.* Virago Books, 1985.

Wood, Jennifer Jenkins. *Spanish Women Travelers at Home and Abroad, 1850–1920: From Tierra del Fuego to the Land of the Midnight Sun.* Bucknell UP, 2013.

INDEX OF NAMES

INDEX OF PARDO BAZÁN'S WORKS